GW00733333

# THE COMPLETE BOOK OF

# CAT CARE

# THE COMPLETE BOOK OF
# CAT CARE

## TIM HAWCROFT
BVSc (Hons), MACVSc, MRCVS

RINGPRESS

I dedicate this book to my father,  Eric Hawcroft

**First published in the United Kingdom by RINGPRESS BOOKS LTD**
A Kevin Weldon Production

Originated by Weldon Publishing, Sydney, Australia
a division of Kevin Weldon & Associates Pty Limited

© Copyright: Tim Hawcroft 1991
© Copyright design: Kevin Weldon & Associates Pty Limited 1991

First published 1991
Ringpress Books Ltd
Spirella House
Bridge Road
Letchworth
Herts SG6 4ET

ISBN 0 948955 71 6

All rights reserved. No part of this book may be reproduced
or transmitted in any form or by any means, electronic or mechanical,
including photocopying, recording or by any information storage and
retrieval system, without permission in writing from the Publisher.

Produced in Hong Kong by Mandarin Offset

# CONTENTS

*A Somali kitten.*

# INTRODUCTION

W hy are cats so popular as pets? Certainly, their independence, cleanliness, size, and soft, furry appearance have a lot to do with their appeal. But, most of all, cats like human company. They like to be touched and stroked, and their need to both receive and show affection greatly endears them to their owners.

The relationship owners have with their cats is often a special one. A cat owner is seldom lonely; the cat is nearly always there, at home or in the garden, offering its companionship, and its friendliness and affection can help its owner to relax and release tension.

Your relationship with your cat is more likely to be mutually satisfying if you remember that your cat is as much of an individual as you are and has more or less the same needs. Its basic need is good health, both physical and psychological. You can help to ensure this by attending to such matters as good veterinary care, nutrition, grooming and housing. As with most rela-

tionships, you will find that the time and patience you invest in your cat will be amply rewarded.

This book provides practical advice and information to help you care for your cat, whether you are an owner, breeder, fancier, student of pet care or member of a cat club.

The first two chapters, 'Choosing your cat' and 'Breeds', give background information to help you make the wisest decision on which breed to choose and so be off to a good start. Chapter 3 deals with behaviour and training, and the next six chapters are all directly concerned with the important topic of health care.

The final chapter is a comprehensive one on breeding. Keep in mind that if owners kept a tighter control of breeding, the feral and stray cat population would diminish and cat lovers would have more peace of mind.

You will find answers to most of your questions about caring for your cat in this book. For any other problems that arise, you should seek advice from your veterinarian.

*Somalis make lively and affectionate companions.*

# CHOOSING YOUR CAT

*Why do you want a cat? — Responsibilities of a cat owner —*
*Boarding catteries — Suitability of family and home for cat —*
*Which breed to choose — What to look for — Where to buy*

## WHY DO YOU WANT A CAT?

IS it to be a companion for yourself, the children or the family? Do you want a cat for showing, for breeding, as a companion in the house, or to control a vermin problem inside or outside the house?

## RESPONSIBILITIES OF A CAT OWNER

When choosing a kitten aged six to eight weeks, you are taking on a commitment for a period of approximately fourteen years, which is the average life span of a cat. During that time you are committed to:

- *Feeding* Your cat needs to be fed at least once a day.
- *Grooming* This task will vary according to the length of your cat's hair. Some longhaired cats require daily grooming. A shorthaired cat requires less grooming time.
- *Housing* If indoors, you need to provide a litter tray, cleaning it regularly and removing soiled litter daily.
- *Health care* It is important for you to arrange annual booster vaccinations and checkup by your veterinarian. A regular worming routine should also be established.

*A cat enjoys companionship.*

9

*An ideal boarding cattery.*

• *Exercise* Cats do not need to be formally exercised like a dog. Most cats will exercise themselves, given access to a garden. Cats can live happily and permanently indoors.

• *Human contact* Most cats seek affection, attention and physical contact. It is important for both cat and owner to have regular contact with one another. Talking to, stroking, nursing and playing with the cat provide opportunities for contact.

• *Desexing (neutering)* If you do not want to have your cat desexed, it is important to take appropriate measures to prevent it from breeding indiscriminately. Having your cat (male or female) neutered helps to reduce the increasing stray cat problem and makes your cat a better companion.

• *Boarding* If you are going away on holidays and cannot take your cat with you, you will need to board it at a cattery or arrange for someone to come to your house, apartment or flat daily to look after it.

## BOARDING CATTERIES

It is a good idea to make arrangements well in advance if you are thinking of booking your cat into a good boarding cattery. Catteries are usually fully booked, especially during holiday periods.

To select a good boarding cattery, it is wise to find out if it holds a current licence. Catteries in many countries are required to be licensed under some such legislation as a Prevention of Cruelty to Animals Act. For the cattery to hold a current licence it has to be checked by some authority such as the Police Department or the local Council.

Do not hesitate to discuss the following with the cattery management:

• Is it a requirement for the cat to have a current veterinary vaccination certificate before being admitted to the boarding cattery? All good boarding establishments demand to see a current vaccination certificate.

If your cat is due for a vaccination (see page 87) around the time of boarding, it is a good idea to attend to this a couple of weeks before it is due to go into the cattery.

• What arrangements does the management have in place for veterinary attention if the cat gets sick while you are away? Leave the name and phone number of your veterinarian in case the cat's health record is required. Also, leave a contact number in case an emergency arises and the management needs to consult you or someone you have nominated.

• Does the management require you to sign a contract form at the time of admission? Does the

*These Maine Coon kittens will make affectionate, companionable pets.*

*Mothers are ever ready to turn a blind eye.*

*A well-located boarding cattery.*

contract clearly state the responsibilities of both parties?

• Is there somebody continually in attendance at the cattery in case of an emergency?

• What kind of food is given to the cats and does the management cater for individual cats that are fussy or require a special diet?

• Ask if you can inspect the cattery. If you are refused permission, it may be wise to seek another cattery to board your cat.

During the inspection of the cattery, check that:

• The cattery is clean, tidy, hygienic, with no unpleasant odour, and well organised. If it is well run, then your cat should be well looked after.

• The cats in the cattery are healthy, happy, bright and alert.

• The pens are adequate for sleeping, eating, exercising and toileting. Cats do not need a large area for exercise and often feel more secure in a smaller space. The pens should be designed so that individual cats do not have any direct physical contact.

• The cattery and pens have good security so that your cat cannot escape while you are away.

• The pens receive good natural light during the day, are well ventilated, dry and insulated from the heat or cold.

*This cattery is well set up for exercise.*

13

*Sunshine is welcome in a cattery.*

Most cats take a few days to become familiar with and feel at ease in their new surroundings, especially with numerous other strange cats. Once they realise they are safe and secure, they usually settle in quite well.

## SUITABILITY OF FAMILY AND HOME FOR CAT

### A cat or a kitten?

A mature, placid cat may be more suitable for an elderly couple who could not cope with a young kitten. Make sure the mature cat is healthy and suitable in temperament before accepting it.

A young kitten six to eight weeks of age would be ideally suited for a young family environment. The children would benefit from the kitten and its playful antics, while the kitten, as it develops into maturity, would adapt itself to family life.

An adult cat admitted into a family may be frightened by overexcited, boisterous children.

### Determining a cat's sex

To identify the sex of your kitten, gently lift its tail. The female (queen) has a vertical, slit-like opening just below the anus. This opening is the vulva, or the entrance to the vagina. The male (tom) has a swelling, just below the anus, known as the scrotum, which contains the testicles. They are not as well developed in the young kitten as they are in the mature male. The circular opening below the scrotum is where the cat's penis is concealed.

A neutered male or female cat makes an equally good companion or family pet. Neutered females are generally less territorial and are more attached to the home.

If you do not have your female cat neutered and take no precautions to prevent it breeding indiscriminately, invariably it will become pregnant. Looking after a queen and her kittens involves a certain amount of time and effort on your part, and furthermore you may be left with some unwanted kittens.

Entire (unneutered) male cats often stray, only coming home for food and rest. Often, they look scruffy as they neglect their grooming and are battle-scarred from fighting. Toms spray strong-smelling urine to mark their territory. It leaves a most offensive odour if sprayed in or around the house and garden. For these reasons, it is wise to have your male cat neutered.

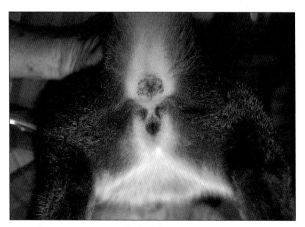

*Female: vagina vertical, slit-like opening just below anus.*

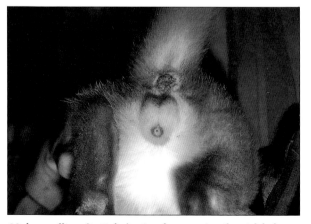

*Male: swelling (testicles); circular opening (penis) below anus.*

14

*These kittens are seven and a half weeks old.*

### Hair length

Longhaired cats require constant grooming to maintain their coat in good condition. If you have limited time to devote to grooming, a shorthaired cat is a sensible choice. Hot, wet climates are more suited to shorthaired cats.

### Temperament

Some cats, such as the Siamese, are demanding of attention and affection, and are often very vocal. For a person or family who wants a vocal cat with plenty of personality, the Siamese would be suitable. On the other hand, Abyssinians are more suited to a person who wants a cat which is gentle, affectionate and not particularly demanding or vocal.

## WHICH BREED TO CHOOSE

Breeds have well-defined characteristics. By choosing a kitten of a certain breed, you will have a good idea of what it will look like and what type of temperament it will have when it matures. Sometimes there is a variation which cannot be predicted.

When choosing a crossbred kitten, its size, shape, hair length and temperament are a little uncertain until it is fully developed. If you know

*Each breed has its own appeal.*

15

*Which one to choose?*

the parents, you will have some indication of what the kitten might be like when it matures.

To help you decide which breed to choose, read the next chapter, 'Breeds'.

## WHAT TO LOOK FOR

Stand back and look at the kitten or kittens from a distance. Look for one that is playful, alert, active, outgoing and friendly. Do not select one that is timid, frightened, aggressive or aloof.

Gently pick up the kitten and have a good look at its eyes to make sure they are clear and that there is no discharge or inflammation (redness). Avoid white cats with blue eyes as they are usually deaf. Also check to see that there is no discharge from the nose. A kitten that sneezes could be incubating cat flu, which may cause it to become a chronic snuffler (see page 166).

Check inside the ears, which should be clean and dry. Heavy wax and/or redness inside the ear is often indicative of ear mites (see page 144).

Carefully pull the lips apart and check to see that the incisor (front) teeth of the upper jaw meet the incisor teeth of the lower jaw when the mouth is closed. Do not select a kitten whose upper jaw protrudes further than the lower jaw. This is known as an overshot jaw. An undershot jaw is where the lower jaw protrudes further than the upper jaw.

Also check the kitten's coat, which should be even, soft and shiny. There should not be any hair loss or broken, scaly, scabby skin. The kitten should be clean around the anus. Dirt around the anus, tail or down the back of the hindlegs could indicate diarrhoea due to worms or infection.

While holding the kitten, you will get an indication of its weight. Avoid choosing a thin, bony kitten and check to see that the legs are not bowed.

Check for swelling around the navel (umbilicus),

*These kittens are playful, alert and active.*

*It is wise to choose a kitten that is friendly, alert and playful.*

*Cats like to bask in the sun.*

*In a sunny climate, a cat with black nose and ears (left) will not develop skin cancer, whereas a cat with white nose and white-tipped ears (right) is susceptible to skin cancer.*

which indicates an umbilical hernia. If prominent, the hernia will need to be repaired surgically at a later date.

Avoid kittens with white ears and nose if you live in a hot, sunny climate. These cats develop skin cancer over years of lying in the sun (see page 165).

Be aware of the following inherited defects when choosing a kitten:
• *Monorchid* One testicle fails to descend.
• *Cryptorchid* Both testicles fail to descend.
• *Umbilical hernia* Swelling around the navel.
• *Deafness* Blue-eyed white cats.
• *Kinked tail* An inherited defect seen in Siamese.
• *Manx (tailless)* Cats may carry a lethal gene causing the birth of dead kittens.
• *Tear duct defects* Some cats, such as Persians, with a pronounced flat or 'pushed in' face constantly have wet facial hair from tears flowing down the cheeks due to malformation of the tear ducts.
• *Cross-eyed* More often seen in Siamese cats.
• *Entropion* Turning in of the upper or lower eyelids or both, causing irritation of the surface of the eye due to the eyelashes rubbing on the cornea.

## WHERE TO BUY

### Neighbours

If you want a crossbred kitten, the best place to acquire one is from a friend or neighbour whose cat has had a litter. The ideal age is about eight weeks. Usually, the litter will have been isolated from contact with other cats, and consequently the kittens are more likely to be disease free.

### Breeders

When buying from a breeder specialising in your chosen breed of cat, you will be able to see what the kitten will look like when fully grown by looking at its parents. Even when buying from a breeder, be aware of the conditions under which the cats are kept. Select a kitten from a breeding establishment that is clean and not overcrowded. The breeder should provide a registered pedigree, vaccination certificate and record of worming.

### Pet shops

Often, the history of where kittens in pet shops came from is unknown. If this information along with details of the parents can be supplied, it will give you an insight into the kitten's health, temperament and what it will look like as a mature adult.

In some countries, pet shops issue a signed health certificate for the kitten you purchase which guarantees a refund of your money within forty-eight hours if a veterinary examination reveals a serious medical problem.

### Animal welfare agencies

Kittens and cats from these sources are abandoned or surrendered by people for all kinds of reasons: behavioural problems, too costly to keep or a medical problem, which made them unsuitable for the family or lifestyle of the former owner.

Ask the agency if the animal has received its vaccinations. With those that have not been immunised and are admitted into a compound of numerous cats, there is a danger that they may pick up a virus: feline panleucopenia (enteritis), or feline respiratory disease (cat flu). These viruses take about ten days to incubate, so there is the possibility that you will not see any symptoms until you have had the kitten home for a week or so.

*Himalayans have the body build of Persians and the colouring of Siamese.*

# BREEDS

*History — Governing bodies — Glossary —
Selection of breeds*

## HISTORY

Whether you want a cat as a companion or family pet, for showing or breeding, you should know a little about different breeds and terminology before making a selection.

When the first official cat show was organised by Harrison Weir in London in 1871, there was no official purebred cat as records were then non-existent. Knowledge of breeding techniques was at a very elementary level and indiscriminate breeding was common. At that first cat show, and those that followed, shorthaired cats were in a majority, but by the turn of the century longhaired cats dominated, especially the Persian breed.

In 1895, an American, Mr J. Hyde, organised a cat show in New York. This proved such a success that it was quickly followed by others, and so what has become known as the 'cat fancy' (see glossary) was launched in the US.

With the growth of cat shows, cat clubs, associations, controlling bodies and the increasing interest of owners and breeders, more attention was given to breeding programs and the quality and variety of breeds, as well as to the keeping of official records.

## GOVERNING BODIES

The approval of breeds and varieties, the standards of excellence associated with them and the registration of pedigrees are recorded by various bodies. In the UK, there is one centralised body,

*A Bicolour Devon Rex kitten.*

*The body type of the Himalayan is described as 'cobby': compact, with a boxy shape.*

the Governing Council of the Cat Fancy (GCCF). In the US, there are about seven such bodies, the largest being the Cat Fanciers' Association (CFA). In Canada, there is the Canadian Cat Association (CCA). In Australia, each state has one or more governing bodies, New South Wales being the first to start a cat fancy. The Royal Agricultural Society (RAS) in Sydney keeps an official record for its own state as well as for breeders in other states who wish to register their cats and kittens.

## GLOSSARY

To help the reader understand some of the terminology used in connection with the breeds of cats, the following simple glossary of terms has been compiled:

*Bicolour(ed)* A British term referring to a cat with two colours, e.g. black and white.

*Cat fancy* A collective term used to cover pedigree cats, cat clubs and cat fanciers.

*Cobby* Describes a compact body with a boxy appearance, such as seen in the Persian: a relatively large, round, short body set low on short, sturdy legs.

*Colour points* The colour markings on the face (mask), ears, tail, legs and paws, being a particular distinctive colour different from the rest of the coat, which is a lighter shade.

*The markings on this cat are called colour points.*

*Foreign* A term used to classify cats such as the Siamese that have large pricked ears, almond-shaped (oriental) eyes, wedge-shaped heads, long slim bodies, long elegant legs and long tails.

*Longhair(ed)* Hair long, as in the Persian, Angora and other breeds. It is becoming the practice in the UK to refer to the Persian varieties as Longhairs, e.g. Black Longhair.

*Mutation* Spontaneous change in the genetic structure which results in a new species , e.g. Balinese.

*Non-self* Not the same colour all over, e.g. Black and White Shorthair. Opposite to 'Self'.

*Self* A British term used to indicate a cat which is the same colour all over, e.g. Chocolate Self Longhair.

*Shorthair(ed)* Hair short, as in the Abyssinian, American Shorthair and other breeds.

*Solid* An American term used in the same sense as the British term 'Self'.

*Ticked coat* Each hair has several bands of dark colour, giving it a glowing, ticked effect, e.g. Abyssinian.

*Tortoiseshell* The Tortoiseshell has three colours — black, with red and cream patches. A desirable feature is a red or cream blaze on the face running from nose to forehead. The name is sometimes

*A silver Abyssinian with a ticked coat.*

*The Siamese is an example of a Foreign type.*

*Somalis are one of the longhaired breeds.*

23

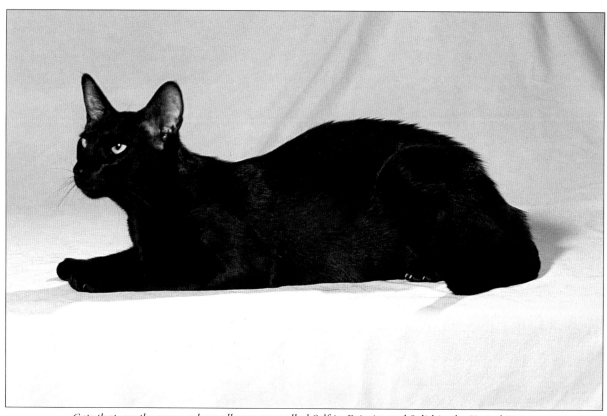

*Cats that are the same colour all over are called Self in Britain and Solid in the United States.*

*A Shorthair.*

shortened to Tortie. If a tortoiseshell cat also has white patches, it is referred to as Tortie and White.

## SELECTION OF BREEDS

A selection of some of the more popular breeds are described to give readers some idea of the variety of cats, along with information that may be helpful when choosing a kitten or cat as a companion and pet.

## ABYSSINIAN

It is thought that the Abyssinian is descended from the sacred cats of ancient Egypt. In 1868, the first of the breed were brought to England from Abyssinia and since then it has been developed into a stylish-looking cat.

It is of foreign type, but not as long or as slender as the Siamese. It has a short, wedge-shaped head, large wide-set pointed ears and almond-shaped eyes of green, gold or hazel. The tail is long, the legs are fine and the feet are oval. The nose is red and the paw pads are black or brown.

The coat is short, fine, close and ticked. The classic type is ruddy brown, while a warm red is also a recognised colour. Several other colours have since been developed — namely, silver, lilac, blue, cream and chocolate.

Mutations with a long coat appeared in litters of Abyssinians and were mated and developed in Canada as a separate breed. They are known as the Somali and are becoming popular (see page 57).

As a pet, the Abyssinian is gaining in popularity not only because of its graceful, attractive appearance, but also because it is gentle, intelligent, affectionate and quiet-voiced.

*This cat has the typical features of an Abyssinian.*

*The classic colour for Abyssinians is ruddy brown (tawny).*

25

*A white Angora with blue eyes.*

*This Balinese shows all the features typical of the breed.*

*Abyssinians are gentle, intelligent and affectionate.*

*A Bicolour Angora.*

## ANGORA

Angoras originated in Turkey and were present in England in the 1890s. Reference was made to them as having silvery, silken fur, with some being almost the colour of a lion. They were indiscriminately bred with Persians, which became most popular, while the Angora breed lost favour and almost died out.

In 1963, several of the remaining Angoras in Ankara (Turkey) were brought into the US and a breeding program was begun. The Angora bred true and in 1970 it was registered by the CFA. This prompted a revival of interest in the breeding of Angoras in the UK.

The Angora is of average size, with a comparatively small head, a long tail and a long, flowing, silky white coat. The eyes are wide-set, large and almond-shaped.

There are three eye colours of the white Angora — orange (amber) eyes, blue eyes and odd eyes (i.e. one orange and one blue eye). The blue-eyed variety is usually deaf, the odd-eyed is usually deaf in the ear on the side of the blue eye, and the orange (amber) eyed is not deaf. The Angora is bred in a range of colours, but only the white is recognised by the CFA for championship competition.

Deaf cats present a problem to moving vehicles and human movement about the home. Otherwise, the Angora breed is healthy, quiet, alert and affectionate. Keep in mind that white cats are subject to skin cancer in hot climates.

## BALINESE

This breed appeared in a litter of purebred Siamese in the US in the 1950s. When bred with a similar mutation, the offspring were lookalikes and were thought of as Longhaired Siamese. From this beginning, a controlled breeding program was followed and the final product was called the Balinese, which was recognised in 1963 by the CFA.

The Balinese has soft, silky, long hair, about 5 cm (2 in) or more in length. It has a graceful, streamlined, muscular body, with long legs, long plume-like tail tapering to a point, wedge-shaped face, large pointed ears, and vivid blue, oriental eyes. Its colour pattern is the same as the Siamese, including the Blue Point, Chocolate Point, Seal Point and Lilac Point. Other colour points are being developed.

It is highly intelligent, affectionate and attractive, but its voice is not as loud or demanding as that of the Siamese.

## BIRMAN

The Birman is often referred to as the sacred cat of Burma. In colour pattern, it is much like the Siamese, with colour points of seal, blue, chocolate or lilac.

One unique feature of its colouring is that the paws are white. The white on the front paws ends in a even line like a glove, while the white on the back paws runs up to a point like a gauntlet.

An interesting story is told on how the Birman got its colour. The temple of some Burmese priests was raided by enemies. One priest, Mun-Ha, with his white cat Sinh beside him, knelt praying for deliverance to the golden statue of Tsun-Kyan-Kse, the goddess of transmigration of souls. Mun-Ha was struck down by the enemies and as he lay dying, Sinh jumped onto his master's body to protect it, at the same time looking into the sapphire blue eyes of the goddess. As it did so, Sinh's eyes turned to blue, its legs, tail, mask and ears turned to brown (the colour of the earth on which the statue stood), its white coat turned to a golden yellow colour (a reflection of the statue's colour), and its paws that had touched its master's body remained white. Mun-Ha's soul had passed into the cat's body. When the next morning dawned,

*White paws are one of the unique features of the Birman.*

*A Bombay.*

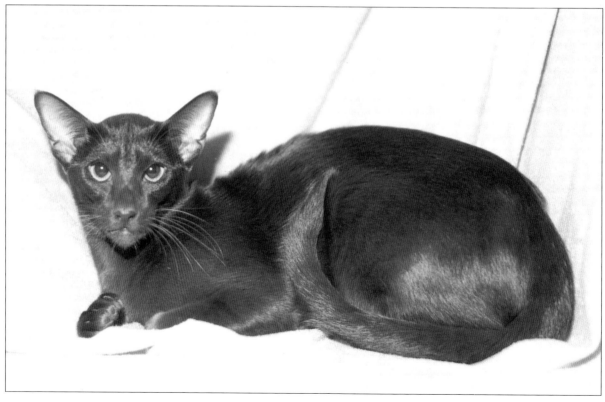

*A Havana Brown.*

the hundred white temple cats had all changed to the same colour and the enemy had retreated in defeat. Within seven days Sinh died and took the soul of Mun-Ha to paradise. From that time the priests regarded the Birman as a sacred cat.

The present-day Birman has long, silky fur and a heavy ruff. Its head is round with full cheeks and rounded china blue eyes. The long yet stocky body is set on short, sturdy legs, and its long tail is bushy. There is a touch of gold in its beige coat.

The Birman is a very attractive cat, affectionate, playful, intelligent and with a pleasant voice.

## BOMBAY

In 1976, the CFA granted championship status to the Bombay, which had been developed in the US by crossing a male Black American Shorthair with a Sable Burmese.

The Bombay is a medium-sized, muscular cat, with tail and legs in proportion to the body. The head is rounded and large, the ears are medium-sized, wide-set and rounded at the tips. The eyes are also wide-set, rounded and yellow to copper in colour. The coat is close-lying, short, fine and satin-like black. The nose and paw pads are black.

The Bombay is companionable, happy to be indoors and a persistent purrer.

## BRITISH HAVANA —AMERICAN HAVANA BROWN

In England in the 1950s, a self or solid-coloured variety, chocolate in colour, was bred from the Siamese. The Havana, as it came to be called because of its similarity in colour to the Havana cigar, was exported to the US in 1958.

In the US, the Havana was placed in a breeding program and gradually an altogether different variety from the British Havana emerged. It was officially recognised and named in North America as Havana Brown. This breed is not allowed to be placed in a breeding program with the British Havana, and if kittens from the British Havana are introduced into North America, they have to be re-registered as Chestnut Brown Foreign in order to avoid confusion.

The Havana Brown has a long svelte body, set on slim legs, with the hind ones being longer than the forelegs. The tail is long. The eyes are almond-shaped and yellowish-green in colour, the ears are large, wide-set and rounded at the tip, and the coat is short, glossy and soft. The coat colour is an even, solid mahogany brown.

Havanas are playful, sociable and elegant. Their voice is a soft cry. They are home loving, affectionate and intelligent pets.

## BURMESE

In North Amercia in 1930, Joseph Thompson set up a breeding program when he brought back from Burma what is now known as a Tonkinese. He mated it with a Siamese, and in the litter were some dark brown kittens, which, when later mated together, bred true to type. They were accepted for registration as Burmese by the CFA.

*Note the beautiful golden eyes typical of the Cream Burmese.*

*A Cream Burmese.*

*A Brown Burmese.*

After World War II, some Burmese were imported into Britain and a breeding program was set up there. Some small differences have appeared between the Burmese breed in the US and the UK. The American Burmese is rounder in the body, head, eyes and feet than its British counterpart.

The Burmese is a medium-sized cat, heavier than it looks, with a straight tail of medium length and slender legs, the forelegs being slightly longer than the hindlegs. The head is rounded, the ears wide-set, of medium size and tilting slightly forward. The eyes are wide-set and slanted. The wedge-shaped face is not as accentuated as it is in the Siamese.

By a process of selective breeding, the original brown (sable) Burmese, with its short, glossy, close-lying coat, has given rise to a whole range of other colours, including blue, chocolate, red, cream, tortoiseshell, champagne and platinum.

The Burmese is an elegant-looking cat, affectionate, playful, intelligent, easy going and happy in a family situation.

### COMMON DOMESTIC CROSSBREED

While this kind of crossbreed is not a pedigree cat, often one will be seen that has some characteristics of a pedigree. There are probably more of these kinds of cats in the world than any other. They come in all kinds of patterns and markings, types and colours. Some veterinarians believe crossbreeds are hardier and less subject to disease than pedigree cats.

They are affectionate, placid, relatively undemanding and make ideal family pets. Possibly the best source for obtaining one is a neighbourhood family whose healthy crossbreed ('tabby' or 'moggy') has had kittens. Knowing the mother and perhaps the father of the kittens, you will have some idea of how your choice will look and behave when it matures.

### EGYPTIAN MAU

The Egyptian Mau is said to be descended from the sacred cats of ancient Egypt. Statues of cats made during the time of the Pharaohs and preserved in the Louvre and British Museum have a marking on their forehead which resembles an 'M' or 'scarab', similar to the marking on the forehead of the present-day Mau.

The Egyptian Mau was first imported into the US in 1953. It is of medium size, well muscled and a graceful mover. The head is rounded and wedge-shaped, the ears are large and pointed, the eyes are almond-shaped, slanted and light gooseberry-green

*Common domestic crossbreeds come in many colours, with different patterns and markings.*

*An Egyptian Mau.*

in colour, and the tail is of medium length.

The Mau has some markings similar to the cross-bred tabby: the 'M' or 'scarab' on the forehead, frown marks between the ears, mascara lines on the cheeks, necklaces on the upper chest and some bars and bands on the legs and tail. Its unique marking is random spots of different size and shape, which should be separate and distinct. There are five coloured varieties — Silver, Bronze, Smoke, Pewter and Black.

The Egyptian Mau is quieter vocally than the Siamese. It is friendly when it gets to know you and accepts the lead when taken out for a walk.

### HIMALAYAN (US) — LONGHAIRED COLOURPOINT (UK)

Originally, the Himalayan was bred by mating a Persian with a Siamese. Its breeding was developed further by mating Himalayan with Himalayan to produce a true breed, Persian in type but with the colour pattern of the Siamese. It is a breed that is progressively becoming more popular.

In the US, the Himalayan, as it is known, was first registered in 1957 by the CFA. In the UK, where it is known as the Colourpoint Persian or Longhaired Colourpoint, it was first registered in 1955 by the GCCF. Present-day colour varieties include colour points of seal, blue, chocolate, lilac, red, cream, tabby and tortoiseshell. All Himalayans have deep blue eyes.

The temperament of the Himalayan or Colourpoint Persian is placid, affectionate, playful and intelligent. Vocally, it is somewhere between the Persian and the Siamese. It needs to be groomed daily.

In general, the Himalayan has the body build of the Persian, the colouring of the Siamese and a temperament that is the best of both.

*Himalayans have deep-blue eyes.*

*The Himalayan is of the same body type as the Persian.*

*A Blue-Point Himalayan.*

*A Korat.*

*A brown tabby classic Maine Coon.*

*A Birman.*

*Maine Coon kittens.*

## KORAT

A rare breed, the Korat originated in Thailand, where it is referred to as the 'good luck' cat. A pair was imported into the US as late as 1959. A careful breeding program was then begun, and in 1966 the CFA accepted the Korat as an official breed.

It is muscular and has a medium-sized, semi-cobby body. The coat is short to medium, fine, glossy and close to the body. The hair colour is solid blue, tipped with silver, which gives it a silvery sheen. The head is heart-shaped, with large rounded ears and large prominent eyes that are brilliant green-amber in colour, round when open and slanted when partly or fully closed.

The Korat is a gentle, even-tempered, intelligent cat, which moves quietly and carefully, and does not talk much. It is an excellent companion.

## MAINE COON

It is believed that the Maine Coon developed from mating between local American domestic cats and longhaired cats brought back to Maine (US) by sailors.

It is a large cat, well proportioned, muscular, with a long body and strong legs. The tail is long and bushy. The head is of medium size, with large, high-set, silky-tufted ears, and the large eyes are wide-set and slant upwards towards the ears. The eye colour is green, gold or copper, with some white cats having blue or odd eyes.

The coat is full and shaggy, silky and smooth, but not as long as the typical longhaired breed. For this reason, the Maine Coon is often referred to as a 'semi-longhair'. The coat colour covers a wide range, somewhat similar to the Persian.

It is an alert, intelligent and clever cat, that shows great affection for its owners.

## MANX

The Manx cat comes from the Isle of Man, located in the Irish Sea, and is known as the cat without a tail. But this is not quite true, as some are born with a tail and are called 'Longies', others are born with a vestigial tail or stump and are known as 'Stumpies', while the standard ideal is born without a tail and is known as the 'Rumpie'.

It has a round head with full cheeks, a rounded muzzle and wide-set, medium-to-long ears. Its characteristic rabbit-like, hopping gait is brought about by a combination of hindlegs that are much longer than the short front legs, a definite rounded rump and a short, arched back associated with a spinal curvature. Its short coat is well padded as its undercoat is soft and thick. The Manx is bred in a wide variety of colours, somewhat similar to the Persian (see page 40).

The Manx cat is affectionate, playful, sturdy, intelligent and a recognised good family pet.

*A cream tabby Manx.*

*Persians have a large head with full cheeks.*

## PERSIAN

One of the more popular breeds, the Persian is said to have its origins in Persia (Iran).

The Persian is of large compact build, its body described as cobby or boxy, being set on legs that are short and sturdy. Its head is large, rounded and with full cheeks. The ears are small and the eyes are round and large. Its tail is short and bushy. The Persian is well covered with long silky hair that stands away from the body. A full ruff frames its face and continues down to between the front legs.

In the UK, the general practice is to group the Persians as Longhaireds; in the US, the name Persian is generally in official use.

In the UK and US, the basic self-coloureds or solid-coloureds respectively that have been accepted by the foremost registering bodies (GCCF and CFA) are Black, White, Blue, Red and Cream. The GCCF has also accepted Chocolate and Lilac. The White is unique in so far as it may have copper eyes, blue eyes or odd eyes, i.e. copper and blue.

The non-self coloureds (UK) or parti-coloureds (US) are classified in a number of groups and varieties. There are the Bicoloured Persians (e.g. Black and White), the Tabbies (e.g. Silver Tabby), the Tortoiseshells (including the Shaded or Cameo varieties), and the Calico Persian (US) which is known as the Tortoiseshell and White in the UK.

Of all the Persian or Longhaired varieties, the Chinchilla is the most photogenic. Its pure white hair is lightly tipped with black on the back, sides, head, ears and tail, giving it a sparkling silvery-white appearance. The nose tip is brick red and the large, round eyes are emerald to aquamarine.

The Peke-face Persian was developed in the 1930s in the US. Its face resembles that of the Pekinese dog. In the US they are recognised in two colours — Red and Red Tabby.

The Persian needs grooming every day as its long silky hair is subject to matting, grass seeds, burrs and the like. Regular grooming is necessary if the coat is to be kept in good condition.

Some Persians can be temperamental and react angrily when crossed or held against their will. Normally they are placid, affectionate, a good companion for the elderly and tolerant of children. They are home loving and quiet to the point of appearing reserved.

*A Persian in repose, showing the short, bushy tail.*

*Of the long-haired varieties, the Chinchilla is the most photogenic.*

*A Chinchilla shows its characteristic brick-red nose tip and large, round eyes.*

*A Blue Persian.*

*A Colourpoint Ragdoll.*

## RAGDOLL

Developed in the US, the Ragdoll is much like the Birman, except that it is larger and heavier, and when held in the arms is limp and floppy just like a rag doll.

It is a semi-longhair, classified in three colour varieties by some American associations: Colourpoint, Mitted and Bicolour Ragdoll.

The Ragdoll is placid and fearless, which often is a source of danger.

It is a rare breed outside the US and is not recognised for showing in Britain.

## REX — CORNISH AND DEVON

Two types of the Rex cat have been named after the English counties, Cornwall and Devon, in which they first appeared in the 1950s. Rex mutations have also appeared in Germany, North America and Holland. The German and Oregon Rexes have similar coats to the Cornish Rex, whereas the Dutch Rex's coat is different.

At first it was thought that the Devon and Cornish Rex coats were each due to the same gene, but later this was proved to be incorrect and they were recognised as two different types.

The main difference between the two is in their fur. The coat of the Cornish Rex is close-lying, short, dense and curly or deeply waved. The coat of the Devon Rex is thinner, shorter, wavy and soft. The fur on the Cornish Rex's tail is well covered and curly, whereas in the case of the Devon Rex its tail fur is short and not as dense. The Devon Rex also has a short nose, ears which because of their shape are often called bat wings and a face that is described as pixie-like. On the other hand, the Cornish Rex has more of a Roman nose, ears that also may be described as bat wings, and a medium wedge-shaped head.

*A brown Cornish Rex.*

*A white Cornish Rex.*

A medium-length, muscular body, with long, fine legs and long, tapering tail completes the picture of the Rex. The Rex comes in a wide range of colours.

The Rex cat is relatively quiet. It is intelligent, inquisitive, easy to train, but some are highly strung and inclined to be sulky. It is an ideal pet for indoors as it does not shed much hair.

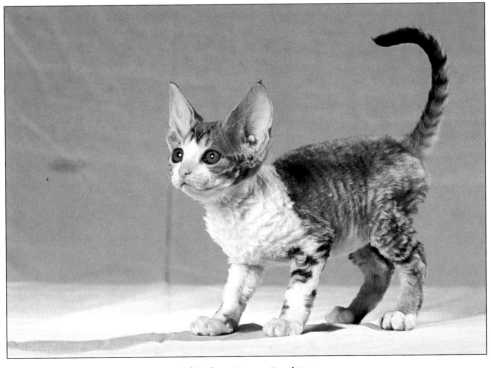

*A bicolour Devon Rex kitten.*

*Note the vivid green eyes
characteristic of the Russian Blue.*

## RUSSIAN BLUE

When the Russian Blue was introduced into England and America, other blue cats were to be found in those countries, as well as in Malta, Spain and elsewhere.

The Russian Blue is a graceful cat, attractive in appearance. It is of foreign type, with a short, wedge-shaped head, long legs, long slender body, long tapering tail and oriental eyes. The eyes are a vivid green in colour, wide apart and almond-shaped to satisfy British standards, or rounded to satisfy American standards. Its double coat of an even shade of blue is short, thick, soft and silky. In some cats the hair is silver-tipped, giving the coat a silvery sheen.

The Russian Blue is shy and gentle, yet friendly, and is spoken of as an excellent pet for flats and apartments. It has a soft voice and when walking appears as if it is walking on its tiptoes.

## SCOTTISH FOLD

This shorthaired, stocky cat, with its distinctive folded ears, first appeared in a litter in 1961 in Scotland.

The Scottish Fold was imported into the US, and there a selective breeding program of mating the Scottish Fold with the American Shorthair (see page 49) has produced a breed in a wide range of coat colours and patterns that was fully recognised by the CFA in 1978. It has a full, round face and generally is similar to the American Shorthair.

The Scottish Fold has a particular appeal to its devotees and steadily is becoming more popular as a pet.

*A Russian Blue.*

*The adult Scottish Fold has a stocky build.*

*A Scottish Fold kitten.*

*A Silver Tabby American Shorthair: a Classic variety of Tabby.*

*This queen and kitten are typical of the Shaded Silver variety of American Shorthair.*

*A Russian Blue.*

*A British Blue.*

*A British Blue.*

### SHORTHAIRS
#### American and British Shorthair

It is believed that these two similar yet different breeds have come from the same stock, i.e. the domestic cats of Britain, which arrived in America with the Pilgrims. While both have common characteristics, there are some differences.

The American Shorthair has a slightly longer nose, its head is not as full, nor is the hair as soft as the British Shorthair. The coat colours and markings cover a wider range and the legs are slightly longer than those of the British Shorthair. In other respects, both types are of strong muscular build, with strong legs and a medium-length tail. The head is broad and rounded with full cheeks, and the large eyes and medium-sized ears are set well apart.

The hair colour of the British Shorthair ranges from Self coloureds, Black, Blue, Cream, White to Tabby to Tortoiseshell to Bicolour, to Blue Cream to Spotted. The American Shorthair is registered in the same coloured varieties with the addition of others such as Red Self, Chinchilla, Shaded Silver, Black Smoke, Blue Smoke, Cameo, Smoke, Blue and Cream Tabby.

The British or American Shorthair is not to be regarded in the same category as the common domestic crossbred shorthaired cat.

The British and American Shorthair are known as ideal pets, noted for their intelligence, sturdiness, gentleness, affection, energy, and being easy to groom.

#### British Blue

The most popular British Shorthair is the British Blue, which is also very popular in the US. It is said to be closest to the official standard for the British Shorthair breed. Its colour is light to medium blue, with no markings or other colour. Its eyes are copper, yellow or orange.

The British Blue is a friendly cat, quiet, intelligent and attractive.

#### Colourpoint Shorthair

This breed was developed in the US by mating a Siamese with an American Shorthair.

The object in mating the Siamese and American Shorthair was to extend the range of colour points beyond the four classic ones — Seal, Blue, Chocolate and Lilac. The objective was achieved and various colour points are to be found within each of the three categories of the breed — namely, Solid Colour Point, Lynx Point and Parti-colour Point.

The Colourpoint Shorthair is attractive, friendly and a very good pet.

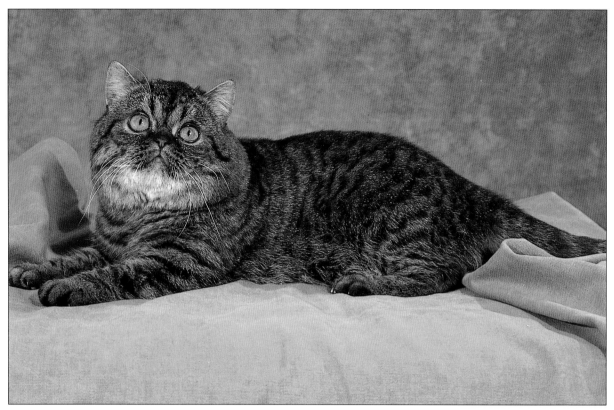

*A Brown Mackerel Exotic Shorthair.*

### Exotic Shorthair

The Exotic Shorthair is not to be confused with the American Shorthair. It has resulted from crossbreeding the Persian with the American Domestic Shorthair, which was the former name given to the American Shorthair. There are now two standards and classes in the US, one for the Exotic Shorthair and one for the American Shorthair.

*A Tabby Oriental.*

### Foreign or Oriental Shorthair

This type includes the Abyssinian, Burmese, Havanas, Rex, Foreign White, Foreign Lilac, Russian Blue, Korat and Siamese. Generally speaking, they all have similar streamlined bodies, with narrow wedge-shaped heads, large alert ears, oriental eyes, long legs and long thin tail.

Grooming is easy and a silk or velvet cloth will give a high sheen to the coat.

### Tabby Oriental

Many domestic, shorthaired cats are referred to as 'Tabbies', but in the strict sense their stripes and markings do not comply with the standards laid down for the pedigreed Tabby Shorthair. The standard of markings applies not only to the Shorthair, but also to the Longhair or Persian Tabby. Of course, in the latter the markings are not so evident because of the long hair.

The accepted standard pattern of markings in the Shorthair are usually referred to as classic, mackerel or spotted. The true mackerel is not so common, the spotted recently has become popular, and the classic is the most common to be seen. Three recognised classic tabby shorthairs are the Silver, Red and Brown Tabby. The Red is more commonly referred to as the Ginger or Marmalade Tabby. In the US, the Blue, Cameo and Cream

*A Foreign White.*

*A Black Oriental kitten.*

*A Silver Tabby American Shorthair. Note the 'scarab' and mascara lines.*

Tabby are also recognised.

The classic pattern of markings, if clearly defined, can be easily identified: the letter 'M' or 'scarab' on the forehead with lines running from it over the head to the shoulder; mascara lines about the eye and cheek; necklaces or mayoral chains about the neck and chest; bracelets on the legs and tail; butterfly wings across the shoulders; oyster shells on each flank, encircled by one or more rings; a line from the butterfly to the base of the tail, running parrallel on each side of the spine; side markings should be the same on both sides.

*A Seal Point Siamese.*

## SIAMESE

The first Siamese to leave their native Siam appeared in England, France and America in the late nineteenth century.

The Siamese is an attractive cat that commands your attention with its intelligent, alert, wedge-shaped head, its refined, streamlined body, its long slender legs and its short, close-lying glossy coat. Its colour adds to its attractiveness. Take, for example, the popular Siamese Seal Point, which is probably the most favoured by owners. Its eyes are the characteristic deep blue, slanting and almond-shaped; its body coat is cream shading to a pale warm fawn on the back; and its seal brown points (i.e. mask, ears, legs, paws, tail) stand out in pleasing contrast. Other examples are the Siamese Blue Point, Siamese Chocolate Point and Siamese Lilac Point.

With the growth in popularity of the Siamese, other varieties were developed by breeders, including the Tabby Point, Tortie Point, Red Point, and self or solid-coloured varieties. In the US, some cat fancy associations, such as the CFA, class the tabby and red series as Colourpoint Shorthairs (as does New South Wales), but the ACFA classifies them as Siamese.

The Siamese is lively, agile, intelligent, affectionate and sociable, but may prove aggressive if aroused. It is a climber, known for its loud, persistent cry.

*A Red Point Siamese.*

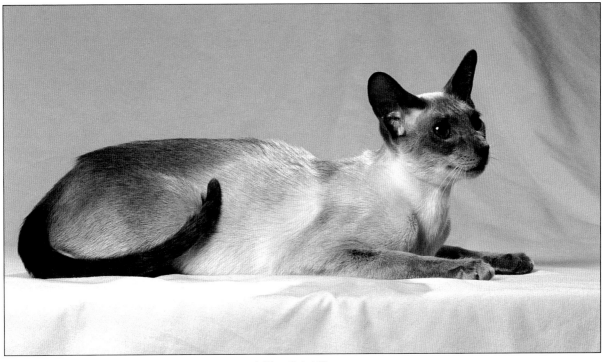

*A Blue Point Siamese.*

*A Cinnamon Somali.*

*This cat has the warm brown coat and dark chocolate markings typical of the Natural Mink Tonkinese.*

*A Somali kitten.*

*A Himalayan*.

## SOMALI

The Somali is a longhaired Abyssinian, first bred and developed in Canada as a separate breed. It is of foreign type.

The head is wedge-shaped, with large, wide apart, pricked ears and large, almond-shaped, expressive eyes, either amber, hazel or gold in colour. The longhaired coat of the Somali is of medium length, fine and dense, and is accepted in two colours, Ruddy or Red. The coat is ticked, which adds a glowing quality to the colour.

The attractive Somali is a lively, alert cat, easy to handle, quiet and affectionate.

## TONKINESE

The Tonkinese was developed in the US from a crossmating between a Siamese and Burmese. When Tonkinese are mated, they will produce Tonkinese or throw back to true Siamese or Burmese. The Tonkinese is of foreign type. It was recognised as a breed in the US in the 1980s, but has not been recognised by all associations in the UK.

The Tonkinese has a medium-sized, lithe, muscular body. The head is a modified wedge shape; the ears, set wide apart, are broad at the base; the eyes are almond-shaped, wide apart and blue-green in colour. The legs are long and slim, and the tail is long and tapering.

The fur is short, close-lying and soft. The colour of the five varieties recognised in the US are warm brown, bluish-grey, ruddy brown, warm beige and soft silver. Their points are not as distinctly defined as they are in the Siamese breed.

The Tonkinese are inquisitive, outgoing and affectionate pets.

## TURKISH VAN

This breed was imported into England in 1955 from the Lake Van district in Turkey. In 1969, the GCCF officially recognised it as a Turkish cat, which is often referred to as the Turkish Van.

It has a distinctive colouring: a long, chalk white, silky fur, auburn markings on the face, and

*A Turkish Van.*

a feathery auburn tail. Some Turkish Vans have an auburn patch on the back. Other varieties being developed are Cream and White, Black and White, and Tortoiseshell and White. The nose pad and the inside of the ears is a delicate shade of pink. Its winter coat is very full, but in summer it loses most of its coat and looks almost like a shorthair.

The Turkish Van's head is short and wedge-shaped, the eyes are large, round and amber, the ears are large and upright, the body is muscular and long, and the legs are of medium length.

The Turkish Van is reputed to be fond of swimming. It is attractive-looking, intelligent, and an affectionate companion.

*Many forms of play are an expression of the hunting instinct.*

# BEHAVIOUR AND TRAINING

***Behaviour****: Aggression — Body language and facial expressions — Clawing and scratching — Grass chewing — Grooming — Hunting — Sleeping — Vocal language — Territory marking — Toilet habits — Wool sucking — Behavioural problems*
***Training****: Litter box or tray — Food and water bowl — Sleeping basket — Clawing post or board — Door flap — Cat and dog relationship —*

## BEHAVIOUR

The behaviour of a cat is influenced by a variety of factors, including breed, learning experience, intelligence, prevailing environment and sex, i.e. whether it is a male (tom), female (queen) or desexed (neuter). The cat is very individualistic in its behaviour, yet it exhibits certain behavioural patterns that are characteristic of cats in general.

### Aggression

Feline aggression ranges from a variety of threats to actual physical conflict. The threats may take the form of a simple chase, body language, facial expressions and vocalisation, examples of which are ears back and flattened, staring, body hair erect, mouth open with teeth bared, growling, hissing and snarling. The physical conflict may be just boxing with the front paws or it may take on a more serious and vicious form of biting, scratching and wounding.

Fortunately, most aggressive confrontations do not end in physical conflict. Before that stage is reached, one cat usually intimidates the other into submission and is recognised as the victor. Normally, the winner will walk away or sit and groom itself, while the loser retires from the scene or lies submissively, lowering its ears and curling in its head.

Whatever form the aggression takes, it may be triggered off by any one of a number of causes, including a challenge for dominance, defence of territory, fear, play, desire for sex and others not so easy to identify.

One of the most common causes of fighting between males is to establish dominance. When cats live in a group, the social order is most complex and difficult to unravel. There appears to be no rigid linear hierarchy; i.e. no tom is No 1 at the top and dominant in all matters, followed by No 2 and so on down the order. It is generally thought that dominance by any one cat over another applies only to the situation that has been in dispute; in another situation the dominance of the victor over the vanquished might be reversed.

The other main cause of confrontation between cats is defence of territory. This may occur when a new cat is introduced into a home where there is already a resident cat, when a strange cat invades the resident cat's territory, or when kittens reach behavioural maturity.

If the resident cat is immediately aggressive

*Aggression: flattened ears and staring eyes.*

*Defensive aggression.*

*Aggressive play.*

towards a newly introduced cat, keep them separated so that they do not see one another. Allow the two cats to meet gradually over the next two to three weeks, at first just by hearing one another meowing or eating their food, then by being allowed a brief look at one another, and finally by letting them sniff each other's living space in the home. Gradually increase the time of these exposures until each cat is happy in the other's company. If this ploy fails, you will have to let the cats establish their own territories, each remaining aloof from the other, with no sign of aggression unless one invades the other's territory. Never try to force the two cats together, as it only consolidates continued aggression and does not bring about reconciliation.

Fear sets up a protective mechanism in cats which takes the form of running away, hiding or defensive aggression. The fear may be induced by such experiences as pain incurred in an accident, a fright from a loud noise or another cat, or its food or kittens being threatened.

When a cat is defensively aggressive it will crouch on the ground, draw in its head and flatten its ears backwards; the pupils will dilate and the body hair will be erect. As the enemy approaches, the defensive cat may roll over onto its back ready

to deliver a paw blow. Biting and scratching may follow. Other defensively aggressive cats may threaten by hunching the back with hair 'standing on end' and hissing and spitting.

Play aggression is linked to the hunting instinct of cats. The urge to paw, stalk, pounce, leap and bite moving prey is sometimes misdirected towards the movement of another cat, the moving feet and legs of its owner or waving curtains and so on. To redirect the cat's attention to more acceptable diversions, it is suggested that the owner play more frequently with the cat (e.g. with a toy felt mouse attached to a piece of string) and provide it with some moving play toys such as a tennis or ping pong ball.

If a queen is not ready to accept a tom's advances, she will move away or perhaps turn on him with a snarl and a flurry of paws. She will distance herself from him if he persists with his advances. At times it may appear that the queen is being hurt by the tom, but there is no cause for alarm as it is just a natural episode in the mating game.

Aggressive kittens usually grow into aggressive cats, so it is best not to choose an aggressive kitten as a pet. If you are in the presence of an aggressive cat or you are uncertain of a cat's attitude towards

*Cats communicate with body language.*

*Cats love to explore the neighbourhood.*

*Cats communicating.*

you, talk to it and try to assess its degree of relaxation before attempting to touch it with the bare hand. Be cautious, otherwise it might redirect its aggression to you. Reprimand an aggressive cat by tapping it on the nose with a folded paper, but do not hurt it. An alternative is to remove the cat from the scene by grabbing it at the right moment by the scruff of the neck, with your hand and arm protected. Usually a cat freezes for a few moments when grabbed in this way — a throwback reaction to the time when it was a kitten and its mother carried it by the scruff of the neck. Other methods suggested for cooling off an aggressive cat are to throw a rug or coat over its head, to make a loud noise or sound, or to spray it with water using an atomiser or water pistol.

### Body language and facial expressions

Apart from communicating with each other and with humans through vocalisation (meowing, purring, snarling and hissing), cats also communicate with body language. For example, sometimes a cat will walk up to you, arch its hindquarters, point its tail upwards with the tip waving to and fro, then move rather stiffly towards you, to rub its head, body and tail about your legs, even curling the tail around them, and perhaps purring. A greeting of

happiness in seeing you is the message being conveyed. At the same time the cat is scent-marking you, to stake out a claim on you so to speak. Scent glands are located along the tail, on the forehead and about the mouth of the cat.

An alert, self-assured cat usually walks confidently, with its tail stretched out backwards and the

*A cat ready to attack.*

63

pupils of the eyes narrowed and slit-like. Whereas a nervous or defensive-aggressive cat usually shows an erect, bristled tail which, as the aggressive component becomes more compelling, may be lowered and pointed towards the ground, the pupils correspondingly becoming rounded and enlarged. The ears are also strong indicators of the cat's attitude. If the ears are erect and pointed towards the sound stimulus, it indicates an alert cat; however, if they are swivelled, pulled downwards to point backwards, then a strong defensive attitude is indicated.

Have you ever noticed what a cat does when it bares its teeth? This is an aggressive, offensive act, but it is accompanied by the defensive act of snarling, growling or hissing. It is an interesting exercise for an owner to study the body and facial language of his/her cat, and to compare observations with those made by other cat owners.

### Clawing and scratching

The cat's claws serve a practical purpose. They are used for climbing, hunting, defending, attacking and territory marking. Sometimes the claws become too long and the old sheaths have to be shed, especially if the cat is a house dweller and is seldom in the garden. The claws can be trimmed at home if you have a pair of nail clippers and the means and ability to restrain the cat. Otherwise, it is a case for the veterinarian.

The indoor cat should be provided with a clawing post or board (see 'Training', page 69); otherwise it will attempt to keep its nails trimmed by clawing the carpet, furniture and so on.

### Grass chewing

Cats sometimes eat grass, particularly fresh shoots. Reasons commonly put forward are that they have a natural need for fibre, or they have a vitamin deficiency, or perhaps they want to vomit because of a stomach or intestinal problem and they know that grass is an emetic. While the sight of a cat vomiting a hair ball or partly digested food may be disturbing to the owner, keep in mind that it is the cat's natural way of correcting a health problem. Try to avoid using dangerous chemical sprays on grass or plants that you notice the cat eats now and then.

### Grooming

Cats are essentially clean animals and spend a fair amount of time each day in cleaning themselves with their tongue. In the process, the barbed tongue catches some of the dead hair, which may be swallowed, eventually forming a hair ball in the

stomach and presenting a health problem (see 'Hair Ball', page 171).

Sometimes cats may resort to grooming other cats or themselves for psychological reasons, such as to relieve tension developed in a stress situation or to escape from boredom.

Apart from the cat grooming itself, there are certain grooming practices which the cat owner should adopt (see 'Health care (grooming)', page 81, for further information).

### Hunting

This characteristic is stronger in some cats than in others. That is why some cats are better vermin catchers. The hunting characteristic has been bred into the cat over thousands of years. It is a primitive instinct or drive which may be difficult to control. Your veterinarian can give help in curbing the hunting drive in your cat by administering drugs or by neutering.

Many of the games and activities that kittens engage in with one another or with their owner are

*A cat hunts for vermin in the garbage.*

*Kittens at play.*

*Hunting.*

*Stalking prey.*

an expression of or provide opportunity for developing the hunting characteristic. If you watch kittens playing with one another or with a ball or a piece of wool or string, you will notice how they crouch, stalk stealthily, lunge, leap or pounce and paw, all of which are basic skills used in the hunting process.

A cat out hunting may return with its prey, dead or alive, and lay it at your feet or on your doorstep. If it is still partly alive, the cat may toy with it before making the final kill. Do not be alarmed, as the cat is just re-enacting the primitive drive that has been bred into it over thousands of years. To you the situation may be abhorrent, but to the cat it is just a natural, instinctive act. You may scold the cat if it is caught in the act, but do not punish it, either during or after the event.

There are several ways in which you can try to curb your cat's hunting drive. Birds can be protected to some extent by placing a collar with a bell attached around the cat's neck. An elasticised collar stretches if it catches on a branch or some

*On the prowl.*

such obstacle and will allow the cat in most cases to struggle free. Keeping yourself hidden and squirting the cat with water while it is actually stalking or playing with its prey might turn what normally is to the cat a satisfying experience into a horrible one. Repetition of this scenario a number of times may implant in the cat's mind the notion that hunting is not a satisfying experience, and so it will be less inclined to hunt in the future. Again, if the kitten for the first six months of its life is not exposed to imitating its mother's hunting characteristics, including playing with, killing and perhaps eating prey, the theory is that its primitive urge to hunt will be more or less submerged.

Caged birds in an outside aviary should be made secure by building a double-wired cavity wall for the cage, assuming the roof is of solid material. If birds are kept inside the home, the cage should be placed out of reach of the cat. Likewise, fish ponds inside or outside the home should be suitably covered.

### Sleeping

Cats engage in two kinds of sleeping — deep sleep and light sleep (catnapping). A cat needs only about four hours' deep sleep per day. In this state of sleep, the cat is very relaxed. Even so, there may be signs of movement such as trembling and jerking, in conjunction with rapid eye movement. In humans, rapid eye movement in the sleeping state is indicative of dreaming. Whether or not cats really dream is an unanswered question. In the early stages of their lives, kittens engage in deep sleep only.

Cats sleep lightly or 'catnap' at frequent intervals for short periods of time. The cat in this state is not fully relaxed; its hearing sense is at the ready, and it appears to awaken at any moment, fully alert.

### Vocal language

Cats make a range of different sounds, each with a different meaning. Some breeds vocalise more frequently and more loudly than others. For example, the loudness of the Siamese breed is in strong contrast to the quietness of the Abyssinian. Some owners are able to recognise the call of the female cat when it is in season and ready to mate, the growl of the tom when in a fight situation, the purr of any cat when it seems to be contented and the meow of the attention-seeking or hungry cat. But most owners fail to recognise the full range of their cat's vocalisation and its meanings. This could be the subject of an interesting exercise for all concerned.

### Territory marking

A cat may reserve for itself a certain area or territory. Other cats may be accepted into it, allowed to pass through it, or are rejected from it. A strange cat is usually allowed to pass through the territory, provided it does so discreetly and presents no threat to the resident cat. Rejection usually takes the form of the resident cat running aggressively towards the intruder with the intention of intimidating it and causing it to retire. There the confrontation ends. If the intruder stands its ground, the resident cat will attack it, striking with its forepaws. Complete physical aggression seldom takes place.

The tom defines its territory by pointing his penis backwards and spraying urine on objects such as a wall or tree to mark the boundary. The urine odour is particularly strong, and many cat owners find it objectionable, especially if the tom has marked his territory inside or around the house.

The queen and neuter also mark their territory by scenting objects, the scent being expressed from glands in the region of the forehead, cheeks, lips, anus, tail and paws. If the queen or neuter is under stress, it may spray urine to reinforce its territory marking. They do not establish a territory as large as the tom's.

If an owner or visitor introduces a strange cat into the household, the stranger may be accepted or rejected by the resident cat. If the stranger is dominant, then the resident cat may have to compromise, whereby new boundaries are set up, allowing each cat to be independent and aloof. (See 'Aggression', page 59, for advice on the introduction of another cat into the household.)

### Toilet habits

One reason for choosing a cat as a pet is its cleanliness. When defecating, the cat usually makes a shallow hollow in loose soil, using it as a toilet bowl, and when finished, covers the faeces with loose soil and debris.

When urinating, the tom's penis points backwards. The urine is particularly pungent due to the presence of chemicals called pheromones in the urine. The queen urinates to the ground. Her urine contains pheromones during the period when she is ready for mating, i.e. when she is in season, on heat, or calling for a male. The pheromones give the queen's urine a particular odour which tells the sniffing tom that she is ready for his advances.

The litter tray or box (see 'Training', page 69) is an essential piece of equipment, particularly if the cat is housebound and does not have free access to the garden.

### Wool sucking

This habit begins as a behavioural characteristic of kittens if they have access to wool, whether it be in the form of a ball of wool or woollen mix garments and curtains. Kittens lick the wool, play with it in their mouth and sometimes swallow it, causing a health problem.

Several theories are advanced to explain why kittens engage in wool sucking. It appears to be more prevalent in the Siamese breed, so it is suggested that it may be genetic in origin. Another theory is that it is due to suckling deprivation when the kittens are weaned. This theory is linked to the fact that wool contains lanolin, which gives off an odour similar to the mother's teats when suckling her kittens.

### Behavioural problems

Besides the behavioural patterns that have been outlined, there are some forms of behaviour that are not common to all cats but which from time to time may be observed in individuals. Examples of such behaviour are moodiness, refusing to eat, going into hiding, a disastrous change in toilet habits, and being destructive when left alone in the home. These forms of behaviour are sparked off by some kind of disturbance to the cat, which may stem from environmental, psychological or physiological causes, or even from causes that cannot be identified. Once the cause is known, an intervention program designed by a veterinarian or an animal behaviour therapist may help to restore the cat's behaviour to normality.

## TRAINING

The cat is not as domesticated as the dog. It is more independent and shows a more instinctive reaction to many situations. Superficially it is tame and

*It may be the lanolin in wool that is so attractive to cats.*

*Cats love to play.*

domesticated, but below the surface the wild animal is still there.

When training your cat, keep the following guidelines in mind:

• Cats vary in intelligence and temperament. Some will accept and cope with a higher level of training than others.

• Begin your training with the kitten. It is difficult to teach an old cat new tricks.

• Short, single command words are more easily understood and are less confusing. The basic vocabulary of words that you might choose from to use with your kitten are: 'out', 'down', 'no', 'come', a single-word name, and a praise-word or short phrase such as 'good' or 'good girl'.

• Always praise correct behaviour when it is taking place. Use the same praise word or phrase each time and accompany it with gentle stroking or a titbit.

• Always use the same command word for a particular form of behaviour; e.g. 'down' is always used to tell the cat to get off your lap or off some article of furniture. 'No' is always used to stop or deter a cat from doing something that you do not want it to do, eg. clawing the carpet, climbing the curtains, and so on.

• Command words should be spoken firmly and with authority. They may be accompanied by an arm movement or by some other physical expression.

• The command word should be given at the time of the misbehaviour, not ten minutes after. In some instances the command word may be accompanied by a gentle tap on the nose with rolled paper or by a squirt of water.

• Be patient, firm, kind, consistent, calm and authoritative in the training or education of your kitten.

• If you tolerate behaviour in your kitten which you consider is unacceptable in an adult cat, you are asking for trouble.

### Litter box or tray

The tray should be large enough to accommodate comfortably a fully grown cat. The sides should be about 8 cm (3 in) high to prevent the litter spilling over and it should be fitted with a plastic liner that can be removed with the soiled litter and replaced. The litter tray should be prepared and ready for the kitten when it is brought home. Place it in a convenient location where the kitten can see it and have access to it.

In the early days of the kitten's training, place it on the litter tray after each feed. Give praise if there is a result. Soon you will find the kitten going to the

tray without your help. If it does not, check the litter. If it is unclean, that may be the reason for the kitten not using it, although the smell of the kitten's urine in the litter often encourages it to use the litter tray again. Other reasons for the kitten not using the litter tray may be that it is placed in a busy area of the household, the kitten may have been punished when on the litter tray or the litter may be of a particular kind that the kitten does not like. The litter may vary in quality and kind. It can be in the form of wood chips, wood shavings, sand, paper, or one of several commercial varieties.

Pregnant women are advised not to touch the soiled litter, as there is a risk of their catching the disease toxoplasmosis (see page 169).

### Food and water bowl

Some kittens in their upbringing are given only milk to drink. Train your kitten to drink water by placing a water bowl, filled daily with fresh water, next to the food bowl within easy access.

### Sleeping basket

A sleeping basket or box which provides warmth and comfort for the kitten should be available for its use when it arrives home. Paper on the floor of the basket, together with a soft toy or two and a lukewarm water bottle wrapped in some soft material should be sufficient to keep the kitten warm during cold days and nights. Place the kitten in the basket every now and then, and it will soon be using it without any encouragement from you.

Cats like to sleep above floor level, so as the kitten grows, think of positioning the sleeping basket in an accessible, elevated site. Some cats will just not use a sleeping basket, so if your cat fits into that category you will just have to accept it.

The sleeping basket should be cleaned and aired regularly so that fleas and worm eggs will not be a problem.

### Clawing post or board

A clawing post is an upright piece of softwood about 5 cm x 5 cm x 30 cm (2 in x 2 in x 12 in) fitted onto a firm heavy base. A clawing board is a flat piece of softwood about 20 cm x 30 cm (8 in x 12 in). The post or the board is covered with carpet or some other suitable material.

Train the kitten to use the clawing post or board by gently but firmly taking its front legs and physically showing the kitten how to claw the carpet on the post or board. During the training process, if you notice the kitten clawing at the lounge suite, curtains, carpet and so on, take it immediately to the clawing post and repeat the

*A post for clawing and scratching.*

*A secure arrangement for a cat travelling in a car.*

process of showing the kitten how to use it. Give praise when it does so. If the kitten has ready access to the garden, you might decide to use some suitable tree as a clawing post to give the kitten the idea that there is an opportunity for clawing in the garden.

### Door flap

Many cat owners find it is convenient to cut a hole in the bottom of a door leading outside to allow the cat to go out or come into the home at will. It is usually covered by a two-hinged flap that swings in and out when the cat gives it a nudge. Most cats usually learn quite quickly how to use it. At first you will need to show the cat how to give it a nudge and pass through. Show the kitten from both sides of the door flap and give praise as it learns to pass through.

In allowing your cat the freedom to go out and come in, make sure that it is familiar with the garden outside and, if it is a queen, that it is not on heat. The door flap may allow a draught to come through, but this can be prevented by attaching a small locking device. Always secure the flap at night when the cat is safely inside, to prevent any stray cat from entering the home.

### Cat and dog relationship

If you have a dog, the new kitten or cat should be introduced to it, kindly and gently, with much praise, after a meal when both are drowsy and well nourished. When you are sure the moment is right, allow them to have minimal physical contact and

*A cat flap.*

70

*Taking a nap together.*

praise them lavishly. When you think a safe physical relationship is established, retire from the scene, but stand where you can watch unseen and quickly return to restore order if the relationship disintegrates.

In some cases a safe cat-dog relationship is never established. If you find this is the case in your home, you just have to accept it.

### Travelling

Never travel in the car with the cat sitting on your lap or on the seat. It could very easily become frightened and set up a dangerous situation. Use a cat cage or carry bag to contain the cat when travelling in a car, but do not use a cardboard box, as a cat in a state of terror may claw its way out. In some countries if you are driving alone in the car with your cat, it is an offence not to confine it to a carrier cage or basket. When travelling long distances, restrict the cat's food and water intake for a couple of hours before beginning your trip; for short distances, such as travelling to the shopping centre, it does not matter. A cat can go for twelve hours without food and water, and no harm is done. Of course in hot weather, the cat will need to have fluid (water or milk) more frequently. If

your cat is prone to travel sickness (vomiting), see page 171.

If your cat is not used to car travel, first sit with it in the car, making it feel at home by talking to it, stroking it and giving it a few titbits. Repeat this procedure until you feel that it is relaxed. The next step is to take it for a short drive around the block, talking to it and praising it. If it is relaxed at the end of the drive, take it for a longer drive next time, but remember to always take it in a cat cage or carry bag.

On a long trip, some nervous cats may need a tranquilliser to travel comfortably. Consult your veterinarian for advice.

Before attempting to transport your cat interstate or overseas, you should contact your local Department of Agriculture or Health to find out about quarantine laws and regulations. Some transport companies specialise in the movement of cats and dogs interstate and overseas. They should be able to advise you about the quarantine laws and regulations of the specific country or state that you are sending the cat to, and can provide you with information on the pick-up and delivery of the cat and how it is transported. Insurance cover and responsibilities of parties involved should also be discussed.

71

*Cats have ways of making their needs known.*

# HEALTH CARE

*Feeding and diet — Grooming — Teeth care — Vaccination program — Worms and worming — The elderly cat*

The old adage 'Prevention is better than cure' applies just as well to cats as it does to humans. A healthy, happy cat results from the owner establishing certain routines, some carried out on a daily basis, others periodically.

Any preventative program of health care for your cat, if it is to be positive, must involve the veterinary surgeon. It is a good idea to contact the veterinarian of your choice to establish some understanding about such matters as hours of attendance, night calls and what to do in an emergency. Then, if your first visit to your veterinarian is a hasty one, perhaps arising from an emergency, you are well prepared for it. Get to know your veterinarian as he/she can be most helpful, not only in the services provided but also in the advice offered.

The following guidelines for daily and periodic cat care are set out for owners, breeders and others who show a serious concern for the cat's health.

## FEEDING AND DIET

It is very important at an early age (eight to ten weeks) to expose your kitten to a wide variety of foods so that it does not become addicted to any one type, which, unknown to the owner, may be one that does not cover the cat's complete nutritional requirements and might put its health at risk. Once a cat develops an addiction for a certain type of food, it can be very difficult, and sometimes impossible, to change it over to another type of diet.

Many owners like to see their cat plump to the point of being overweight. Remember, slim is

*Feeding.*

73

healthy. Overweight cats may be difficult to slim down because the two components of a weight-reducing program are sensible diet and exercise. While the owner may be able to control the cat's diet, it is extremely difficult to control its exercise. In the wild, the cat must hunt for its food, and that is how it gets its exercise. The domestic cat does a negligible amount of hunting and in the main is fed by the owner, so that its exercise is minimal.

The nutritional requirements of cats vary according to individual needs and are determined by such factors as maintenance, growth, exercise, pregnancy, lactation, disease and age. The basic ingredients of any sound nutrition program are protein (amino acids), carbohydrates, fats, vitamins and minerals.

Because the cat is a carnivorous animal, it cannot obtain certain food requirements from plant products like humans and dogs can. While humans and most animals can convert carotene found in plants into vitamin A, the cat must obtain its vitamin A needs from its diet. Liver, milk and cod liver oil are recognised sources of vitamin A. Commercial dog foods are not suitable for cats. If you feed a cat dog food over a period of time it will lead to nutritional deficiencies and eventually death.

Cats cannot metabolise essential fatty acids, such as linoleic and linolenic acid, which are found in plants, to arachidonic acid. Consequently, the cat requires arachidonic acid to be supplied in its diet. Meat is a good source. Niacin, one of the water-soluble B vitamins, cannot be manufactured by the cat; it has to be supplied in the diet. It is found in abundance in liver and meat. Taurine, which is one of the essential amino acids needed by the cat in its diet, is virtually absent from plant products, but is found in relatively high concentrations in milk, meat and fish.

## TYPES OF CAT FOOD

### Meat

This is a good source of protein as well as being highly palatable. However, cats cannot live on a meat diet only. Meat is very high in phosphorus and very low in calcium, and does not contain enough iron, magnesium, copper, sodium or iodine. The ratio of calcium to phosphorus in the cat's diet should be in the order of 1.2 - 2.0 calcium to 1.0 phosphorus. Meat diets have a calcium to phosphorus ratio of approximately 1:20. Cats, especially those four to six months of age, fed only on a meat diet develop a disease called nutritional secondary hyperparathyroidism (see page 78).

Iodine deficiency in the pregnant queen due to being fed a meat diet only can cause birth difficulties and deformities in the kittens, such as cleft

*Eating commercially prepared food.*

palate, open eyes (see 'Deformities', page 192) and thyroid abnormalities. Such kittens have little hair, thickened skin and poor growth.

Meat should not exceed 20-25 per cent of the cat's total diet.

## Milk

This is a good source of protein, fat, vitamin A, vitamin D, vitamin B12, calcium, phosphorus, potassium and iodine.

In the wild, when kittens are weaned from their mother, they never drink milk again. Once kittens are weaned, milk is not necessary for their growth or maintenance of a healthy state. Even queens feeding a litter of suckling kittens do not need it. Many cats older than twelve weeks of age cannot metabolise milk and consequently suffer from diarrhoea, because they lack an enzyme called lactase.

Those cats that do have the enzyme lactase and can drink milk without developing diarrhoea may be fed milk as part of their diet.

## Liver

This is a good source of protein. It is very high in phosphorus and vitamin A, low in calcium and a good source of vitamin B1, niacin, choline and cobalt.

Cats fed exclusively on a liver diet develop a disease called hypervitaminosis A (see page 170). This disease leads to excess bone growth involving the vertebrae (spinal column) and the elbows of the forelimbs.

During pregnancy and lactation, the queen can deplete her store of vitamin A by up to 50 per cent. During that period it is recommended that occasionally she be fed liver.

## Fish

This is a good source of protein, magnesium, iodine and selenium.

Raw fish contains an enzyme called thiaminase, which destroys vitamin B1 (thiamine). Cooking the fish will destroy the enzyme thiaminase. Thiamine or vitamin B1 deficiency leads to brain damage. Early signs are not eating, weight loss, vomiting and weakness of the hindquarters, followed by irritability, wobbliness and walking with claws extended and the head and neck bent downwards.

Excess fish can result in the diet being high in unsaturated fatty acids. This can cause a disease called steatitis (see 'Yellow fat disease', page 173).

## Eggs

These are an excellent source of protein, vitamin D, vitamin B12, choline, sulphur and iron. Raw egg white contains an enzyme which destroys biotin. Biotin deficiency causes dry, flaky skin and dry hair. Raw egg yolks are not a problem. A cooked egg is an excellent source of protein for the cat.

## Kidney

This is a good source of protein, very high in phosphorus and very low in calcium. It is also a good source of vitamin B1 (thiamine) and cobalt. Cats fed only on a kidney diet develop a disease called nutritional secondary hyperparathyroidism (see page 78).

## Bones

These are a good source of calcium, phosphorus and copper. Unlike dogs, many cats are not attracted to bones. Chewing on a bone is a good exercise that helps to maintain healthy gums and removes plaque and tartar from the teeth. The risk with bones, though only slight, is that they may become caught in the teeth or throat or may cause a blockage of the intestine if swallowed. Do not offer your cat poultry bones as they could splinter and choke the animal.

## Water

Cats do not drink much water. An adult cat's water intake is about 25 mL (5 teaspoons) per day. Cats do not have sweat glands and they have the ability to concentrate their urine, so that their water loss from the body is minimal. The other source of water is in the food eaten by the cat.

Water intake can be increased by adding just sufficient salt to the diet to increase thirst without making the diet unpalatable or by adding water to the food.

## Vitamin-mineral supplement

If the cat is on a complete diet — that is, one which covers all of its nutritional requirements — then the addition of a vitamin-mineral supplement may be harmful. This applies particularly to excess vitamins A and D, calcium and phosphorus. If not harmful, the additional vitamin-mineral supplement may be of no benefit whatsoever.

A vitamin-mineral supplement should only be fed if the diet is deficient in those areas or if the cat has some metabolic problem or disease. Seek the advice of your veterinarian.

When purchasing a vitamin-mineral supplement, it is important to ensure that it contains the whole range of vitamins and minerals in correct balance. Read the label carefully. It is not sufficient for it to list what is included in the contents of the container; the precise quantity of each vitamin and mineral should also be included. Only then can you evaluate the quality and economic value of the product.

### Cod liver oil

This is a concentrated source of vitamins A, D and E, which are harmful in excess. Addition of cod liver oil to an already complete, balanced diet is unnecessary and may cause hypervitaminosis A (stiffness of the joints and lameness). Excess vitamin D may cause calcification of the soft tissues, reduced appetite, vomiting, bloody diarrhoea, lethargy, rapid breathing, excessive tear production and deformed jaws and teeth. Excess vitamin E may cause reduced thyroid activity and may affect the blood-clotting mechanism by slowing it down.

Excess cod liver oil in association with a high intake of fish can result in a diet high in unsaturated fatty acids. This can cause a disease called steatitis (see 'Yellow fat disease', page 173).

## WHAT SHOULD YOU FEED YOUR CAT?

If you wish, you may feed your cat a home-cooked meal, commercial pet foods (canned or dry) or a combination of both. Needless to say, a meal prepared at home can be time-consuming and you will need to know the cat's nutritional requirements and what foods provide the necessary proteins, fats, carbohydrates, vitamins and minerals to satisfy those requirements.

Your cat may reject a meal you have prepared because it is not palatable, or it may select the meat only and leave the rest.

Commercial preparations are palatable, easy to use, readily available and reasonably priced. Some provide a complete and balanced diet while others need to be supplemented if the cat is to obtain all its nutritional requirements.

When purchasing the commercial pet food, read the label carefully to check if it is complete or incomplete. Well-known brands of commercial cat foods are made by reputable companies and what they claim on the label has to be substantiated in law.

### Canned food

There are numerous varieties of canned foods that are attractive, palatable, nutritious, economical and convenient. They consist of a mixture of meats or fish in a jelly, with all the essential vitamins and minerals added. Read the label carefully to make sure that it is a complete and balanced cat food. If it is incomplete, it will require supplementation.

Feed your cat a variety of canned foods to prevent it from developing a taste for one type and

*Water is offered here with dry food.*

refusing all others. When feeding your cat a number of different types, mix them thoroughly together, otherwise it may eat the one it prefers and leave the others.

If 80 per cent of the cat's total diet is made up of a complete and balanced canned food, it will not suffer nutritionally if the other 20 per cent is made up of table scraps, meat or other highly palatable titbits.

### Dry food

Dry food comes in various shapes and sizes, from a round pellet to a biscuit-type form. Check the label to ensure that it is a complete cat food. If it is, the cat can live a healthy life on the dry food diet only.

The cat's requirement for water increases ten times with dry food. Make sure that fresh water is always readily available. Dry foods contain salt, which increases the voluntary water intake. They should be introduced gradually so that the cat can adjust its drinking habits. If your cat is drinking very little water, the dry food can be moistened before feeding.

Cats with a history of crystals in their urine (see 'Feline urological syndrome', page 150), particularly neutered male cats, should not be fed more than 20 per cent of dry food in their total diet and even then the food should be moistened before feeding. Magnesium is implicated in the formation of struvite (sand-like) crystals in the urine. In most dry foods, the magnesium level has been reduced to a low level to minimise such formation.

## FEEDING ROUTINE

When kittens are eight weeks old, they can be fed canned food and/or dry food. Provide four small meals a day until the kitten is four months old, then reduce it to three times a day. At nine months of age, reduce the number of meals to twice daily. Stale food and water should be disposed of so that the food and water bowls are always kept thoroughly clean.

### Amount of food required by your cat

The amount of food that a cat requires varies according to growth, maintenance, exercise, lactation, pregnancy and disease. The following table is only a guide. Some cats require more food than others and some require less.

The canned and dry food referred to in the Diet Chart is a complete cat food; that is, one which will supply the cat with all the nutritional requirements for good health.

The cat may be fed a mixed diet of canned and

| DIET CHART | | | | | |
|---|---|---|---|---|---|
| Age | Weight | | Canned food | Dry food | No. of times daily |
| | kg | lb | 415 g can per day | Table-spoons per day | |
| 2 months | 0.8 | 1.7 | 1/10 or | 1/4 | 4 |
| 4 months | 2.0 | 4.4 | 1/5 or | 3/4 | 3 |
| 6 months | 3.0 | 6.6 | 1/4 or | 1 | 3 |
| 9 months | 4.0 | 8.8 | 1/2 or | 1 1/2 | 2 |
| Adult | 5 | 11 | 1/2 or | 2 1/2 | 2 |
| Queen (last 3rd of pregnancy) | 5 | 11 | 1/2 or | 2 | 3 |
| Queen (lactating) | 4 | 8.8 | 1/2 or | 2 | 3 |

dry food or one type only.

### How much to feed your kitten or young cat

A young cat's nutritional requirements are far greater than that of an old mature cat. A young cat needs food for maintenance, growth and exercise. An old mature cat lying around most of the day in the warmth of the sun or next to a heater or an open fire only needs food for maintenance and very little exercise.

If your kitten or young cat is healthy but leaves its food or some of it, even though it is palatable, then you are feeding it too much. If it eats all the food, quickly or slowly, and it still looks thin, then you need to give it more. If it eats everything, is steadily growing and gaining weight, then you can assume that you are feeding it the correct amount. If it eats everything and looks fat and maybe lazy, then you are feeding it too much.

## SPECIAL HEALTH PROBLEMS RELATED TO DIET

### Feline urological syndrome (FUS)
(see page 150)

This is an inflammation of the bladder (cystitis) and the urethra, together with the formation of crystals or stones. In females, because the urethra is shorter and its lumen wider, obstruction from crystals is rare. In males, because the urethra is long with a bend and a narrow lumen, obstruction of the urethra is more common.

Prevention of FUS can be achieved by using ammonium chloride or DL methionine to acidify the urine. Inflammation and crystal formation occur more frequently in an alkaline urine.

Another approach is to reduce the cat's dietary intake of magnesium by feeding it no more than 20 per cent of dry food in its total diet. Magnesium takes part in the chemical composition of struvite crystals, which are the most common crystals found in cases of FUS. For this reason, the magnesium level in dry food is minimal and the salt content has been increased to 2 per cent approximately, thereby increasing the cat's thirst and voluntary intake of fluid. In this regard, make sure that clean, fresh water is always available. The increased fluid intake stimulates urination which has a good flushing effect on the bladder, thus helping to get rid of the crystals. Fluid intake can also be increased by adding water to the dry or canned food.

### Diarrhoea (see page 140)

Many cats, once they are older than twelve weeks, do not produce an enzyme called lactase in the intestine. Lactase is essential to digest lactose in milk. Cats deficient in lactase develop diarrhoea, when given milk due to fermentation of lactose by bacteria in the intestine. In these cases, do not give the cat milk or dairy products.

Cats with diarrhoea should be fed a fat-free diet while they have the complaint and until their faeces (motions) return to normal. Boiled chicken, lean grilled meat, grilled fish and boiled rice are relatively fat free. Reduce the volume of food by two-thirds. Fresh water should be readily available.

### Kidney disease (see page 157)

Kidney disease is one of the most common medical problems in cats. The kidneys filter waste products from the blood, and when diseased they either stop filtering or do so inadequately. Waste products then become concentrated in the blood and have a toxic or poisoning effect on the cat.

There are diets specifically formulated with reduced amounts of high quality protein, sodium and phosphorus. By reducing the amount of protein, the amount of waste product in the blood is reduced for the kidneys to filter. Excess sodium and phosphorus have a detrimental effect on kidney function.

Do not feed eggs, meat or cheese to the cat.

### Nutritional secondary hyperparathyroidism

The ratio of calcium to phosphorus is important for good bone formation and skeletal development. Meat-only diets are high in phosphorus and low in calcium, iodine, magnesium and some vitamins.

Cats (particularly kittens) that are on high meat diets have such problems as poorly formed bones, bowed legs, flat faces, an overall stunted appearance, lameness, joint pain, deformed spinal column and pelvis. The bones are very susceptible to fracture.

The cat's diet should be changed to one based on complete and balanced canned and/or dry food. Add calcium to the diet daily for about a month in the form of calcium carbonate, gluconate or lactate at the rate of one tablet or one teaspoon of powder per 5 kg of body weight. It is most important that the calcium supplement does not contain any phosphorus such as calcium phosphate because the imbalance in the calcium-phosphorus ratio will not be rectified.

### A sick cat with poor appetite

Make sure the cat's diet is complete and balanced. In addition, there are specially designed vitamin-mineral supplements which also should be given. They contain the whole range of vitamins, minerals and trace elements in correct balance. When purchasing these supplements, read the label carefully. It is not sufficient for them to list what is included in the contents; the precise quantity of each vitamin, mineral and trace element should also be included. Only then can you evaluate the quality and economic value of the product.

These supplements can be administered by injection, or orally in a tablet, powder, liquid or paste form.

Feed the cat small amounts of food frequently, three to four times a day. Sick cats often lose their sense of smell and taste. Give them foods with plenty of flavour and odour, such as sardines. Warm the food, as this makes it more appetising and heightens the flavour and odour. Hand-feeding will often encourage a sick cat to eat. Smearing food in a paste form around the cat's mouth or on the hair of the forelimbs will often encourage it to lick the food off.

In cases where the cat does not eat or drink for two days, contact your veterinarian as the cat will start to dehydrate, which will exacerbate the illness. If the cat is dehydrated but will still drink, an electrolyte formula can be purchased from your veterinarian to add to the water to help prevent dehydration. If the cat refuses both food and fluids, it may be fed with an eye-dropper (syringe), stomach tube or an intravenous drip administered by your veterinary surgeon.

### Pregnancy and lactation in the queen

Pregnant queens require extra food in the last third of pregnancy for the rapid growth of the kittens during this period. Increase the volume of food at this stage by 25 per cent, otherwise the queen will

*Healthy cats groom themselves regularly.*

*Longhaired cats need extra grooming.*

metabolise her own body tissue and lose weight. Queens that are lactating require extra food for milk production and to make up for the loss of nutrients in the milk to the feeding kittens. If she is not fed adequate amounts of good quality food, her milk supply will decrease and consequently the kittens will suffer.

## GROOMING

### Grooming equipment

• Short, pure bristle brush — to brush shorthaired and longhaired cats.
• Short, flexible, wire bristle brush — to brush shorthaired and longhaired cats.
• Pointed scissors — to deknot longhaired cats and trim hair.
• Cotton buds — to clean ears.
• Cotton wool balls — to clean eyes and control bleeding if nails are cut too short.
• Nail cutters — designed to cut the nails of cats.
• Fine-toothed comb — for general grooming.
• Wide-toothed comb — to comb out knots in longhaired cats.
• Ferric chloride — to control bleeding if nails are cut too short.
• Insecticidal rinse or shampoo — one recommended for cat use.

• Baby shampoo or medicated shampoo — one recommended for cat use.
• Powder — baby powder or flea powder for cats.
• Towel — a suitable drying cloth.

## COAT CARE

Cats devote lengthy periods of time to grooming themselves using their tongue and paws. Their tongue is covered with short spikes, which make it a very efficient tool for grooming. Some cats develop a fetish about grooming themselves, and the usual result is loss of hair (bald patches) and abrasion of the skin (see 'Overgrooming, page 162). It seems that licking their coat and sometimes the coat of other cats is not purely for the purpose of cleaning, but also for some sort of pleasure acquired from this activity.

Cats that are old or sick and some toms do not pay attention to grooming themselves. The grooming of these cats as well as the longhaired breeds needs more attention from owners than does the grooming of shorthaired breeds.

Shorthaired breeds should be brushed gently but firmly and thoroughly twice weekly with a flexible wire bristle brush. the Tex and Sphynx breeds do not require brushing because of their sparse hair cover.

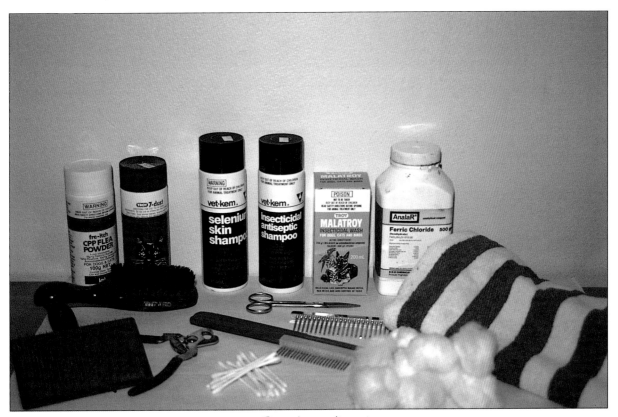

*Grooming equipment.*

*The matting of hair can be prevented by brushing.*

intestine, causing constipation and occasionally a bowel blockage (see 'Hair ball', page 171).

Longhaired cats need their coats combed and brushed daily to prevent the hair becoming matted. Mats tend to form around the neck, under the belly, along the sides and in the tail. Cats that are badly neglected can develop matted hair practically all over the body, which looks and feels like a thick dense carpet. Once this happens, these cats are impossible to groom with a brush or comb. Loose hair sometimes catches around the teeth of longhaired cats when grooming themselves, causing gingivitis (inflammation of the gums, see page 153) and an unpleasant odour from the mouth.

### Brushing and combing

Start grooming your kitten at about three months of age so that it becomes accustomed to the feel of the brush and/or comb. Do not be too vigorous, otherwise the kitten will resent being groomed. Most cats enjoy being brushed and combed, and grooming your cat at an early age makes your task much easier as the cat gets older.

Shorthaired cats should be brushed twice weekly using a brush with flexible wire bristles or short natural bristles. Brush the hair in the direction it falls. Cats often resent having their face brushed. In these cases, wipe the face with a moist cloth. When brushing around the face, be careful not to accidentally damage the eyes.

A short flexible wire bristle brush and a wide-toothed comb should be used for grooming the longhaired cat every day. Longhaired cats should have the hair combed away from the body to remove any small knots, followed by a thorough brushing in the direction that the hair falls. Knots

Grooming keeps the coat clean, prevents matting of the hair, stimulates circulation and removes loose hair. If the loose hair is not removed by brushing, it often gets caught on the spikes of the cat's tongue and is swallowed. Loose hair at the back of the throat may cause coughing. In many cases, loose hair is swallowed and accumulates in the stomach in the form of a wad. It may remain in the stomach for weeks or months, stimulating vomiting, especially after eating. The wad of hair in the stomach, if small enough, may pass into the

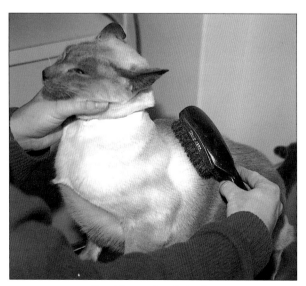

*Brushing a shorthaired cat.*

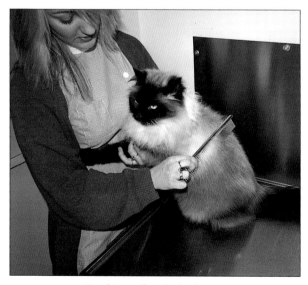

*Combing a longhaired cat.*

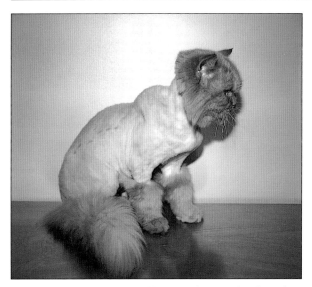

*When a cat's hair is badly matted, it can be shaved.*

large areas of badly matted hair. The best method is to get your veterinarian to sedate or in some cases anaesthetise the cat, so that the matted hair can be shaved off with electric clippers.

### Washing

Cats only require washing if they are dirty, have a skin problem or live in a warm climate where ticks and fleas are prevalent. Some cats hate water, so if you think it will be necessary in the future to wash your cat, it is a good idea to start washing your kitten at about three months of age. The best place to do the washing is in a large laundry tub. Shut the laundry door and place the kitten or cat in an empty tub, holding it by the scruff of the neck. Do not place the cat in a tub full of water or under a jet of water from a tap, because it will become frightened and may be impossible to handle.

that cannot be combed out may be teased out or broken down by using a pair of pointed scissors, followed by combing. If the knots cannot be teased out or broken down with scissors, then they can be very carefully cut out. To do this, cut a few hairs at a time just under the knot until it is free, otherwise, if you try to cut out the knot impatiently, you may take out a section of skin with the hair.

It is impossible to groom longhaired cats with

Begin by gradually wetting the cat's coat until it is saturated, then apply sufficient cat shampoo to achieve a good foaming lather as you gently massage the shampoo into the coat. Use only shampoos recommended for cats or if unavailable use baby shampoo. Keep holding the cat by the scruff of the neck. Only shampoo the head if it is necessary. Be careful not to get shampoo into the cat's eyes or ears.

Once a good foaming lather is achieved, rinse

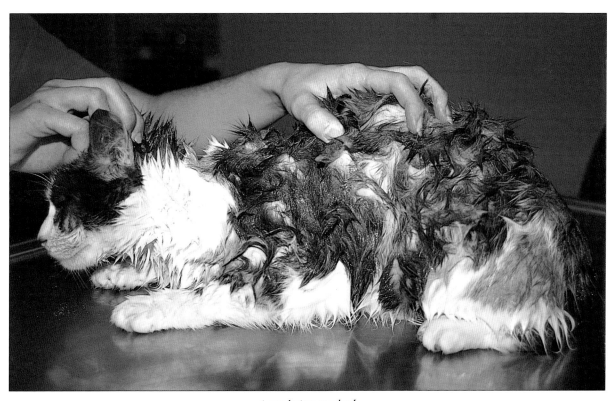

*A cat being washed.*

83

the coat thoroughly and gently with clean water. Using your hand, squeeze the water out of the coat. Lift the cat out of the tub onto a bench and towel-dry it. Some cats will allow the drying process to be completed with a hairdryer. It is important with longhaired cats to comb and brush the hair as it dries, to prevent knots from forming.

## EYE CARE

Except for those breeds with a flattened face, as found in certain lines of Persians, a healthy cat rarely, if ever, requires its eyes to be cleaned. Longhaired breeds with a flattened face often have tear ducts that are kinked or too narrow and do not allow tears to flow down the duct and out of the nose. Instead, the tears flow out of that corner of the eye closer to the nose, causing a wet stain in the hair on either side of the nose.

Tear staining may also be due to excessive tear production caused by entropion — that is, turning in of the eyelid, with the eyelashes rubbing on the surface of the eyeball (see page 144) — or by conjunctivitis (see page 191). Long hair close to the corner of the eye near the nose can act like a wick. By carefully clipping and keeping the hair short in this area, it will help to keep the area dry and prevent staining.

If tear staining continues, consult your veterinarian, who may flush the tear ducts under a general anaesthetic. If the tear ducts are narrowed or blocked due to the flattened shape of the face, flushing will not improve the situation. Your veterinarian may prescribe an antibiotic (tetracycline), which will eliminate the reddish stain produced by the tears.

If the eyes require cleaning, use a moist cotton wool ball.

*Cleaning the eyes.*

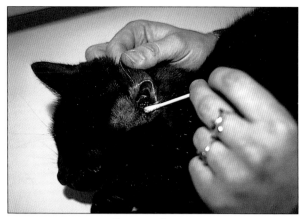

*Cleaning the ears.*

## EAR CARE

Check the inside of the ears regularly for dirt, wax and foreign bodies such as grass seeds. Like humans, some cats produce more wax in their ears than others. Wax is a suitable breeding ground for ear mites (see page 144), bacteria, fungi and yeast. The wax also can irritate the cat and cause partial, temporary deafness if it blocks the ear canal.

If there is no sign of dirt or wax, do not clean the ears, because overzealous cleaning irritates them and sets up an infection.

To clean the ear, place the cat on a table, then take hold of the ear in such a way that you expose the inner side. With a cotton bud moistened in diluted peroxide or in a special cleansing agent obtained from your veterinarian, clean carefully in and around the folds of the ear as well as the opening of the ear canal. Be careful not to push any wax or dirt deeper into the canal, thereby compounding the problem.

If there are signs of the cat scratching its ear, holding its head to one side, redness inside the ear or of discharge in the canal, then seek your veterinarian's advice.

## NAIL CARE

Cats wear down their nails during their daily routine by walking, running, hunting and climbing. Some cats wear down the nails of their front paws by deliberately scratching at the base of a tree or some other object, such as a scratching post provided by the owner.

Cats that are sedentary, old or confined inside a carpeted apartment or house should have their nails checked regularly, especially those of the front paws. If the nails are not checked regularly they could grow too long, sometimes growing in the shape of a hook and back into the pad, causing lameness and infection.

The degree of difficulty met in cutting the cat's

*Infection at the base of the nail.*

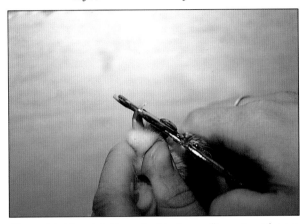

*The quick (the pink tissue inside the nail) must not be cut.*

nails depends on the temperament of the cat and on the owner having a suitable pair of nail clippers designed for cats. Scissors or human nail clippers are not satisfactory and tend to split the nail.

By having someone else hold the cat, you can make the nail protrude by using the thumb and forefinger to squeeze the toe at the base of the nail. It is important to get a good view of the nail so that you can identify the quick, (the pink-coloured tissue inside the nail), which contains blood vessels and nerves. If you cut the quick, it will hurt the cat and the cut may bleed freely for a short time. Cut the nail a short distance from where the quick ends. If the nail bleeds after cutting, apply pressure with a cotton wool ball for a few minutes. Ferric chloride applied to the bleeding nail will stop the bleeding almost immediately.

Cutting the nails will not prevent the cat from scratching and damaging furniture in the home. If possible, give the cat plenty of access to the garden, where it can do no real damage by scratching. If the cat lives inside your home, introduce it to a scratching post when young. By hanging a toy from the top of the post, the kitten pawing at the toy will soon catch on to the idea of scratching the post.

If a cat persists in damaging furniture by scratching, consult your veterinarian. In some countries it is legal to declaw cats, provided the owner makes a statutory declaration that the only alternative to declawing is having the cat put to sleep.

## TEETH CARE

The cat is a predator which uses its canine teeth (fangs) to catch and hold its prey. The incisor (front) teeth are used to tear the flesh off its prey, while the premolar and molar (back) teeth are for chewing the food in preparation for digestion. The cat usually chews the food to reduce it to pieces of a size that can be swallowed.

### Eruption of teeth

Like humans, the cat has two sets of teeth in a lifetime — namely, the temporary or deciduous set (milk teeth) and the permanent set. The teeth erupt through the gum in pairs; when one incisor appears on one side of the jaw, the corresponding incisor appears on the other side.

Temporary teeth begin erupting between the second and third week after birth, the first to appear being the incisors. By the fourth to sixth week, all temporary teeth except the third molars have erupted. The total number of temporary teeth is twenty-six.

| TIME OF ERUPTION OF TEMPORARY TEETH | | |
|---|---|---|
| **Teeth** | **Number** | **Time of Eruption** |
| Incisors | Top Jaw 6 Bottom Jaw 6 | 2-3 weeks |
| Canines | Top Jaw 2 Bottom Jaw 2 | 4-6 weeks |
| Molars | Top Jaw 6 Bottom Jaw 4 | 4-6 weeks |

| TIME OF ERUPTION OF PERMANENT TEETH | | |
|---|---|---|
| **Teeth** | **Number** | **Time of Eruption** |
| Incisors | Top Jaw 6 Bottom Jaw 6 | 4 months |
| Canines | Top Jaw 2 Bottom Jaw 2 | 5-6 months |
| Pre molars | Top Jaw 6 Bottom Jaw 4 | 5-6 months |
| Molars | Top Jaw 2 Bottom Jaw 2 | 7 months |

The time of eruption of temporary and perma-

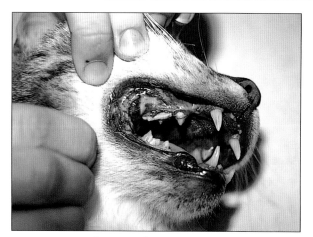

*Plaque and tartar on teeth.*

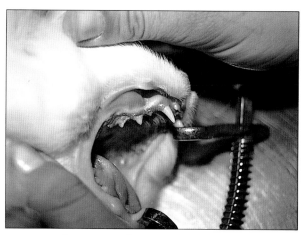

*Gingivitis: inflammation of the gums.*

nent teeth can help you determine a cat's age up to about seven months. Beyond this stage, unlike the horse, the cat's teeth are of no help in determining age.

Kittens do not appear to have any real discomfort when cutting their temporary or permanent teeth.

## TEETH PROBLEMS

### Retained temporary teeth

This is not common in the cat. Occasionally, the permanent canine teeth erupt alongside the temporary canines. The temporary canines remain firmly embedded in the gum, leaving the cat with extra teeth, sometimes referred to as supernumerary teeth. This usually occurs in the upper jaw on both sides. Food collects between the teeth, causing plaque and tartar to form on the teeth and the gum to become infected and inflamed.

If the temporary teeth are still firmly embedded in the gum by the age of six months, see your veterinarian, who will distinguish the temporary teeth from the permanent ones, give the cat a general anaesthetic and then extract the temporary teeth.

### Undershot jaw

The normal occlusion or bite is one where the upper and lower incisor teeth meet when the mouth is closed.

The common malocclusion is the overshot jaw, the upper jaw being longer than the lower jaw. This is more common in the longhaired, short-faced breeds such as Persians.

### Broken teeth

The canine teeth, being long, tapered and more exposed, are prone to being chipped or broken. The common causes are fights, falls and being struck by motor vehicles.

If the end of the tooth is chipped or broken, it usually remains healthy. However, the sharp, jagged edge of the tooth may irritate the lip, causing an ulcer. In these cases, the cat is given a general anaesthetic and the end of the tooth is filed to make it round and smooth.

If the fractured tooth becomes discoloured, the pulp cavity is exposed, the gum at the base of the tooth is inflamed or if it is causing the cat discomfort, then the tooth including the root should be extracted under a general anaesthetic.

### Plaque and tartar

Cats carry large numbers of bacteria in their mouth because they have no oral hygiene and groom themselves by licking their skin and fur. The bacteria develop on food particles in and around the teeth and combine with saliva to form plaque. Plaque is a yellow-brown scum which eventually becomes calcified to form a hard, cement-like mass called tartar. Tartar is found mostly on the outside of the canine, premolar and molar teeth at the junction of the tooth with the gum. Over a period of time, the gum recedes from the tooth; eventually the tooth becomes loose and falls out.

*Signs*

Drooling saliva, bad breath, reluctance to eat hard food, difficulty closing the jaw if tartar build-up is excessive and rubbing the mouth on objects or with a paw.

If you pull the lips back, you will notice a yellow-brown scum or a hard, cement-like brown substance stuck to the canine, premolar and molar teeth at the tooth-gum margin. The odour from the mouth is offensive.

*Treatment*

See your veterinarian, who will give the cat a general anaesthetic, provided it has not eaten or drunk for eight hours, and will remove the plaque and tartar with an ultrasonic scaler. After the tartar is removed, the teeth are polished to provide a smooth surface, which slows down the reformation of plaque.

The teeth cannot be scaled properly unless the cat is anaesthetised. If the gums are inflamed or infected (gingivitis) they are treated at the same time. After the tartar is removed, the teeth are inspected and any loose, decayed or broken teeth are extracted.

Cavities caused by decay are not common. If a tooth cavity is extensive, extraction is the preferred method, otherwise the cavity can be filled.

*Prevention*

The cat's diet should include:

• Dry cat food; its hard, crunchy nature has an abrasive effect on the teeth, helping to remove some of the plaque.

• Strips of meat so that the cat has to chew its food into suitable sized pieces for swallowing.

• Bones with meat on them to encourage chewing. This is likened to a person eating an apple; it has a cleansing effect on the teeth and a massaging effect on the gums. The risk of bones, though only slight, is that they may become caught in the teeth or throat or they may cause a blockage of the intestine if swallowed. Do not offer your cat poultry bones as they could splinter and choke it.

The temperament of some cats will allow you to clean their teeth using your finger covered with gauze dabbed in bicarbonate of soda. Rub the teeth firmly, concentrating on the area of the tooth near the gum. Some cats may allow you to use a child's toothbrush. Cats will not tolerate the taste or foaming action of toothpaste.

No matter what you do, eventually the plaque and tartar will build up, so a checkup by your veterinarian every six to twelve months followed by ultrasonic scaling if necessary is the best way to maintain the health of your cat's teeth and gums.

## VACCINATION PROGRAM

Young kittens are temporarily protected for up to sixteen weeks against many diseases by the antibodies received through their mother's first milk (colostrum). The young kitten will respond to vaccination when these maternal antibodies decline to a sufficiently low level. This decline may occur at any time in the six to sixteen week period after birth, varying from kitten to kitten, even from the same litter.

The only effective method of preventing your kitten from catching a viral disease is vaccination. Vaccines stimulate the kitten's immune system to produce antibodies against specific viruses. The antibodies remain in the bloodstream for varying periods of time; it is important that regular booster

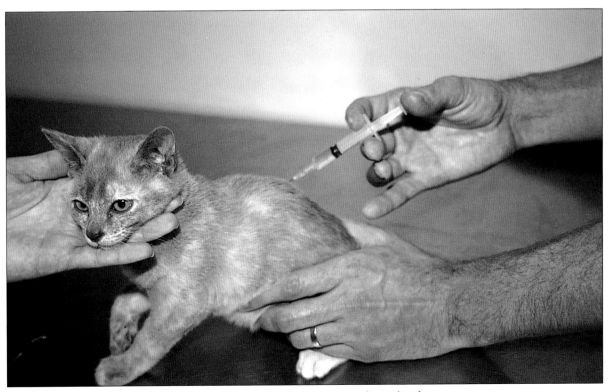

*A kitten being vaccinated at six to eight weeks of age.*

vaccinations are given throughout the cat's life.

Vaccination at six to eight weeks, twelve to fourteen weeks and sixteen to eighteen weeks of age will ensure that the kitten is protected over that period.

About 50 per cent of kittens have low levels of maternal antibodies at six to eight weeks of age, and if they are not vaccinated until sixteen weeks of age, they will have no protection against viruses. They run the risk of catching a viral infection unless they can be completely isolated from other kittens or cats during that period.

Immunity after vaccination may take up to ten days to develop.

## VACCINES

### Infectious feline enteritis vaccine

There are two types of this vaccine, either killed or modified live virus. The latter acts more quickly to give protection and immunity lasts longer.

The vaccination procedure for kittens, adult cats and queens is as follows:

Kittens — Vaccination with either killed or modified live vaccine at six to eight weeks, twelve to fourteen weeks and sixteen to eighteen weeks.

Adults — An annual booster vaccination with either killed or modified live vaccine.

Queens—Vaccination of pregnant queens using killed vaccine in the last third of pregnancy will produce high levels of antibody in the first milk (colostrum). Provided the kittens suckle soon after birth, they will have strong temporary immunity. The use of modified live vaccine for pregnant queens is not recommended.

### Feline respiratory disease complex vaccine

This disease complex is caused by two separate viral diseases, often incorrectly referred to as 'cat flu', though it is not caused by influenza viruses. One causal virus is feline viral rhinotracheitis (FVR) and the other is feline calicivirus (FCV).

The vaccines for these two virus diseases are combined in the one injection. They are available in the modified live virus or killed form.

The vaccination procedure for kittens, adult cats and queens is as follows:

Kittens — Can be given the killed or modified live vaccine at six to eight weeks, twelve to fourteen weeks and sixteen to eighteen weeks of age.

Adults — Adult cats should be given a booster vaccination annually with killed or modified live vaccine.

Queens—Can be vaccinated in the last third of

pregnancy with the killed vaccine. This increases the level of antibodies in the colostrum, giving the kittens strong temporary immunity. Modified live vaccine should not be used on pregnant queens.

### Rabies vaccine

Rabies is a viral disease of warm-blooded animals and is transmitted by biting. It can be transmitted to humans by a bite from a rabid cat. **In most cases, the disease is fatal.** (The only positive determination for rabies is an autopsy.)

Rabies occurs worldwide, except in the UK, Ireland, Japan, the Netherlands, Australia, Norway, Sweden and New Zealand.

There are both killed and modified live virus vaccines to combat this disease. Some vaccines for dogs are unsuitable for use in cats. The vaccine is not available in countries that do not have the disease.

The vaccination procedure for kittens and adult cats is as follows:

Kittens — First vaccination at three months of age.

Adults — Booster vaccination annually.

### Tetanus vaccine

Tetanus is rare in cats, and they are not routinely vaccinated because of their apparent resistance to the disease. It is caused by a bacteria, *Clostridium tetani.* There is a vaccine, Tetanus Toxoid, which can be administered to kittens older than four months; two vaccinations within a month, then a booster annually.

### Feline leukaemia virus (FeLV) (see page 148)

There is a vaccine available in the United States.

## WORMS AND WORMING

All cats have worms, with kittens having a higher worm burden than mature cats. Worms in cats can be transferred to humans and may be dangerous. It is very important to ensure that your cat is worm free, not just for the cat's health but also for the health of yourself and your family, especially young children.

While the cat is subject to many types of worms, only the four most common ones dealt with in veterinary practice are discussed in this section.

### Signs of worms.

These are fairly obvious and include weight loss, dull harsh coat, poor appetite, tail rubbing, dragging of hindquarters along the ground, lethargy, diarrhoea, anaemia (pale mucous membranes around eyes and gums), coughing and, in heavy worm infestation, you may observe worms in the cat's faeces.

However, signs or symptoms alone do not necessarily indicate that a cat has worms. Numerous other health problems, such as poor nutrition, teeth and gum problems, may produce similar symptoms. Even healthy-looking cats may have worms.

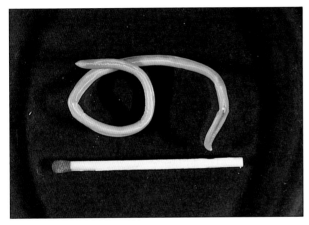

*Roundworm.*

| COMMON TYPES OF WORMS | | | |
|---|---|---|---|
| **Worm** | **Length** | **Colour** | **Shape** |
| **Round-worm** | 3-10cm (1.2-4in) | White | Slender with tapered ends |
| **Hook-worm** | 5-12mm (0.25-0.48in) | Greyish-White Red (if full of blood) | Thin with tapered ends |
| **Tape-worm** | i) Up to 30 cm (12in) ii) Segments 5mm (0.25in) | White | i) Flat, made up of segments ii) Segments look like flattened grains of rice |
| **Lung-worm** | 7-9mm (0.28-0.35in) | Greyish-White | Slender with tapered ends |

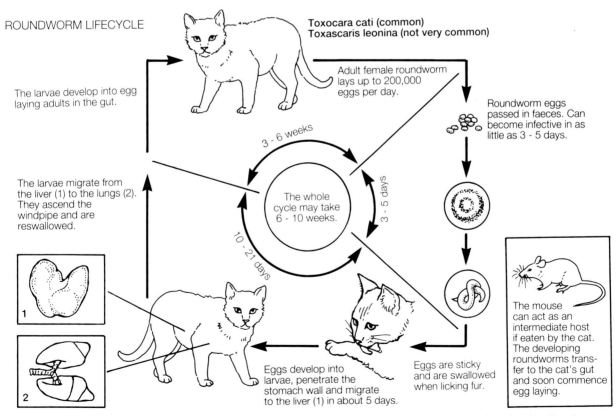

ROUNDWORM LIFECYCLE

Toxocara cati (common)
Toxascaris leonina (not very common)

The larvae develop into egg laying adults in the gut.

Adult female roundworm lays up to 200,000 eggs per day.

Roundworm eggs passed in faeces. Can become infective in as little as 3 - 5 days.

3 - 6 weeks

The larvae migrate from the liver (1) to the lungs (2). They ascend the windpipe and are reswallowed.

The whole cycle may take 6 - 10 weeks.

3 - 5 days

10 - 21 days

1

2

Eggs develop into larvae, penetrate the stomach wall and migrate to the liver (1) in about 5 days.

Eggs are sticky and are swallowed when licking fur.

The mouse can act as an intermediate host if eaten by the cat. The developing roundworms transfer to the cat's gut and soon commence egg laying.

Note: Growth of reswallowed larvae is rapid. Large immature worms can be present again within 2 - 3 weeks of treatment. Toxocara cati can sometimes be passed to kitten through the milk of the mother.

### Worm eggs and larvae

The female roundworm and hookworm lay their eggs in the intestine of the cat, and they are passed into the environment via the cat's faeces. The mature tapeworm segments contain eggs, which are released when the segment ruptures or disintegrates in the intestine or in the environment. Each of these three types of worms — round, hook and tape — has a distinct type of egg, so an inspection of the egg found in the faeces will indicate the type of worm in the intestine. Also, the number of eggs found in the faeces gives an approximate indication of the number of worms in the intestine.

In the case of tapeworm infestation, look for segments in the faeces or in and around the cat's anus.

The female lungworm lays its eggs in the lung tissue, and they develop into larvae (see 'Life cycle of lungworm' page 91). The lungworm is identified by the appearance of larvae in the cat's faeces.

Worm eggs and larvae are microscopic, and positive diagnosis can only be made in the veterinarian's laboratory.

### Treatment

If you suspect your cat has worms, there are various courses of action that you can take.
• Seek your veterinarian's advice and diagnosis on the signs and symptoms evident in the cat.
• Have the cat's faeces tested in the veterinarian's laboratory to find out if your cat's condition is due to worms. If worms are present, your veterinarian can identify them, give an estimate of the number present and prescribe appropriate treatment.
• Worm the cat with a worm preparation and wait to see if it improves. This is not as advisable as the two previous approaches because it may take some time before you can expect any change, and during

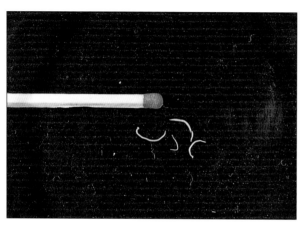

*Hookworm.*

HOOKWORM LIFECYCLE

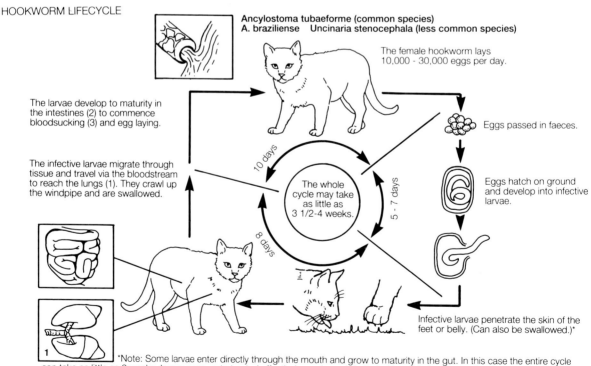

**Ancylostoma tubaeforme (common species)**
**A. braziliense   Uncinaria stenocephala (less common species)**

The female hookworm lays 10,000 - 30,000 eggs per day.

The larvae develop to maturity in the intestines (2) to commence bloodsucking (3) and egg laying.

The infective larvae migrate through tissue and travel via the bloodstream to reach the lungs (1). They crawl up the windpipe and are swallowed.

10 days

The whole cycle may take as little as 3 1/2-4 weeks.

5 - 7 days

8 days

Eggs passed in faeces.

Eggs hatch on ground and develop into infective larvae.

Infective larvae penetrate the skin of the feet or belly. (Can also be swallowed.)*

*Note: Some larvae enter directly through the mouth and grow to maturity in the gut. In this case the entire cycle can take as little as 3 weeks. In any case, cats treated effectively can be re-infected with egg laying mature hookworms 18 days later. Hygiene measures are therefore important.

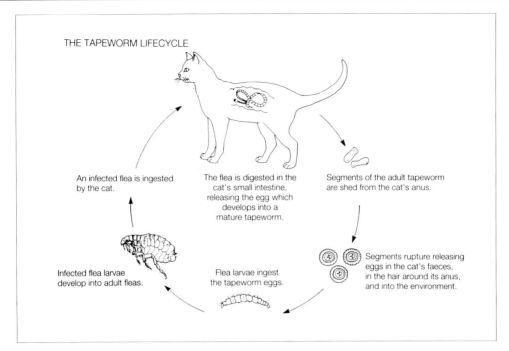

THE TAPEWORM LIFECYCLE

An infected flea is ingested by the cat.

The flea is digested in the cat's small intestine, releasing the egg which develops into a mature tapeworm.

Segments of the adult tapeworm are shed from the cat's anus.

Infected flea larvae develop into adult fleas.

Flea larvae ingest the tapeworm eggs.

Segments rupture releasing eggs in the cat's faeces, in the hair around its anus, and into the environment.

that time your cat's condition may deteriorate if its symptoms are due to some cause other than worms.

### Methods of worming

Worm syrup is usually used with young kittens, four to six weeks of age, because it is easier to administer than other worm preparations.

Worm paste is ideal for kittens older than six weeks of age and also for mature cats that resist the administration of tablets. It can be mixed in with

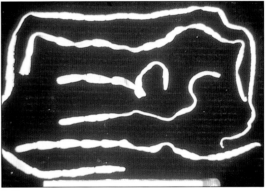

*Tapeworm.*

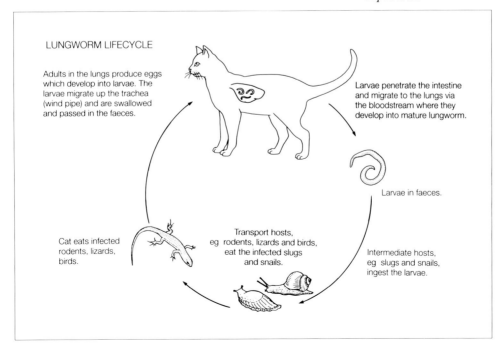

LUNGWORM LIFECYCLE

Adults in the lungs produce eggs which develop into larvae. The larvae migrate up the trachea (wind pipe) and are swallowed and passed in the faeces.

Larvae penetrate the intestine and migrate to the lungs via the bloodstream where they develop into mature lungworm.

Larvae in faeces.

Cat eats infected rodents, lizards, birds.

Transport hosts, eg rodents, lizards and birds, eat the infected slugs and snails.

Intermediate hosts, eg slugs and snails, ingest the larvae.

some highly palatable food, smeared on the fur of the front legs or around the mouth, or put directly into the mouth.

Tablets put into the cat's food, either whole or crushed, are usually rejected. In most cases, when you adopt this method, you can assume that the cat has not eaten the tablet and therefore is not wormed.

Cats that will accept tablets placed in the mouth may be wormed in this manner; it is quick, direct and effective.

*Worm paste has been added to this cat's food.*

When the cat has been given a worming preparation by any of these methods, it does not automatically mean that the cat is worm free.

• Some worms have developed a resistance to certain worming preparations.

• Worming preparations are effective only against adult worms. The migrating, immature larvae in other areas of the body at the time of worming are not affected, and consequently mature into adult worms.

• A worming preparation may be very effective against one type of worm, but only partially effective against other types.

A worming preparation that is effective against all intestinal worms should contain pyrantel, praziquantel and febantel.

Lungworm can only be treated successfully by your veterinarian.

Some worm preparations, in particular those used for dogs, may not be suitable for cats and could have a toxic effect.

### Worming program

Start worming the kittens at three weeks of age and worm the mother at the same time. Then worm the kittens four times at two-weekly intervals. The reason for worming kittens so frequently is that they usually have a heavy worm burden and

*Worm paste being smeared on the fur of the front leg.*

*A cat licking worm paste off its front leg.*

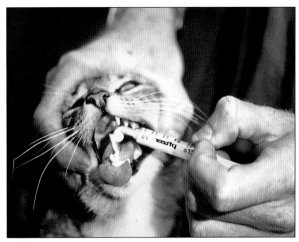

*Administering worm paste directly into the mouth.*

numerous migrating larvae. Repeated worming kills not only the adult worms in the intestine, but also those that develop from the migrating immature larvae. Continue worming the growing kitten and young cat every three months. Maintain this practice even when the cat has reached maturity. Make sure that you use an effective worming preparation. If you follow this worming program, you can assume that your cat is worm free and poses no threat to your health.

Pregnant queens should be wormed when they are four and seven weeks' pregnant. Queens being sent to a breeding establishment should be wormed two weeks before going to the stud and four weeks after returning home.

Cats going to a boarding establishment should be wormed two weeks before being boarded and two weeks after returning home.

### Worm prevention precautions

The following precautions against worms should be taken:
• Remove the faeces daily from the cat litter tray, then burn or wrap securely and dispose of them in the rubbish bin.
• Clean the litter tray thoroughly with boiling water.
• Wash the cat thoroughly and groom it regularly to minimise accumulation of worm eggs in its coat.
• Clip the hair away from the anus of longhaired cats to minimise contamination of the hair with faeces and worm eggs.
• Avoid crowding too many cats in the one area. Overcrowding results in heavy contamination of the environment with worm eggs, greatly increasing the risk of infection and reinfection.
• Keep your cat(s) flea free, as the flea plays a part in the tapeworm's life cycle (see page 91).

• Restrict your cat's hunting drive and eradicate rodents. This will help to prevent hookworm and roundworm infection.
• Roundworm and hookworm eggs can survive for long periods in moist, warm surroundings. In a cattery or boarding establishment, runs with a concrete base that can be thoroughly cleaned and kept as dry as possible will help to prevent infection or reinfection.

### Risks to humans

The usual worms that infect humans, especially children, should not be confused with cat worms. Humans can pick up the cat's roundworm eggs from the environment or from the cat's contaminated fur and transfer the eggs via their unclean hands to the food that they place in their mouth. The roundworm eggs are swallowed and develop into larvae in the human's intestine. The larvae migrate through the intestinal wall into the liver or lungs and may stay there. In small numbers, they may not cause any obvious damage, but in large numbers the damage caused to the liver or lungs could be quite severe. While it is rare, larvae migrating to the optic nerve of the eye have been known to cause blindness in that eye. The migrating larvae of the roundworm in humans is known as visceral larva migrans. Migrating larvae in humans are not affected by routine worming preparations.

To minimise the risk associated with cat worms, humans should take the following precautions:
• Pet cats should be wormed frequently with an appropriate worming preparation (see 'Methods of worming', page 91).
• Cats should not be allowed to sit on kitchen benches and the dining table.
• Cats should not be kissed, or fondled with the face.

• Thoroughly wash your hands after handling, cuddling or caressing cats and before eating or handling food.

• Keep cats out of bedrooms and off beds.

• Cover children's sandpits to prevent cats defecating in them.

## THE ELDERLY CAT

The average life span of a cat is approximately fourteen years. At about ten years of age, cats begin to show signs of ageing.

### Signs of old age

The signs vary with individual cats and may develop so slowly that they go unnoticed until they are advanced and obvious. Common signs are:

• Reduced sense of sight and hearing. The cat may not respond to your call and/or it may bump into objects and appear disorientated.

• Reduced appetite, which may be due to reduced sense of smell and consequently taste.

• Weight loss, which may be due to eating less as well as loss of muscle mass due to reduced exercise. Old cats spend much of the day snoozing.

• Loss of coat colour, dull sheen, and unkempt, dirty appearance, due to less time spent in grooming.

• Bad breath due to plaque, tartar and gingivitis (see pages 86, 153).

• Constipation (see page 137).

• Urinary incontinence (see 'Bed-wetting', page 170).

• Diarrhoea (see page 140).

*An elderly cat.*

• Susceptibility to certain diseases such as arthritis (see page 134), cancer (see 'Skin cancer', page 165, and 'Lymphosarcoma', page 140), diabetes (see page 139), heart disease (see page 153), nephritis (see 'Kidney disease', page 157), respiratory diseases (see 'cat flu', page 148) and worms (see pages 88-94).

### Care of the elderly cat

As a cat gets older, its ability to digest and absorb nutrients is reduced, so it should be fed smaller meals of high quality food more frequently. Highly palatable prescription diets, with reduced amounts of high quality protein, phosphorus, sodium, magnesium and calories, are available. Excessive amounts of protein, phosphorus and sodium may worsen kidney and heart diseases.

Elderly cats need fewer calories because they exercise less and expend less energy. If obesity or a tendency to put on weight is a problem, then a diet containing fewer calories is recommended. However, if your cat is too thin, consult your veterinarian as the problem may be more complex than a simple dietary one.

The diet should contain greater amounts of vitamins, zinc, essential fatty acids and fibre. Add a specially formulated cat vitamin and mineral supplement to the diet. Do not use a human vitamin-mineral supplement, as a cat's requirements differ.

Regular grooming helps the cat to look and feel better, as well as preventing constipation and/or vomiting due to the ingestion of loose hair. It also helps to prevent skin problems associated with a matted, dirty coat.

Exercise is important to maintain muscle tone and joint flexibility. It also stimulates the cat to urinate and defecate, which assists in preventing cystitis (see page 138) and constipation (see page 137). You can encourage exercise by putting the cat outside regularly or by taking it for a walk.

Provide an area for sleeping which is warm and draught free in winter and provides shade and protection from the elements in summer.

Worming every three months (see page 92) should ensure that the cat is worm free.

Take your cat to your veterinarian regularly for a check up and its annual vaccination, particularly against feline enteritis (see page 147) and feline respiratory disease (see 'cat flu', page 148).

The risk of disease increases with age, so careful observation of any alteration in your cat's daily habits together with regular examinations by your veterinarian will aid in the early diagnosis of a possible life-threatening disease. An early diagno-

*An elderly, arthritic cat.*

sis may enable the disease to be treated successfully. If the disease cannot be treated, a decision on euthanasia ('putting your cat to sleep') can prevent unnecessary and prolonged suffering.

### Euthanasia

There comes a time when you feel a decision about putting your old cat to sleep should be made or at least should be discussed with your veterinarian.

Some people are reluctant to approach their veterinarian on this matter. Rest assured that your veterinarian is there to assist and advise you, and that he/she has discussed the same problem with clients many times before. Do not hesitate to discuss the matter with your veterinarian.

Just because the cat is old is not a sufficient reason in itself to justify euthanasia. But if the cat is old, its quality of life is unacceptable and there is no hope of improvement, then a decision about euthanasia should be made.

Over the years you become emotionally involved with your cat and understandably sometimes your emotions can cloud your reasoning. Some people will not or cannot make the decision to put their old cat to sleep because the thought of it hurts them too much to arrive at that final decision. In not making the decision they are unnecessarily putting their old cat through further discomfort and pain. When your veterinarian advises you to put your cat to sleep, he or she is thinking of what is the kindest thing to do for the cat and of shielding you from the stress of watching your cat over a short or lengthy period of time going through pain or discomfort from which it is not going to recover.

Once the decision to put your cat to sleep has been made, you may wish to stay with it while this is being done. It is a painless and peaceful procedure. A concentrated anaesthetic is injected into a vein, and the cat literally goes peacefully to sleep within seconds.

Following euthanasia, you may wish to bury your cat at home, have your veterinarian take care of the burial or have the cat buried or cremated at a pet cemetery. The decision is a personal one.

After the death of a cat, the owner usually suffers a sense of loss and grief. Some allow time to heal their hurt, but others take a more positive step; they acquire a new kitten and a new caring, loving relationship begins. In that sense life is renewed.

*Regular veterinary care helps to keep your cat healthy.*

# WHEN TO CALL YOUR VETERINARIAN

*Call immediately — Call same day — Wait twenty-four hours before calling*

The following brief checklist of conditions and symptoms will help you decide how serious your cat's condition is and what course of action you should take. If you are not sure about when to take your cat to the veterinarian, telephone first and explain the symptoms.

## CALL IMMEDIATELY

• *Choking*
Appears distressed; extends head and neck; salivates; coughs; paws at the mouth.

• *Collapse or loss of balance*
Overreaction to external stimuli; depression; staggering/knuckling over; walking in circles; unable to get up; general muscle tremor; rigidity; paddling movements of legs; coma.

• *Continual straining*
Attempting to defecate (pass a motion) or urinate with little or no result.

• *Heavy bleeding*
From any part of the body; will not stop; apply pressure to stop the bleeding on the way to the veterinarian.

• *Difficulty in breathing*
Gasping; noisy breathing.

• *Birth difficulties*
No kitten appears after straining for an hour; if after straining for a period of time the queen gives up; if part of a kitten appears, e.g. head but nothing else appears after twenty minutes of straining.

• *Injury*
Severe continuous pain; severe lameness; cut with bone exposed; puncture wound, especially to eye, chest or abdomen.

• *Pain*
Severe, continuous or spasmodic.

• *Poisoning*
Chemical, snake, spider or plant; retain specimen for veterinarian to identify quickly type of poisoning.

• *Vomiting and/or diarrhoea*
Evidence of blood; putrid, fluid diarrhoea.

• *Urine*
Obvious blood in the urine.

• *Itching*
Continual, uncontrollable scratching, biting, tearing at the skin; skin broken and bleeding.

## CALL SAME DAY

• *Abortion*
• *Afterbirth*
If retained for eight hours.

• *Breathing difficulties*
Laboured breathing; rapid and shallow breathing with or without cough.

• *Diarrhoea*
Motion fluid and putrid.

• *Vomiting*
Evident on a number of occasions; associated with some other symptom such as lethargy.

• *Eye problem*
Tears streaming down cheeks; eyelids partially or completely closed; cornea (surface of eye) cloudy, opaque or bluish-white in colour.

• *Injuries*
Not urgent but liable to become infected; a cut through full thickness of skin which needs stitching; puncture wound in leg or head; acute sudden lameness.

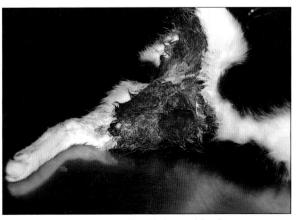

*A severe wound, with heavy bleeding.*

*Swollen conjunctiva covering the eye.*

*This kitten is holding a front leg off the ground.*

• *Itching*
Self-mutilating; biting; scratching; hair loss; skin red and inflamed.
• *Not eating*
Depressed; in conjunction with other signs such as laboured breathing, diarrhoea, lying down, pain.
• *Swelling*
Hot, hard and painful or discharging.
• *Burns*
Often difficult to assess the depth and extent.

• *Frostbite and/or hypothermia*
Low body temperature associated with sub-zero temperatures.
• *Mismating*
Termination of an unwanted pregnancy can be done safely and harmlessly within twenty-four hours after intercourse.
• *Swallowed object*
Better to assess early rather than wait until a possible life-threatening situation develops.

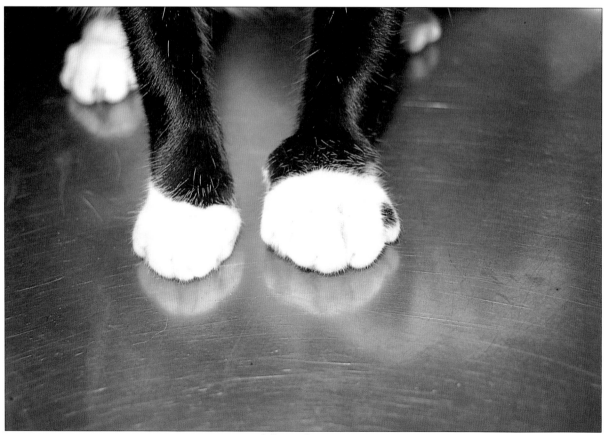

*A painfully swollen paw.*

*A healthy crossbreed.*

*A Russian Blue kitten.*

## WAIT TWENTY-FOUR HOURS
## BEFORE CALLING

• *Diarrhoea*
No indication of abdominal pain; no sign of blood; no straining.
• *Itching*
Moderate; no apparent damage to the skin by self-mutilation.

• *Lameness*
Ability to bear weight on leg; not affecting eating or other functions.
• *Not eating*
No other sign or symptom.
• *Vomiting*
On two or three occasions; no other symptoms.
• *Odour*
Unpleasant odour; other than a soiled coat.

*Cats love to climb trees.*

# FIRST AID

*First aid kit—Approaching, handling and assessing an injured cat Allergic reaction—Artificial resuscitation—Bleeding—Choking— Fish hook caught in the lip—Fit or convulsion—Fracture— Heatstroke—Low temperature (hypothermia)—Paint on the coat— Poisoning—Puncture wound—Shock—Snake bite—Spider bite*

Injury and accidents to cats appear to be fairly common, possibly because of their inquisitive nature and tendency to be active during the night.

## FIRST AID KIT

- Antiseptic wash (e.g. chlorhexidene)
- Cat carry basket
- Hydrogen peroxide 3%
- Roll of cotton wool
- Roll of adhesive bandage 2.5 cm (1 in) wide
- Roll of gauze bandage 2.5 cm (1 in) wide
- Scissors
- Thermometer
- Tincture of iodine
- Tweezers

## APPROACHING AN INJURED CAT

Approach with caution, as an injured cat in pain or frightened can give you a nasty bite or scratch. Before handling the injured cat check to see if:
- it is conscious or not;
- there is any obvious blood on the cat or on the ground nearby;
- there are any obvious wounds or broken bones;
- its breathing appears to be normal or laboured, rapid and shallow;
- it shows an aggressive reaction to your approach.

## HANDLING AN INJURED CAT

If the cat shows no reaction to your approach, rub the back of your hand behind its ears and then turn your hand to take a good handful of the scruff of the neck. This grip gives you good control of the cat, particularly its head, and prevents you from being bitten when placing it into a cat basket or cage.

If the cat reacts to your approach by hissing with open mouth, drawing back its ears and/or dilating its pupils, do not touch it. Instead, take a blanket or towel, continue talking reassuringly to the cat, then quickly but gently place the blanket completely over it. Touch the blanket about the head region of the cat to assess its reaction. If it does not appear to be aggressive, then take hold of the cat with both hands, holding it behind the shoulders. With the blanket still tucked around it, lift the cat into a suitable cat basket from which it cannot escape. Take it to your veterinarian. If there is no suitable cat carry basket or box available, then lift

*A first aid kit.*

*An injured cat, secure in a cat basket.*

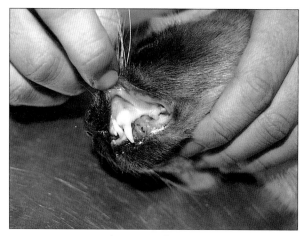

*Pale gums indicate shock.*

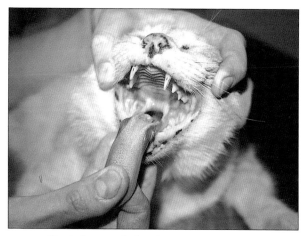

*Check the mouth for obstruction of the airway.*

the cat into the boot of the car, where it will not suffocate, nor can it cause any injury to the driver or passenger if it panics.

## ASSESSING AN INJURED CAT

Look at the colour of its gums. If they are pale or white, the cat is probably suffering from shock or blood loss. Take the cat to your veterinarian immediately. If the gums are pink, then it is a good sign that there is no major blood loss externally or internally.

Carefully run your free hand over the cat's body, looking and feeling for a wound, swelling or painful area. Check the movement of the limbs and note if there is pain, swelling, a grating sensation, a floppy limb irregular in appearance, or any inability to move one or more limbs. Any of these signs indicate that the limb, pelvis or spine may be broken (fractured) or the joint dislocated. In such cases or if the cat is unconscious, take it to the veterinarian.

If everything seems to indicate that the cat is sound, prop it up on its four legs and encourage it to walk. If it flops down, walks on three legs and carries the fourth, limps, staggers, refuses to move, cries frequently as if in pain or breathes in a laboured, panting fashion, wrap the cat in a blanket to keep it warm and to counteract shock, place it in a cat carry basket and take it to your veterinarian immediately.

## ALLERGIC REACTION

Being inquisitive, cats usually investigate something moving in the garden with their nose or front paw. In the event of a bite or sting, the first thing you will notice is a swollen face or paw and the cat rubbing its face with its paw or against some object. If the paw is swollen, the cat may bite it to relieve irritation. Usually it is difficult to determine what

has caused the allergic reaction. If the cat is not distressed and the swelling is small and local, investigate the swollen area for a sting or bite mark and apply a commercial preparation such as calamine lotion. If the swelling is extensive and the cat is distressed, take it to your veterinarian.

## ARTIFICIAL RESUSCITATION

If the cat is in a state of collapse, not breathing and perhaps has a blue tongue, feel for a heartbeat by placing a finger and thumb on either side of the chest just behind the elbow. If there is a heartbeat:
• Check the mouth for any food or foreign body obstructing the airway. If there is a blockage, take the cat by the hindlegs, hold it upside down and shake it vigorously to dislodge the obstruction. Lay the cat on its side and check the mouth again. If still obstructed, use a pair of tweezers or long-nosed pliers to remove the foreign body or food. Do not use your finger.
• With the neck extended, pull the cat's tongue out

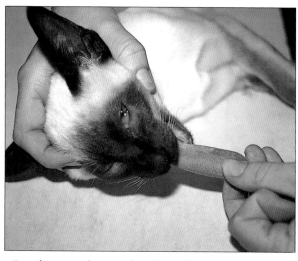

*Breathing can be stimulated by pulling the cat's tongue.*

*Cats love to climb, but this Himalayan kitten may need help.*

*A cat will make itself comfortable almost anywhere.*

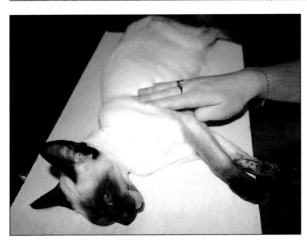

*Artificial respiration.*

## BLEEDING

Do not panic and just stand there and watch the cat bleed to death. Immediately apply direct pressure on the wound and stop the cat from moving around.

If the cat is bleeding freely from a wound, two persons are needed to assist: one to take hold of the cat firmly by the scruff of the neck, the other to control the haemorrhage (bleeding).

If the blood is slowly oozing from the wound, apply direct pressure to the site by means of a piece of clean gauze or sheeting held between the fingers. Do not dab or wipe the wound; this tends to promote further bleeding. Hold the pressure on the wound for ten seconds, then remove the hand holding the gauze or sheeting and evaluate the depth and breadth of the wound. If the bleeding recommences, apply further pressure.

If the blood is flowing freely, take a wad of gauze or suitable absorbent material and apply heavy pressure to the wound with your clean hand. If you press too hard, the cat may resent it. Over the wad of gauze wrap firmly but not too tightly a 2.5 cm (1 in) wide adhesive bandage and leave it in place for about thirty minutes. Then remove the bandage and evaluate the wound. Do not use cotton wool because small, fine fibres tend to collect in the wound, acting as a foreign body and

as far as you can. This often stimulates the cat to breathe and opens up the airway.

• Place your fingers on the chest and press down firmly to compress the chest and expel the air. Release the pressure quickly and repeat every five seconds until spontaneous breathing resumes.

If spontaneous breathing does not resume after five minutes and if the gums and tongue are blue, there is no heartbeat, the pupils of the eyes are dilated, and there is no blinking of the eyes when you touch the cornea (surface of the eye) with your finger, then the cat is dead.

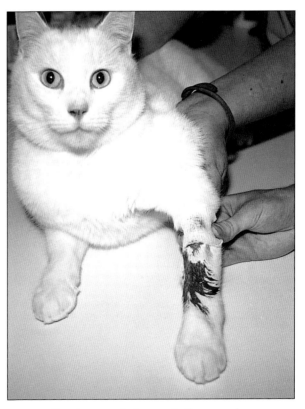

*This cat is bleeding freely from a wound.*

*Pressing a pad of gauze to the wound.*

107

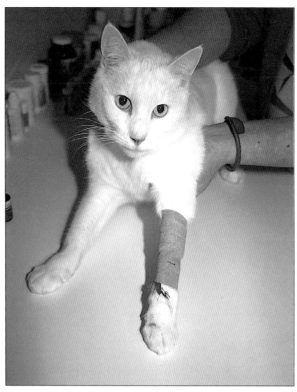

*Applying an adhesive bandage over gauze.*

slowing down the healing process.

In cases of arterial bleeding, the blood is normally bright red and spurts out with a pulsating action. Apply heavy pressure with gauze in hand directly over the site of the bleeding. Then wrap a 2.5 cm (1 in) wide adhesive bandage tightly around the gauze. Not only does the bandage apply pressure, but it also immobilises the edges of the wound, thereby helping to stop bleeding. Keep the cat calm and quiet, preferably wrapped in a blanket, and place it in a cat carrying box or cage. Leave the bandage in place and take the cat to your veterinarian. If the blood is coming through the

bandage, do not remove it; apply more adhesive bandage more firmly over the top.

If the cat is bleeding from an inaccessible area, such as inside the nostrils, restrict its movement then apply a cold compress to the area (e.g. ice packed in a towel or some suitable container).

When a pressure bandage to control haemorrhage of a limb is left on for any length of time, always check the limb below the bandage. If it is swollen, cold to the touch or does not react to pain when pinched, then remove the bandage immediately. If necessary, apply a new bandage less tightly.

Tourniquets are not recommended. They are often difficult to apply and, if applied incorrectly, can accentuate rather than retard blood loss.

## CHOKING

If the cat is choking, one or more of the following signs may be evident:
• retching,
• mouth open and cat does not appear to be able to close it,
• saliva dribbling from the mouth,
• clawing at the mouth with the front paws.

These signs often indicate that a foreign body is stuck in the throat, or across the roof of the mouth and between the teeth. If the cat is breathing reasonably freely, take it to your veterinarian immediately.

If the cat is on the verge of collapsing and its tongue is going blue, wedge something such as the rubber handle of a screwdriver between the molar teeth on one side of the mouth. Inspect quickly between the teeth, the roof of the mouth and in particular the back of the throat for a foreign body. With a pair of long-nosed pliers or the fingers, carefully pull the tongue out. This may reveal a foreign body over the back of the tongue. Remove

*Bleeding from the nostrils.*

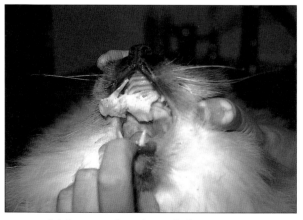

*A fish bone stuck in the roof of a cat's mouth.*

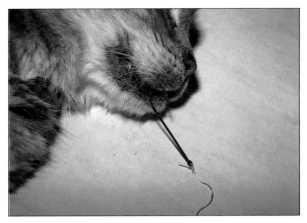

*A fish hook caught in the lip.*

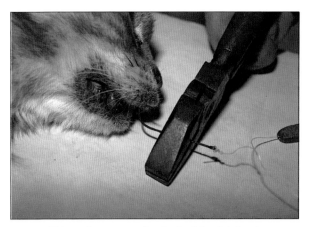

*Using pliers to cut the shaft of the fish hook.*

it with the pliers or, if the cat cannot close its mouth and bite your finger, get your finger behind it and lever it out. The same applies to a foreign body in the roof of the mouth.

If you are unable to remove the foreign body or if after removing the foreign body the cat's tongue is still blue, then take hold of the cat by the scruff of the neck in one hand and both hindlegs in the other. Hold the cat upside down and shake it vigorously to dislodge the foreign body and clear the airway.

## FISH HOOK CAUGHT IN THE LIP

Do not try to push or pull the hook. If the cat is quiet and the barbed end of the hook is protruding through the lip, seek the help of an assistant. Wrap the cat up in a blanket so that you can hold it by the scruff of the neck and allow its head to protrude. The assistant, with a pair of pliers, can cut through the hook between the barb and the skin, allowing the rest of the hook to be removed relatively easily.

If the cat is agitated or the barbed end of the hook is embedded in the lip or mouth, seek veterinary assistance.

If you notice a fishing line or perhaps cotton thread disappearing into the cat 's mouth, open the mouth, and if it appears to disappear over the back of the tongue, pull the line or thread gently. If it will not budge, do not persist with the pulling and do not cut the line or thread. The line or thread could be very useful to the veterinarian in locating the hook or needle and could assist in its removal. Take the cat immediately to your veterinarian.

## FIT OR CONVULSION

Usually the cat is lying on its side unconscious, paddling with its legs, champing its jaw, frothing at the mouth and twitching. Though you may be concerned that the cat will swallow its tongue, do not try to take hold of it, as you may be badly bitten by the unconscious cat champing its jaw.

Observe the cat, but do not touch it. Touching the cat while it is having a fit may aggravate and prolong the situation. Usually the fit lasts for about five minutes and then the cat recovers, although it may seem a little disorientated temporarily. Once it has recovered make an appointment to see your veterinarian.

If the condition lasts beyond five minutes, you need to take the cat to your veterinarian immediately. Have a cat basket or heavy duty, sealable cardboard box ready near the cat. If there is a break in between fits, pick up the cat by the scruff of the neck with one hand and place it into the cat box gently and close the lid quickly and quietly. If the cat is impossible to handle, phone your veterinarian.

## FRACTURE

The majority of fractures (broken bones) in the cat involve the limbs, pelvis, lower jaw or spine. When handling a cat with a fracture, try not to increase any pain or trauma it may be suffering and avoid being bitten or scratched.

Because the cat's limbs are relatively short and angular, particularly the hindlimbs, it can be difficult to apply a splint to immobilise the fractured limb and to prevent pain and further damage. When a cat fractures a limb, it usually holds the leg off the ground, indirectly immobilising and protecting it.

The sudden onset of one or more of the following signs may indicate a fracture.
- swelling,
- pain,
- holding the limb off the ground,
- the limb appears to be at an odd angle,
- collapsing in both hindlimbs, but able to move them,
- unable to move the hindlimbs and no response to pinching the toes (indicates fractured spine).

*Cats like being above floor level.*

*Kittens are naturally inquisitive.*

*How to carry a cat with a fractured forelimb.*

*How to carry a cat with a fractured hindlimb or pelvis.*

### Fracture of a limb

If a forelimb is fractured, pick up the cat by the scruff of the neck in one hand and support its body by cupping the other hand around the hindquarters.

If a hindlimb is fractured, pick up the cat by the scruff of the neck with one hand and support its body by placing the other hand under the chest. Pick up the cat in the same way for a pelvic fracture.

### Fracture of the spine

If the cat cannot use its hindlimbs and there is no pulling away of the limbs when pinching the toes, suspect a middle to lower spinal injury.

If the cat cannot use the fore and/or hindlimbs and there is no response to pinching the toes, suspect a neck injury.

If the cat is lying quietly, place a flat board beside it. Take the cat by the scruff of the neck and gently pull it onto the board.

Transport the cat to the veterinary hospital with minimal movement of its spine to prevent any further damage to the spinal cord.

If the cat cannot use its hindlimbs, but is trying to drag itself around using its forelimbs, then pick it up by the scruff of the neck with one hand and, using the other hand to support its back, lift it into a large box and close the flaps or lid. Often, it will try to drag itself out of the box, so for this reason it must be contained.

## HEATSTROKE

Like dogs, cats can only regulate their body temperature by panting; they have no sweat glands. They are inefficient at getting rid of body heat, especially in hot weather; whereas they are efficient at retaining body heat and can tolerate very cold conditions.

Common causes of heatstroke are being locked in a car in very hot weather or being confined in a poorly ventilated cat basket and being left in the sun. The signs of heatstroke in a cat are:
• panting with mouth open, gasping for air,
• distressed,
• often unable to stand,
• moving about in an agitated and uncontrolled fashion,
• gums are deep red.

Immediately cool down the cat by wetting it thoroughly with cold water and placing it in front of a fan or air conditioner. When the cat appears to have recovered, move it to a cool, shady area with easy access to water.

If after ten minutes the cat does not appear to be responding to treatment, contact your veterinarian. Prolonged heatstroke can lead to coma and death

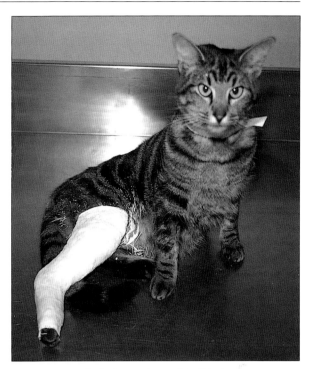

*A plaster cast on a hind limb.*

or brain damage.

Never leave your cat confined in a poorly ventilated area (e.g. car, cat box etc.) in summer. In very hot weather provide a cool, shady area with access to water.

## LOW BODY TEMPERATURE (HYPOTHERMIA)

In cold conditions, a healthy cat should not suffer from hypothermia. It is mainly seen in the newborn, geriatric or sick cat (see 'Care of newborn kittens', page 187).

## PAINT ON THE COAT

In such an event, it is important to remove paint from the cat's coat, otherwise it will more than likely lick the hair and ingest some of the paint. Water-based paints, while still wet, can be removed from the coat by thorough rinsing with water.

Oil-based paints, while still wet, can be very carefully wiped from the surface of the coat using a cloth dampened with the appropriate paint solvent, e.g. turpentine. *Under no circumstances allow the solvent to contact the skin.* Immediately after wiping the paint off the hair, wash the affected area with warm water and soap, and rinse thoroughly to get rid of the solvent, otherwise it will inflame the skin, causing the cat to scratch violently and lick it vigorously, with the possibility of being poisoned.

If the oil-or water-based paint has dried, remove it by carefully cutting away the affected hair.

## SPECIFIC TREATMENT FOR POISONS GENERALLY FOUND IN THE HOME AND GARDEN

| POISON | SOURCE | SIGNS | TREATMENT |
|---|---|---|---|
| Antifreeze (ethylene glycol) | Used in motor vehicle radiators; cats like taste; will seek out and drink. | Wobbling, vomiting, depression, convulsions, coma. | If sure that cat has ingested antifreeze, induce vomiting; take cat to your veterinarian, who will inject ethyl alcohol to block effect of antifreeze and administer further supportive treatment. |
| Arsenic (vermin poisons, insecticides, herbicides) | Ingestion of grass sprayed or rodents poisoned with arsenical preparations; licking fur covered with insecticidal or herbicidal spray. | Salivating, thirsty, vomiting, fluid diarrhoea with blood, abdominal pain, collapse, death. | Induce vomiting in early stages (see page 171) immediately contact your veterinarian, who will administer antidote. |
| Aspirin (acetylsalicylic acid) | Usually administered by owner without veterinary advice to alleviate pain or discomfort; single large dose or a series of small doses can be poisonous. | Vary according to period of time during which dosage administered; poor appetite, depression, pale gums, vomiting, blood-tinged vomitus, staggering, falling over. | If recently administered, induce vomiting, give sodium bicarbonate (baking soda) solution by mouth; contact your veterinarian. |
| Benzine hexachloride (lindane, gammexane, chlordane, dieldrin, aldrin) | Insecticidal rinse safe for dogs; cats absorb it through skin and are poisoned. | Agitated, restless twitching, convulsions, coma, death. | If no sign of convulsions, wash with soap and water; rinse thoroughly; contact your veterinarian. |
| Carbon monoxide | Motor vehicle exhaust fumes; cat exposed to fumes if kept in garage. | Legs wobbly, breathing difficult, gums and mucous membrane around eyes (conjunctiva) bright pink. | Remove cat from poisonous environment to fresh air; if unconscious give artificial resuscitation (see page 104) ; immediately contact your veterinarian, who will administer oxygen directly to lungs with an endotracheal tube and give a respiratory stimulant. |
| Kerosene | Heating fuel and cleaning fluid; has a burning effect on cat's skin; cat licks affected area, thereby ingesting kerosene. | Red, inflamed skin, vomiting, diarrhoea, possible convulsions, inflamed and ulcerated tongue. | Wash the cat's skin with soap and water; give it 20-30 ml (2 tablespoons) of olive oil; contact your veterinarian. |
| Lead | No longer used in paint manufacture; some old houses still covered with lead paint; soil around lead mines polluted with lead; cat becomes poisoned by licking its coat contaminated with lead. | Poor appetite, weight loss, vomiting, anaemic, diarrhoea. Depending on degree of lead poisoning, cat may show signs of hyperexcitability, convulsions, depression, blindness, paralysis, coma. | Lead poisoning shows up over a period of time; consult your veterinarian, who will confirm lead poisoning by a blood or urine test and will treat your cat with an antidote as well as for any presenting symptoms. |
| Metaldehyde | Snail and slug poison in powder or pellet form; some cats like the taste, actively seek it out. | Tremor, salivation, diarrhoea, wobbling, convulsions. | If cat observed at time of ingestion, induce vomiting; contact your veterinarian immediately; recovery rate very good. |

| POISON | SOURCE | SIGNS | TREATMENT |
|--------|--------|-------|-----------|
| Oil, grease | Cat lying under a motor vehicle or accidentally falling into a container. | Covered in grease or oil; depressed. | Wash with warm water and soap; if unable to remove see your veterinarian. |
| Organo-phospate carbamate | Snail and slug poison in pellet form; some cats like the taste, will actively seek it out. | Tremor, salivation, diarrhoea, wobbling, convulsions. | If observed at time of ingestion, induce vomiting; contact your veterinarian immediately; recovery rate very good. |
| Paracetamol | Household pain reliever; may be administered to cat by owner. | May appear hours to days after ingestion. Include lethargy, gums may range from pale (anaemic) to yellow (jaundiced) to bluish, breathing difficult, swelling of lips and face. | Induce vomiting if recently ingested; contact your veterinarian. |
| Phenol (carbolic acid) | A potent disinfectant, poisonous to cats by ingestion or absorption through skin; after skin contact, cat may ingest by licking the contaminated fur and skin. | Cat smells of phenol; vomiting, diarrhoea, severe abdominal pain, shock, collapse. | Remove phenol from fur and skin with soap and warm water; give 20-30 ml (2 tablespoons) of olive oil orally; contact your veterinarian. |
| Strychnine | Rat poison; often used deliberately to poison animals with a bait. | Restless, twitching, general stiffness, convulsions with head and neck arched and limbs stretched out; convulsions can be set off by a touch or noise, become continuous, followed by death. | If cat has ingested strychnine, but shows no symptoms, induce vomiting immediately. If showing symptoms, carefully place cat in basket or secure box, take to veterinarian immediately. In transit, do not touch cat or make a noise. If cat dies, strychnine can be confirmed by chemical analysis of stomach contents. |
| Thallium | Rat, cockroach and ant poisons; cat can be poisoned by eating poisoned rat. | Vary according to amount ingested and period of time in cat's system. Redness of skin followed by a crust, peeling and hair loss; starts on ears and lips, progresses to head, feet, limbs and body. Further symptoms are weight loss, vomiting, diarrhoea, wobbling, convulsions. | Veterinarian can confirm by testing for thallium in urine. If cat has just swallowed thallium, induce vomiting; see your veterinarian, who will administer a drug to bind thallium and prevent its absorption through intestine. |
| Turpentine (turps) | Paint solvent, wrongly used to remove paint from cat's fur or to dab on embedded tick. Never use turps on cat's fur or skin as it can poison through skin. | Red, inflamed skin, cat vigorously licks skin affected by turps, vomiting, diarrhoea, abdominal pain, restlessness, hyperexcitable, wobbly, coma. | Wash skin and fur with soap and water, rinse thoroughly; see your veterinarian. |
| Warfarin | The cat may eat the poison itself or eat a dead rat that has been poisoned with warfarin, which stops blood from clotting. | Lethargy, pale gums, membrane around eye, weakness, laboured breathing, maybe signs of haemmorhage in gum tissue, collapse, death. Signs may be slow to develop and vary according to time and amount ingested. | If recently ingested, induce vomiting; treat for shock (see page 116); see your veterinarian, who can administer an antidote; success rate very good. |

## POISONING

Unlike dogs, cats are generally very careful about what they eat. Consequently, they are rarely poisoned by eating a 'bait' — food that has been deliberately laced with a poison with the intention of killing an animal. Cats tend to eat small quantities of food at any one time, so it is unlikely that they will eat large quantities of poisoned food.

Because of their inquisitive and hunting nature, cats are more likely to be bitten by venomous snakes or spiders.

It is important to note that some drugs, such as aspirin, which are perfectly safe if the correct dosage is administered to humans or dogs, may be lethal to cats.

Cats can be inadvertently poisoned by deliberate or accidental contamination of their coat with insecticides, disinfectants, paint, tar and other toxic substances. The poison is not so much absorbed through the skin as it is by ingestion when the cat meticulously goes about cleaning itself by licking its coat. The fact that many cats spend most of their life confined to their owner's home reduces their exposure to many poisons, although there are numerous household disinfectants, cleaning agents, insecticidal sprays, herbicides and pesticides which, if ingested, are highly poisonous. Fortunately, most of these products are unpalatable and it is very unlikely that the cat would ingest them.

Most countries throughout the world have poison information centres with information on hundreds of thousands of potentially poisonous substances. Always keep your poison information centre's phone number in an accessible place so that you can contact them quickly in case of an emergency.

If your cat is ill, you can only suspect that it is poisoned unless you have actually observed it eating, drinking or coming into contact with a poisonous substance.

### General rules for treatment of poisoning

1. .Initiate treatment immediately you are sure that the cat has been poisoned.
2. Induce vomiting if:
* *you are sure* that the cat has eaten some poisonous substance;
* *you are sure* the poisonous substance is not petrol, kerosene, turpentine, an alkaline or acidic cleaning fluid, or a corrosive material such as paint thinners;
* *the cat is conscious and able to vomit* (if the cat is semi-conscious or unconscious when induced to vomit, it may inhale some of the vomitus into the lungs, causing death by asphyxiation or by inhalation pneumonia).

Induce vomiting by administering:
* 10-20 mLs (2-4 teaspoons) of salt solution (3 teaspoons of salt to half a cup of warm water); or
* syrup of ipecac (average adult cat dosage is 8 mL).
3. If the hair and skin is contaminated with a poisonous substance wash the cat with warm water and soap, then rinse thoroughly and repeatedly.
4. If the cat is convulsing intermittently, wait until it stops then carefully pick it up by the scruff of the neck with one hand and support it under the chest and stomach with the other hand. Place it carefully into a cat basket, close the basket securely and take the cat to your veterinarian immediately.
5. If the cat is convulsing continuously, try to protect it from injuring itself and phone your veterinarian. Be careful to avoid being bitten or scratched.
6 . Contact your veterinarian and take the cat there as quickly as possible. Take the container of suspected poison with you to aid in identification of the poison and antidote.

Recovery depends on the type of poison, amount of poison in the body, the period of time lapsed after poisoning and before treatment is started, and whether or not a specific antidote is available.

## PUNCTURE WOUND

Fighting cats may bit one another and inflict a puncture wound with their canine teeth. The common sites for puncture wounds are the head, forelimbs and around the base of the tail.

If you hear cats fighting outside during the night, check your cat carefully the next morning, feeling and looking for puncture wounds, a painful spot or blood matted in the hair. Invariably, these puncture wounds become infected because of the large number of bacteria in the cat's mouth. Often, the puncture wound looks clean and neat, whereas the tissues under the skin can be badly torn and smouldering with infection.

If you find a puncture wound, carefully clip the hair away from the hole, clean the area with 3 per cent hydrogen peroxide and dab the wound with tincture of iodine. If the puncture penetrates through the full thickness of the skin into the tissues underneath, take your cat to your veterinarian. The usual course of treatment is an antibiotic to clear up the infection and prevent it from developing into a more serious infection or abscess.

## SHOCK

Shock is a term used to describe a state of collapse following many forms of serious stress, such as a car accident, massive haemorrhage, heavy fall, overwhelming infection (septicaemia), intussusception (intestinal blockage) and dehydration. The symptoms can vary depending on the cause and may include depression, prostration (lying down), rapid breathing, pallor of the gums and conjunctiva (membrane around the eye), and cold to the touch.

Take the cat to your veterinarian immediately, but in the meantime:

• keep the cat warm, but not too warm (maintain the normal body temperature; warmth can be overdone to the point of accentuating the shock if the cat becomes too hot);

• control any bleeding (see page 107);

• keep the cat calm and quiet — put it in a cat carry basket with a blanket draped over it or it may be preferable to hold the cat wrapped in a blanket.

## SNAKE BITE

In most instances of snake bite, you will probably not see the cat get bitten and will not know if the snake was venomous or non-venomous. If you do witness it, try to visualise a good description of the snake. In many case, you will find the cat in a stunned state, staring with unblinking eyes and lying on its side or chest with little movement of its limbs. Take the cat to your veterinarian immediately.

In cases where the cat is bitten on a leg, apply a broad bandage with firm pressure over the bite and about 5 cm (2 in) either side of the fang marks. Keep the cat quiet in a cat basket, and immediately take it to your veterinarian. The purpose of the pressure and immobilisation of the cat is to slow down blood flow from the site of the bite and to minimise spread of the poison.

Do not apply a tourniquet, as it can be difficult to apply and, if applied incorrectly, can aggravate the problem. Do not cut the skin at the site of the bite, as this will increase the blood supply to and from the bite, helping to spread the poison. If the cat is

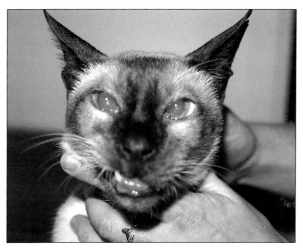

*This cat is suffering from snake bite.*

bitten in an area such as the face which cannot be readily bandaged, apply ice to the site of the bite to constrict the blood vessels in the area and to prevent spread of the poison. Take the cat to your veterinarian immediately. There are antivenoms available, some of which are effective against a number of different types of snake poisons. The veterinarian will treat the cat according to its symptoms.

## SPIDER BITE

In most cases, you will not witness the cat being bitten by a spider. If in your presence the cat cries out, hisses and appears to be in pain, and you see a spider in the vicinity of the cat, you may assume that it has been bitten. Collect the spider in a sealable container and take it with the cat to your veterinarian. The spider will be identified by the veterinary surgeon, and if it is a poisonous variety the cat will be kept under observation and treated according to symptoms as they develop.

If you are not aware of what has bitten your cat or even that it has been bitten, but you notice that it appears to be in a state of shock, take it to your veterinarian immediately.

*There is nothing wrong with this little fellow!*

# ADMINISTRATION OF MEDICATION

*Tablets— Liquids— Pastes— Eye ointments and drops — Ear drops — Injections*

There is nothing more worrying and frustrating than your cat refusing to take its medication. If the medication is not administered correctly, the cat's condition will not improve and may even worsen, and in most cases the medicine is wasted.

If the cat's condition is serious and you find it impossible to administer medication, call your veterinarian, who will medicate the cat in a professional manner. If the treatment needs to be given regularly, it may be preferable to hospitalise the cat.

Whether the medication is given orally, by stomach tube or by injection depends upon the type of medicine and its palatability, the condition and temperament of the cat, and the temperament of the owner.

The following is a guide on how to administer medication efficiently and successfully.

## TABLETS

1. *Via the food* Some tablets are palatable, and the cat may accept them without fuss either whole or crushed in the food. However, most cats are very fussy about their food and are highly suspicious of any foreign material introduced into it. Most tablets are unpalatable and often when a cat is sick it will not eat anyway.

In most cases, if you place a tablet, whole or crushed, into the food, you can reasonably assume that the cat is not getting the medication.

2. *Via the mouth and over the back of the tongue* The surest way of getting a cat to take a tablet is to place it over the back of the tongue. Before you can do this, however, you must know how to open the cat's mouth.

### Opening the cat's mouth

Move the cat into a small room such as a laundry and shut all the doors. Put the cat up on a bench at a comfortable height. You can try to open the cat's mouth by yourself or you can get someone to

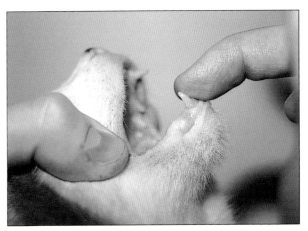

*One method of opening a cat's mouth*

hold the cat firmly to stop it moving or attempting to scratch you with its front paws.

Take hold of the cat's head between your fingers and thumb. Tilt the cat's head back so that it is looking at the ceiling. As you tilt the head back, press into the cheeks firmly with your fingers and thumb. The mouth will automatically open. Using the middle finger of your free hand press the lower jaw down to open the mouth wider. Do not try to open the mouth too wide as the cat will become distressed.

An alternative method is to pinch as much skin as you can between the ears using the fingers and thumb. Then tilt the cat's head back so that it is looking at the ceiling. The mouth will automatically open.

### Placing the tablet in the mouth and over the back of the tongue

1. *Using a pill popper* With the tablet placed in the pill popper in one hand, use the pill popper to press on the lower jaw to open the mouth wider. Quickly and smoothly pass it into the back of the mouth and press the plunger to release the tablet over the back of the tongue. It is important to release the tablet over the back of the tongue, otherwise if it is put on

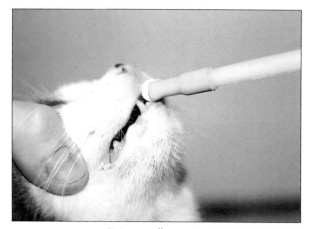

*Using a pill popper.*

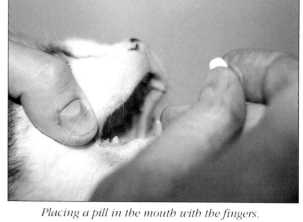

*Placing a pill in the mouth with the fingers.*

*Using a spoon.*

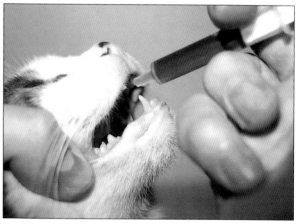

*Using a syringe to administer liquids.*

the front of the tongue the cat will spit the tablet out. The most common cause of failure is due to not putting the tablet far enough over the back of the tongue. Keep the cat's head tilted so that it is looking at the ceiling. When you see the cat lick its upper lip with its tongue, this is a signal that the tablet has been swallowed.

2. *Using the fingers* With the tablet between your thumb and index finger, open the mouth wider by pushing the lower jaw down with your middle finger. Drop the tablet onto the back of the tongue, then with your index finger quickly push the tablet over the back of the tongue. Remove your finger before the cat closes its mouth. You can use a pencil with a rubber on the end to poke the tablet down if you do not wish to use your finger.

3. *Using a spoon* Place the tablet on a teaspoon and get the cat to open its mouth wider by inserting the spoon into the mouth and pressing down firmly on the lower jaw. Push the spoon into the mouth, tilting it to release the tablet onto the back of the tongue. Then use the spoon to push the tablet over the back of the tongue. Keep the head tilted back until the tablet is swallowed.

## LIQUIDS

Hold the cat's head and tilt it slightly backwards so that the liquid will run towards the back of the throat rather than towards the open mouth (lips). Using a syringe or eye-dropper, slowly dribble the liquid directly onto the tongue. If the cat does not swallow, tilt the head back a little more and dribble more liquid onto the tongue. If you tilt the head back too far, the liquid may flow into the windpipe, causing the cat to cough and splutter.

If the taste of the liquid is unpleasant, the cat may salivate profusely, causing saliva with most of the liquid to dribble out of the mouth.

*Using a stomach tube* Administration of liquids to an adult cat via a stomach tube should be left to your veterinarian as it takes professional knowledge, skill and restraint.

With kittens, you can use plastic tubing 2 mm (1/12 in) in diameter (see 'Orphan kitten', page 188); this diameter is small enough to allow the tubing to pass freely into the oesophagus, but too large for it to enter the larynx of a kitten up to ten days old.

*A crossbreed cat makes an ideal family pet.*

*Crossbreed cats come in all kinds of patterns and markings.*

*Administering eye drops.*

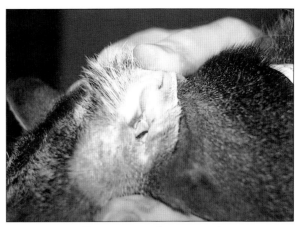

*How to expose the ear canal.*

## PASTES

Paste usually comes in a syringe. You can administer the paste directly from the syringe onto the cat's tongue. The paste adheres to the rough surface of the tongue and is swallowed. If it is unpalatable, the cat will salivate, causing a mixture of paste and saliva to pour from the mouth.

If the paste is palatable, it can be mixed with the cat's favourite food or it can be smeared on the hair of the forelimbs or around the mouth, and the cat will lick it off.

## EYE OINTMENTS AND DROPS

Generally, two people are required: one to hold the cat firmly and the other to administer the medication. If the cat is held too tightly, it will struggle and may become aggressive. If held too loosely, it will tend to move about and escape from your grasp. The person holding the cat should tilt the head back slightly. The person administering the drops should hold the eyelids apart with the index finger and thumb and put two drops directly onto the eyeball. Keep the head tilted back for twenty seconds, otherwise the cat will drop its head forward, and the eye drops will roll out and be wasted.

Many eye ointments are solid and are designed to melt at body temperature. Pull the cat's lower lid down with the thumb and lay a strip of eye ointment inside the lower lid along its full length. Then close the eyelid and the ointment will melt, forming a film over the eyeball and conjunctiva. Alternatively, pull the upper eyelid up and lay the ointment under it.

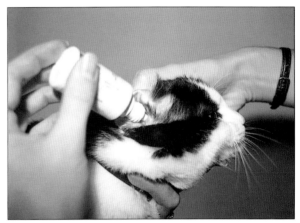

*Squirting drops into the ear canal.*

## EAR DROPS

One person should hold the cat firmly while the other person administering the drops takes hold of the ear with the index finger and thumb and pulls it towards the other ear. This helps to open up the inside of the ear and makes the opening of the ear canal obvious. Squeeze four to six drops into the ear canal. Continue to hold the ear tightly, otherwise the cat will shake its head vigorously and spray the drops everywhere. With your free hand, massage gently below the ear to work the drops down the ear canal.

If the cat is fidgety, do not worry about trying to count the drops, just put the nozzle of the container in the ear canal and give it a squirt. Stop when you see the drops starting to well up out of the cat's ear canal.

*These three kittens are in excellent health.*

# DISEASES AND HEALTH PROBLEMS A-Z

*General signs of illness — Specific diseases and health problems  A-Z*

## GENERAL SIGNS OF ILLNESS

Cats are creatures of habit and any variation or departure from their normal habits should be viewed with suspicion. It is advisable for all cat owners to develop the habit of following a routine checklist in assessing their cat's health. In doing so, they may become aware of a health problem in its early stages, which they may be able to treat, or if not, to refer the problem to their veterinarian before it becomes too serious.

A health checklist should include at least the following:

### Activity

Cats range from being slow and languid to very active and alert. Observe what is the norm for your cat. If it is normally very active and suddenly one day it is inert and lying around, indications are that something is wrong. If your cat is normally lethargic, it may be difficult to pinpoint its inactivity as indicating something is wrong.

### Appetite

Loss of appetite is one of the first signs of illness. If your cat has eaten very little compared with what it usually eats or has not eaten anything at all, try to find a logical explanation for this behaviour before calling your veterinarian. Keep in mind that cats can be fussy about their food, so check its palatability and whether or not there has been any change in quality or type. If your cat continues to be off its food for twenty-four hours and you cannot find any logical explanation for it, call your veterinarian.

### Coat

The condition of a cat's coat will vary according to its breed, the time of year, housing, grooming and washing. If the coat is dry, harsh, broken, sparse, mottled, patchy, matted, knotted, or wet in a local area because of excessive licking, it is usually a sign of illness.

### Condition (weight)

A cat's condition (weight) varies with diet, exercise and breeds. Condition can also vary within a breed; some cats may be well-muscled, others may be fat or thin. A thin cat is not necessarily an unhealthy one. A cat on the same ration doing the same amount of exercise will remain at a certain weight for years. If suddenly or over a short period of time it loses weight, the change in condition should alert the owner to check the cat carefully.

Weight loss, especially in association with some other sign, such as poor coat, diarrhoea, poor appetite or lethargy, is indicative of a health problem.

### Demeanour

Demeanour in different breeds and in individual cats varies tremendously. A sharp change in demeanour, such as from being quiet to excited, alert to dull, placid to aggressive or relaxed to restless, is a sign that should alert the owner to the fact that the cat may have a health problem.

### Droppings (faeces)

Many cats are modest about their toilet habits and you may never see them in the act of defecating (passing their droppings) or any evidence of their

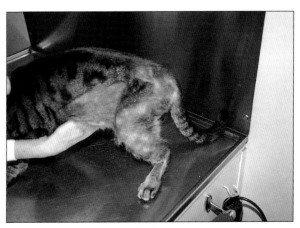

*A sparse, broken coat.*

*This cat has one floppy ear.*

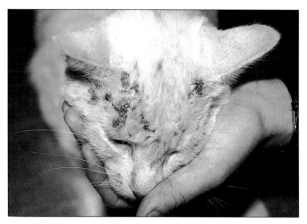

*A cat with broken, red, scabby skin.*

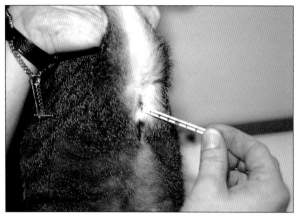

*Checking a cat's temperature.*

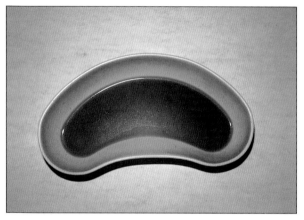

*A sample showing blood in a cat's urine .*

faeces. If you happen to notice your cat defecating, observe it and inspect the faeces.

If your cat is straining excessively for a lengthy period of time or more frequently than usual and is passing nothing or just some small amounts of hard or fluid-like faeces, it is a sign of illness. If the faeces contain worms, mucus, blood, undigested food or are small in volume, hard or fluid-like or black, white or yellow in colour, then a health problem is indicated.

When cats urinate or defecate, they adopt the same position. This may mislead owners when they observe their cat straining frequently or for longer periods than usual. They may think their cat is constipated, when in reality it has a bladder infection or perhaps a blockage of the penis (males) or urethra (females).

### Ears

Normally the ears stand erect in an alert position. A health problem may be indicated if there is a sign of discharge, redness, swelling, scratching or rubbing, heavy build-up of wax from the ear or if one ear flops down.

### Eyes, nose, mouth

Call your veterinarian if:
• a discharge from these areas is excessive in volume and/or yellow in colour;
• odour from the mouth is foul and offensive;
• the mucous membrane lining the eyes, nose and mouth (normally glistening pink in colour), is white, yellow, bluish or brick red.

### Respiration

Rapid, shallow, heavy or noisy respiration is abnormal and requires veterinary attention.

### Skin

The state of the skin may be a telltale sign of illness, especially if it is broken, red, dry, scabby, scaly, tight when pinched or there is evidence of raised lumps.

### Temperature

A normal thermometer can be used to take the temperature of a cat. Make sure you shake down the mercury before using it. Insert the thermometer for two-thirds of its length via the anus into the cat's rectum, so that the bowl of the thermometer rests

*Check your cat regularly for signs of ill-health.*

*This cat has a healthy, shiny coat.*

against the rectal wall. Leave the thermometer in position for approximately one minute.

If the cat's temperature is outside the range of 37.8° to 39.2° Celsius (100° to 102.5° Fahrenheit), it could indicate that the cat is ill and your veterinarian should be contacted.

### Urine

A cat's urine is normally clear, colourless to yellow, of a water-like consistency and with a strong, pungent, offensive odour. If the cat is frequently straining to urinate and passes a little urine often or not at all, or if the urine is reddish-brown or blood tinged, you should call your veterinarian.

If you suspect there is something abnormal with the urine, collect a sample if possible. Try sliding a clean flat dish, (disposable) under the cat. Pour the urine sample into a clean screw-top jar and keep it in the refrigerator. Take the cat and urine sample along to the veterinarian as soon as possible.

## SPECIFIC DISEASES AND HEALTH PROBLEMS A - Z

**Abnormal labour** (see page 181)

**Abortion** (see page 178)

**Abscess**

An abscess is a collection of pus enclosed in a sac embedded within the tissues of the body.
*Causes*
Abscesses that can be seen or felt under the skin are caused in most cases by fights with another cat. A tooth or claw penetrates the skin, causing damage to underlying tissue. Bacteria are deposited in the tissue at the time of penetration. Foreign bodies such as a splinter of wood or a grass seed are not a common cause of abscesses in cats. Sometimes cats develop internal abscesses on the liver, lungs and elsewhere. These are associated with a generalised bacterial infection.

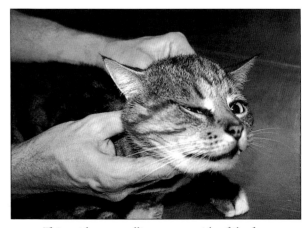

*This cat has a swelling on one side of the face.*

*A swelling which is closing the eye.*

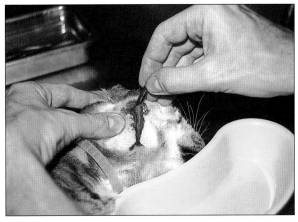

*Opening an abscess.*

*Draining pus from the abscess.*

*A wound left open to allow further draining.*

## Signs

In the early stages, as the abscess forms, the swelling is diffuse, painful, hard and may not be noticed. Often you are not aware that your cat has been in a fight unless you see a puncture wound or some blood on the fur. The first sign that you may be aware of is when the cat cries or hisses as a reaction to being touched on the painful spot. If you rarely touch the cat, the first sign observed may be a bloody, purulent discharge oozing into the hair and in some cases matting it.

As the abscess matures, it becomes more localised, softer, less painful and forms a point. At this stage, when pressed by a finger, often it will momentarily leave a pit or indentation. Depending on the size and position of the abscess, the cat may be lethargic, off its food, and/or have a temperature.

## Treatment

In the early stages, if a puncture site is obvious, thoroughly cleanse the wound with an iodine-based scrub or chlorhexidene, removing any dirt, debris or dead tissue. Check the wound to see that no foreign body remains embedded in it. Carefully cut the hair away from the opening.

Take the cat to your veterinarian, who will administer antibiotics and recommend that you bathe the cat's wound with water that is as hot as you can tolerate. Hot-bathe the area for ten minutes, twice daily, gently squeezing any discharge if present from the puncture hole. Any apparent swelling may disperse and disappear or it may form into a mature abscess, in which case return to your veterinarian.

After examination, the veterinarian will give the cat a general anaesthetic and open the abscess to drain out the pus, as well as administering antibiotics. The wound should be kept open as long as possible to provide continuing drainage.

If there is a large pocket after the pus has been drained out, it should be irrigated twice daily by a syringe full of 3 per cent peroxide. Drainage can be aided by gently pressing from the outer extremities of the abscess towards the opening. This treatment should continue until the opening is almost closed.

## Prevention

Cats prowl at night and that is the time when they

131

usually engage in a fight. To minimise this possibility, keep your cat locked up at night and have it desexed.

If you hear cats fighting nearby, check your cat thoroughly next morning for any wounds. If you find one, take your cat to your veterinarian, who will administer antibiotics which may prevent an abscess forming.

If your cat is aggressive, your veterinarian can give it an injection of medroxy progesterone acetate, which helps to reduce its aggressiveness for about five months and has no tranquillising effect on the cat.

### Acne (feline)

*Causes*
The point of the cat's chin is an area where fleas often congregate and which regularly comes into contact with dirt, vegetation and food. The skin may become irritated, producing excess oil, which combines with dirt and blocks the pores of the skin.

*Signs*
Blackheads, pimples, pustules and small abscesses on the point of the chin and around the margins of the lower lip.

*An irritation on the point of the chin.*

*Small abscesses on the point of the chin.*

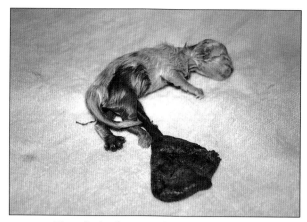

*The afterbirth is attached to this kitten.*

*Treatment*
Take your cat to your veterinarian, who will administer antibiotics. Some persistent cases will need a general anaesthetic to have the small abscesses lanced and drained.

*Prevention*
Strict flea control and clean the chin once or twice a week with an antibacterial shampoo which contains chlorhexidine. Make sure that you rinse off the shampoo and pat dry, otherwise it can act as an irritant.

### Afterbirth (placental membrane)

The afterbirth is normally expelled with the birth of each kitten or immediately after. Often the queen will eat the afterbirth, which does not seem to do her any harm, although in some cases it may cause a mild form of temporary gastroenteritis, with symptoms of vomiting and diarrhoea.

If the afterbirth is not expelled within eight hours after the last kitten is born, contact your veterinarian. If the retained afterbirth is obvious, it is usually removed by manually pulling on it with firm, even tension. If this fails, the use of a drug will be necessary to aid in the separation of the afterbirth from its attachments in the uterus. In this situation, antibiotics are often administered to prevent infection of the uterus.

**Aggression** (see page 59)

**Allergic bronchitis** (see page 135)

**Allergic reaction** (see page 104)

**Allergic sneezing** (see page 166)

### Anaemia

Anaemia is not a disease; it is a symptom of some underlying cause. It is essential to find the causal factor(s) before treatment is initiated.

Anaemia is a decrease in the haemoglobin or red

blood cells or both to below the normal level, thus reducing the oxygen-carrying capacity of the blood.

Because the lifestyle of mature cats is generally an inactive one, anaemia in cats will not be as immediately obvious as it is in other, more active domestic animals.

*Causes*

Anaemia may be caused by:

• haemorrhage, which may be acute due to internal bleeding from a ruptured blood vessel or external bleeding from a wond, or it may be chronic due to blood loss associated with blood-sucking parasites;

• destruction of red blood cells, which may be due to infection (e.g. a blood organism, *Haemobartonella felis*, destroys the red blood cells; this disease is known as feline infectious anaemia);

• depression of red cell production, which is associated with chronic infections, nephritis with uraemia, malignancies, nutritional deficiencies and poisons.

*Signs*

The colour of the tissue around the eye (conjunctiva), gums and tongue reflects the status of the red blood cells in cats. The normal colour is pink; white indicates severe anaemia. In many cases the colour of the mucous membranes falls in the range from pink to white. In these cases a full blood count is essential. The purpose of the blood count is to:

• recognise the not-so-obvious anaemic cat;

• indicate the degree of anaemia;

• diagnose the cause.

Other signs of anaemia which may be evident are lethargy, laboured breathing, restlessness, loss of appetite, loss of condition and a rough coat.

*Treatment*

The results of the blood count will determine the type of treatment to be given. The treatment will vary according to the cause and severity of the problem, and is best left to your veterinarian.

*Prevention*

Some cases of anaemia can be avoided by good nutrition and a regular worming program.

## Anal gland blockage/infection

There are two small glands on either side and just below the anus. They are scent glands that produce a foul-smelling fluid. The anal glands may play a part in the 'communication system between cats'. The act of defecating (passing a motion) also causes the foul-smelling scent or fluid to be discharged from the anal glands. This scent may serve a purpose in the cat's normal behaviour of marking its territory.

*Cause*

The opening of the anal gland sometimes becomes blocked and results in a build-up of the fluid inside. The fluid may become infected or the pressure from it may cause irritation and inflammation.

*Signs*

• Licking around the anus.

• Scooting along the floor or ground on the anus.

• Lying down, suddenly jumping up, running a few paces and then lying down again.

• Swelling of one or both anal glands.

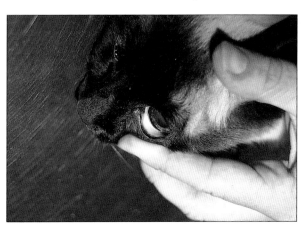

*This cat has a pale conjunctiva.*

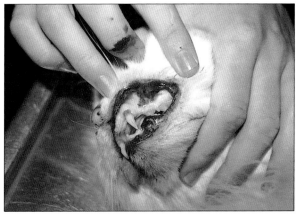

*White gums indicate severe anaemia.*

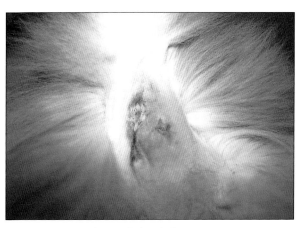

*An anal gland abscess.*

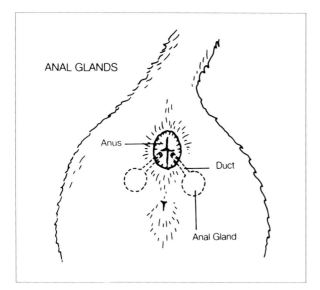

ANAL GLANDS

Anus

Duct

Anal Gland

• An anal gland abscess, indicated by a red, painful swelling on one side of the anus, which may have ruptured to release a bloody fluid.

*Treatment*

Consult your veterinarian, who will squeeze the discharge from the glands and, if necessary, administer an antibiotic injection to clear up any infection, and an anti-inflammatory injection to alleviate the irritation. If the ducts of the anal glands are blocked repeatedly, then surgical removal of the glands is recommended. This operation can be performed readily without any adverse effect on the cat.

*Prevention*

Prevention can be partially achieved by feeding the cat on a diet whereby its motions are firm. The act of passing a firm motion causes fluid to be expressed regularly from the gland, thus helping to prevent the duct from becoming blocked. If you are so inclined, your veterinarian may show you how to express your cat's anal glands when there are signs of anal irritation.

### Arthritis

Arthritis is inflammation of a joint, which is made up of bones, cartilage, ligaments and a joint capsule. The joint capsule produces fluid that lubricates the joint. Arthritis, which may be either acute or chronic, is not common in cats.

*Causes*

Inflammation of the joint is caused by:

• trauma, which may be due to a fall, penetration by a foreign body, bite or blow (e.g. motor vehicle accident);

• infection, which may localise in the joint from a general infection or it may enter the joint through a wound;

• poor conformation, placing abnormal stress on a joint;

• nutritional deficiencies such as lack of calcium.

*Signs*

In acute arthritis all the signs of inflammation are evident. The joint is warm, painful to the touch and swollen. The cat limps or holds its affected limb off the ground. Acute arthritis may subside, leaving a normal joint, or it may lead to chronic arthritis.

Chronic arthritis is associated with a joint that has been swollen for a long time. Compared with the acute form, the swollen joint is firm or hard, usually not warm to the touch and not as painful. In many cases movement of the joint is restricted permanently. The cat will limp or hold its affected leg off the ground. If the arthritis involves joints in several limbs, the cat may move slowly and with difficulty, and may also find it difficult to lie down and get up. There may be muscle wasting in the affected limb(s).

*Treatment*

Treatment varies according to the cause. Your veterinarian is best able to diagnose arthritis and pinpoint the cause. In many cases, an X-ray needs to be taken. If an infection is present, antibiotics will be administered and hot and cold foments applied.

Anti-inflammatory agents such as cortisone can be administered orally, intramuscularly, or by direct injection into the joint and may prove to be very effective.

If the cat is overweight, some reduction in weight may contribute to an improvement in its condition.

### Artificial resuscitation (see page 104)

### Black spot on cornea

A central area of the cornea, approximately 2 mm (1/12 in) in diameter, dies and forms a black plaque, which acts like a foreign body and sets up inflammation of the cornea around it. The problem is seen more commonly in Persian cats.

*Cause*

Unknown

*Signs*

Tears streaming down the cheek from the affected eye.

• Eyelid(s) may be partially closed.

• Closer examination may reveal the eye to be cloudy, with blood vessels running through the cornea to an oval-shaped brown area, which in time becomes darker and eventually turns black.

*Treatment*

Surgical removal of the black plaque, followed by prolonged treatment with eye ointment.

### Bleeding (see page 107)

## Blocked tear duct

Tear ducts are located in the inner corner of the upper and lower eyelids, and are connected to the nasal cavity.

*Cause*

The tear duct may be blocked by pus due to an infection. Certain breeds of cats, such as Persians, with bulging eyes, flat faces and pushed-in noses, are prone to blocked tear ducts. In some cases the tear duct may be narrow or kinked.

*Signs*

Tears streaming from the inner corner of the eye. Often both eyes are involved. The facial hair on either side of the nose is continually wet, leaving a reddish-brown stain in light-haired cats.

*Treatment*

Take the cat to your veterinarian, who will put some fluorescent dye on the eye. If the tear duct is open, the dye will flow from the eye down the duct and appear at the nose within ten minutes.

Be careful to see that the cat does not lick away the dye when it appears at the nose. If the dye is not obvious at the nose, wipe the nose with a white tissue and check for a smear of dye. If there is none, it would suggest that the tear duct is blocked.

In these circumstances the veterinarian would give the cat a general anaesthetic and insert a fine cannula into the opening of the tear duct. A syringe containing saline solution would be connected to the cannula and the tear duct flushed out to remove the obstruction. Some tear ducts remain permanently blocked and cannot be cleared by flushing.

## Breast lumps (see page 159)

## Broken teeth (see page 86)

## Bronchial asthma (allergic bronchitis)

*Cause*

House dust, pollens and other irritants found in the house or garden. Cats that have had a history of feline respiratory disease may be more susceptible due to damage to the mucous membrane lining the bronchial tubes.

*Signs*

Sudden onset of coughing associated with wheezing. Breathing may be laboured. The cough may begin with dry coughing and progress to moist coughing.

*Treatment*

See your veterinarian, who will give your cat a detailed examination to eliminate other causes. Treatment includes antibiotics, antihistamines and cortisone. The response to treatment is usually rapid.

## Calcium-phosphorus imbalance (see page 78)

## Cancer of the kidney

If primary cancer is diagnosed in one kidney and it has not spread to other parts of the body, the kidney can be removed surgically and the cat can live a healthy, happy life with one kidney.

## Cataract

A cataract results from crystallisation of the lens of the eye, causing the lens to become cloudy (see diagram). Light eventually cannot pass through the cloudy lens to the retina at the back of the eye; this results in blindness. Fortunately, cataracts are not an inherited disease in cats.

*Causes*

Congenital defects, injury, infection, chronic inflammation and diabetes are all known causes of cataracts, which can form in one or both eyes.

*Signs*

An immature cataract is one which partly or wholly clouds the lens but permits some light to penetrate through to the retina, so that sight is not completely lost. A mature cataract is dense, silvery-white and fills the entire pupil, which is usually dilated. Light

*A cancerous kidney which has been removed.*

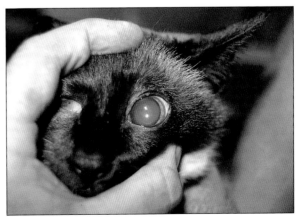

*A mature cataract in a cat's eye.*

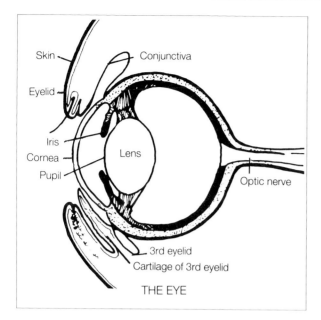

THE EYE

cannot penetrate the opaque lens, so the result is total blindness.

A cat that is totally blind in one eye will often walk into objects on its blind side. If you touch it from the blind side, it may react suddenly in fright.

A cat totally blind in both eyes will walk into objects and will be tentative in its movements. If it walks into a corner, it may become confused and unable to find its way out.

A cat partially blind in one or both eyes may balk unnecessarily at objects or it may have difficulty negotiating its way around objects when the light is subdued, such as at dusk.

*Treatment*
Generally, cats with immature cataracts can live a happy life. The development of an immature cataract associated with diabetes can be slowed down with insulin injections.

If the cat is blind because of mature cataracts in both eyes, its sight can be restored by surgical removal of one or both cataracts.

### Cat leprosy

Cat leprosy is not transmissible to humans.
*Cause*
It is caused by a bacteria which is linked with rat leprosy.
*Signs*
Sores up to 3 cm (1.2 in) in diameter, mainly in the head and neck region. They do not appear to cause any real discomfort.
*Treatment*
Consult your veterinarian, who will make a definite diagnosis by taking a biopsy for pathological examination. Surgical excision or the use of drugs is generally successful.

**Choking** (see page 108)

**Chronic kidney disease** (see page 157)

### Coccidiosis

This is a parasitic infection of the intestine, mainly affecting kittens. Kittens and young cats are more severely affected than mature cats. It is found in Australia, Europe and North America.
*Cause*
Coccidia, which is a single-cell parasite, microscopic in size.
*Signs*
Symptoms are loss of appetite, dehydration, lethargy, diarrhoea and weight loss. In severe cases there may be blood and mucus in the diarrhoea. Your veterinarian can make a diagnosis on the presenting symptoms and by a microscopic examination of the cat's faeces to check for coccidia oocysts.
*Treatment*
Consult your veterinarian, who will treat the cat with one of the sulphonamides. The disease is self limiting in many cats because they develop an immunity. To prevent spread of the disease or reinfection, faeces should be removed daily and litter trays should be disinfected with boiling water or an ammonia solution.

### Conjunctivitis

The conjunctiva is the membrane lining the inside of the eyelids, seen when you pull the upper or lower eyelid away from the eyeball. Conjunctivitis is inflammation of the conjunctiva.
*Causes*
• Foreign bodies such as grass seeds.
• Injury (fight wounds).
• Infection, both bacterial and viral.
• Allergies.
• Chronic irritation of a cat's white eyelids by the sun and chemicals, for example.insecticidal

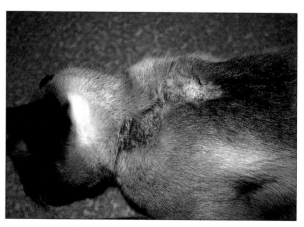

*This cat is suffering from leprosy.*

*A red and swollen conjunctiva.*

*Thick, yellow-green pus in the eye.*

shampoos, rinses and sprays.

*Signs*

The conjunctival membrane is very red and swollen. It produces a discharge varying from copious amounts of clear, watery fluid that runs down the cheek to thick, yellow-green pus that lies in the corner of the eyelids, sometimes matting them together. If one eye is involved, it usually indicates an injury or foreign body; if both eyes are involved, the cause is often a viral infection or allergy.

*Treatment*

Make an appointment to see your veterinarian. In the meantime, bathe the eye for ten minutes, four times a day, with hot water that is as hot as your hand can tolerate. While bathing the eye, wipe away any discharge adhering to the lashes or lids. Keep the cat out of the wind and direct sunlight. If you can see a foreign body in the conjunctiva, remove it, provided that it can be done readily. If not, leave the eye alone, as you may increase the irritation and even damage the eyeball.

There are numerous eye ointments, all of which have a specific purpose. They should not be used indiscriminately for conjunctivitis as some can worsen certain conditions. If there is ulceration of the cornea (surface of the eyeball) and it is incorrectly treated, the result may be a permanently damaged eye or even blindness.

**Conjunctivitis (kitten)** (see page 191)

**Constipation**

This is relatively common in cats. Often the owner is not aware the cat is constipated until it is noticed that the cat is sick and showing signs of straining. By this time the cat is usually severely constipated and needs veterinary attention quickly.

*Cause*

• Accumulation of hair in the bowel brought on by the cat's habit of grooming.

• Eating bones or ingesting prey, e.g. a bird.

• Pelvic deformity due to secondary hyperparathyroidism (see page 161) or a fracture following a motor vehicle accident.

• Damage to nerves supplying the bowel or recurring bouts of constipation, causing the bowel to lose its muscle tone and become permanently stretched.

*Signs*

The cat strains vigorously, producing a small amount of hard faeces, fluid faeces which may be mistaken for diarrhoea, or nothing at all. Once the cat strains vigorously, it is usually severely constipated. In these cases it may refuse food, be lethargic and vomit because of the absorption of toxins from the constipated mass in the bowel. In some of these cases the cats are not constipated but have cystitis or FUS (see page 150). Beware if a male cat is straining; it may have a blocked penis, which needs to be rectified quickly otherwise it could be fatal.

*Treatment*

Simple cases can be treated with 5-15 mL (1-3 teaspoons) of paraffin oil in the food or administered orally in conjunction with dioctyl sodium sulphosuccinate (a faecal softener, one to two tablets daily for two to three days). More advanced cases may be treated with a mixture of coloxyl and danthron. The dioctyl sodium sulphosuccinate softens the faeces, while the danthron stimulates the bowel to contract and expel the faeces (one to two tablets daily for two to three days).

In advanced cases of constipation see your veterinarian. Generally, when you recognise your cat is constipated, it is most often an advanced case. Your veterinarian may treat the cat conservatively with drugs or may anaesthetise the cat and remove the faeces by giving it an enema.

In some cases the faecal mass is so hard and large that surgery has to be performed for its removal.

*Prevention*
This will vary according to the cause. In cats that are prone to repeated bouts of constipation, it is important to observe how often the cat defecates and the volume and consistency of the faeces.

Milk, canned cat food and liver have a laxative effect. Paraffin oil (5-15 mL/1-3 teaspoons) given two to three times a week is helpful. Bran mixed into the food may be beneficial. Careful use of dioctyl sodium sulphosuccinate tablets with or without danthron twice weekly can also help to prevent constipation.

**Convulsion** (see page 109)

**Coughing** (refer to the following)

Allergic bronchitis (see page 135)
Bronchial asthma (see page 135)
Choking (see page 108)
Pneumonia (see page 162)

**Cystic kidneys**
A condition in which cysts develop in the kidney, destroying the tissue as they grow larger. In most cases cysts are found in both kidneys.
*Cause*
Unknown. It is suspected that it might be a genetic (inherited) characteristic.
*Signs*
The kidneys may be so large that they distend the abdomen and can be easily palpated. Depending on the extent of the cysts and the amount of kidney damage, some cats may not show signs, while others show signs of kidney failure.
*Treatment*
There is no known treatment that will cure this condition. Those cases showing signs of kidney failure should be put to sleep.

**Cystitis**
Cystitis is inflammation of the bladder. It is a common disease in cats.
*Cause*
In male cats, cystitis is usually associated with feline urological syndrome (FUS — see page 150). In females, cystitis may be due to FUS or to contamination of the vulva by bacteria during the act of defecating. The bacteria find their way up the urethra to the bladder.

Cats that are removed from their normal urinating place may hold their urine for a much longer time, until it is absolutely necessary for them to urinate. Stale urine in the bladder is a good breeding ground for bacteria, and crystals can form in the bladder. Cats in this predicament are usually ones that find their litter tray is unclean and

objectionable to use, or have the run of the garden to urinate but for one reason or another are confined in the home without a litter tray, or are boarded in a cattery where the environment is strange and perhaps frightening to them.
*Signs*
• Squatting frequently to urinate.
• Passing small amounts of urine in places where the cat normally would not urinate.
• The cat may frequently lick its genital area.
• The urine may be clear, tinged slightly with blood (pink), or practically all blood.
• The urine may have a more pungent odour than usual.
• The cat may strain frequently, leading the owner into thinking that it is constipated.
*Treatment*
See your veterinarian, who will collect a urine sample from the cat and test it before commencing treatment, which usually involves antibiotics and urine acidifiers if the urine is alkaline. In an acid urine, crystals tend to dissolve and bacterial infections clear up more readily.

Increase your cat's fluid intake by having clean water readily available. Add water to canned food and milk, although not too much, as you may make it unpalatable to the cat. Add a small amount of salt to the food to increase the cat's thirst, but take care not to make the food unpalatable. Take the cat off dry food or reduce it to less than 20 per cent of the daily intake.

If the cat urinates outside, encourage it to go out frequently or give it free access to the garden. If the cat is confined inside, make sure the litter tray is clean. The cat's urine should be checked about a week after the antibiotics finish, as some cases of cystitis are persistent. If cystitis is still present, the urine can be swabbed and cultured to identify the infection and determine the best antibiotic to use.

An X-ray will help to determine if the cystitis is due to stones (calculi) or a tumour.

**Dandruff**
*Causes*
• It may be the after-effect of inflamed skin caused by an allergy, e.g. fleas or vegetation. Once the inflammation subsides, the superficial skin cells die and flake off.
• Deficiency of saturated and unsaturated fatty acids in the diet.
• Washing the cat in a shampoo that is too harsh or not rinsing the cat thoroughly after shampooing.
• Mange, which is caused by a mite (see page 160).
*Signs*
Dry, white skin flakes on the surface of the skin and

in the hair, especially along the back, around the neck and head.

*Treatment*
• Wash the cat in 0.5 per cent Malathion (maldison) solution to get rid of any fleas or mites.
• Add a saturated and unsaturated fatty acid supplement to the diet.
• Use a special medicated shampoo for dry skin and make sure you rinse it off thoroughly.

### Deafness

Deafness in cats may be easily overlooked. If testing your cat for deafness, make sure that it is not responding to visual stimulation or to vibrations felt through its body or that it is just ignoring any sounds that you may be making.

*Cause*
• Genetic (inherited) deafness, as in the case of blue-eyed white cats that are deaf from birth.
• Infections.
• Deterioration of the cat's hearing apparatus, more evident in the ageing cat.
• Administration of certain drugs such as the antibiotic Streptomycin.
• Ear canals blocked with wax.

*Signs*
It does not appear to hear such noises as:
• a dog barking,
• a car engine,
• a loud whistle,
• a tapping on an empty tin with a spoon,
• the owner calling it by name.

*Treatment*
Syringing the ears under a general anaesthetic can restore hearing to cats with blocked ears. The use of antibiotics and anti-inflammatory agents can cure inflamed, infected ears. Deafness from birth or associated with old age cannot be treated.

### Deformities (kitten) (see page 192)

### Diabetes (mellitus)

There are two types of diabetes: diabetes mellitus, which is commonly known as sugar diabetes, and diabetes insipidus, which is known as water diabetes. The latter is rarely seen by the small animal veterinarian, while sugar diabetes is seen occasionally. Sugar diabetes is caused by decreased insulin production in the body. This in turn allows the sugar level in the body to rise and the well-recognised signs of sugar diabetes to appear.

*Cause*
The pancreas contains cells called islets of langerhans, which produce insulin. If the pancreas is diseased (pancreatitis) and the islets of langerhans

*This cat is deaf in the ear on the side of its blue eye.*

are involved, the production of insulin is either reduced or stopped. There are other causes of diabetes which are not well understood.

*Signs*
• Thirst, drinking and urinating excessively.
• Ravenous appetite and weight loss.
• Bowel motions are often of a putty colour and consistency.
• Appetite may decrease as the disease progresses.
• Cat may become depressed.

*Treatment*
See your veterinarian, who can confirm the diagnosis by doing a blood sugar test and a urine test. The blood sample should be taken from the cat approximately twelve hours after eating. Treatment involves hospitalisation to stabilise the cat's blood sugar level by administration of insulin injections. This may take four to seven days, then your veterinarian will show you how to inject the insulin, which has to be done daily. The injections are relatively painless and easy to give. The diet need not be changed, but the times at which the cat is fed after the insulin injection are important. Your veterinarian will supply you with insulin, needles, syringes and sticks for testing the sugar level in the urine. Regular monitoring of the cat's blood sugar by your veterinarian is important.

Note: Diabetic cats can enjoy a healthy life for years, provided they have their daily insulin injection.

### Diaphragmatic hernia

*Causes*
A fall, blow to the body or a motor vehicle accident. The diaphragm tears, allowing some or almost all of the abdominal contents (liver, stomach, spleen and intestines) to pass into the chest. The abdominal organs, when in the chest cavity, compress the lungs and thus adversely affect the cat's breathing.

*Signs*
The extent of the effect on the cat's breathing will

depend on the amount of abdominal content that has passed into the cat's chest cavity. Occasionally, the abdominal content does not always pass immediately into the chest cavity following the accident. Months later it may do so, causing the cat's breathing to become distressed.

The cat maintains a sitting position, refuses to lie down and may refuse to eat or drink. Its breathing is rapid and shallow.

*Treatment*

Surgical repair by your veterinarian.

### Diarrhoea

Diarrhoea in cats is characterised by faeces (motions) which are of a porridge- or fluid-like consistency, often with a very offensive odour. Normal faeces are of a formed, putty-like consistency, usually with an unpleasant odour.

*Cause*

• Diet
— milk,
— change of,
— excessive eating.
• Parasites.
• Infection
— bacterial,
— viral.
• Other Causes
— lymphosarcoma (FeLV),
— pancreatitis.

DIET

*Milk* Some cats do not have the enzyme lactase to digest the lactose in milk. The lactose ferments in the intestine, causing diarrhoea, a condition most often observed in young kittens after weaning (see page 194).

*Change of diet* Cats do not need variety in their diet like humans do. If you observe your cat's bowel motions to be normal on a certain type of diet, do not change it. Change in diet, such as offering leftover food, especially exotic foods such as lobster, prawns and liver, can cause diarrhoea.

*Excessive eating* Some cats do not know when to stop eating, and if you continue to provide food they will continue to eat it. Often, eating in excess of their normal diet or drinking an excessive amount of milk will cause diarrhoea.

PARASITES

Parasites include round, hook and tape worms, and also protozoan infections such as coccidia, toxoplasma (see pages 136, 169) and giardia.

INFECTION

*Bacterial* There are a number of different bacterial infections such as salmonella that can affect the intestine, causing diarrhoea.

*Viral* The most common and most dangerous viral infection causing diarrhoea is the feline panleucopenia virus (see page 147).

OTHER CAUSES

*Lymphosarcoma* Feline leukaemia virus (FeLV) (see page 148) may form lymphosarcoma, a malignant tumour involving the intestine and associated lymph nodes. This affects intestinal function, causing diarrhoea.

*Pancreatitis* This is not as common in the cat as in the dog. The inflamed or infected pancreas does not produce sufficient enzymes for proper digestion of the food, particularly fat.

*Signs*

The signs will vary according to the cause and severity of the diarrhoea. The cat often appears well and may want to eat normally. The bowel motion may be porridge- or fluid-like, with a very offensive odour. The colour may vary from green, yellow, grey to black, with or without the presence of blood. The cat will defecate more frequently and in areas such as inside the house or apartment where it would not normally do so. The cat may strain and have an inflamed anus, with faeces matted in the hair around the anus, tail and hindlimbs. Dehydration occurs as a result of severe or ongoing diarrhoea.

*Treatment*

If the cat is bright and alert, do not feed it for twenty-four hours. Provide water only, making sure it is always available. If the cat has not passed a motion or the motion appears firmer, then offer a small amount of boiled chicken or lean grilled meat, but only a quarter of what it would eat normally in a day.

Large volumes of food aggravate an already inflamed or infected intestine, so keep the volume of food down. As fat or dairy products aggravate diarrhoea, they should be excluded from the cat's diet until it has fully recovered.

As the bowel motion improves, increase the volume of chicken or grilled meat. Once the motions have been normal for three to four days, slowly reintroduce the cat's normal diet.

If the diarrhoea persists for more than twenty-four hours, take your cat to the veterinarian. On the other hand, if you notice your cat has diarrhoea in association with some other symptom, such as blood in the motion, lethargy, vomiting, loss of appetite or straining, see your veterinarian as soon as convenient. If possible, also take along a sample of the cat's bowel motion for examination by your veterinarian.

### Diarrhoea (kitten) (see page 191)

*A Ragdoll kitten.*

*Older cats need regular check-ups.*

## Ear diseases and problems
(refer to the following)

## Ear haematoma

An ear haematoma is an enclosed swelling of the ear flap containing blood (i.e. a blood blister).

*Cause*

Rupture of a blood vessel in the ear flap caused by a bite, blow, infection or ear mites. Infection or ear mites cause the cat to scratch the ear or shake it vigorously to the point where a blood vessel in the ear flap is ruptured.

*Signs*

• Swelling of ear flap. The swelling can vary in size, involving the whole or a part of the flap.

• Swollen ear in early stages is soft to the touch but usually not painful.

• Soft swelling if tapped gives you the impression of tapping a fluid-filled cavity.

*Treatment*

In the early formation of a haematoma, an ice pack will help to stop the internal bleeding and reduce the swelling. If a blood-filled cavity has formed, take the cat to your veterinarian, who will give it a general anaesthetic in order to drain the blood from the ear and to stitch a splint to the back of the ear flap. This procedure will stop the drained cavity from refilling with blood and aid the ear to heal in its original shape.

If the haematoma is not opened and drained,

*An infected ear, showing a discharge matting the hair.*

the blood is converted into a hard, fibrous swelling over a number of weeks. The ear contracts and is distorted in shape; it is often referred to as a cauliflower ear.

The initiating cause, such as an infection or ear mites, is treated at the same time.

## Ear infection

This condition is technically known as otitis externa and is often referred to as canker. It is an infection associated with inflammation of the external ear canal.

*Causes*

All cats have a right-angled bend in the ear canal. The glands in the wall of the canal secrete wax, which lies in the canal and does not drain readily because of the bend. Consequently, the warm, waxy environment provides a breeding ground for bacteria, fungi and yeasts. The membrane lining the ear canal becomes inflamed, producing more wax.

Fight wounds, foreign bodies (e.g. grass seeds) and ear mites are often the initiating cause. Over-zealous cleaning of the ears can also be responsible.

*Signs*

• Shaking the head.

• Scratching of one or both ears.

• Skin inflamed behind the ear with hair missing.

• Odour from the ear.

• Discharge from ear canal, brown and waxy to creamy pus, which may be blood-tinged. Often matted in the hair around the opening to the ear canal.

• Skin inflamed inside the ear.

*Treatment*

Look inside the ear. Remove any foreign body such as a grass seed. If you are unable to remove the foreign body or there is evidence of pus or heavy, waxy discharge, take the cat to your veterinarian.

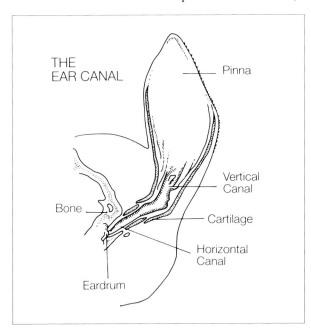

THE EAR CANAL

Pinna

Vertical Canal

Bone

Cartilage

Horizontal Canal

Eardrum

On examination, he or she will prescribe a particular ear drop to administer which may be anti-inflammatory, antibacterial or antifungal, or a combination of all three. If the discharge is thick and dry, an ear drop with an oil base to soften the wax will be prescribed; if the discharge is moist to wet, an ear drop with an alcohol base to dry the secretion will be prescribed.

If the infection is persistent, a swab may be taken and a culture done to identify the type of infection so that the most effective antibiotic for treatment can be prescribed.

When the ear is badly infected, a general anaesthetic is often necessary to enable the veterinarian to clean the ear in order to see more clearly the cause and site of the problem. He or she can then prescribe the right treatment and administer it to the crucial area.

Some chronic infections require a surgical procedure known as an ear resection. In this procedure, the vertical section of the ear canal is excised, thus providing permanent drainage.

### Ear mites

Ear mites are found in cats of all ages, but their presence is more common in kittens. Sometimes, signs of their presence are not obvious to the untrained eye and the problem goes undetected for a long time.

*Cause*

The mite, *Otodectes cynotis*, living in the ear canal can be seen with the naked eye. It is very small, white in colour and sensitive to light, causing it to move away from any light rays that might penetrate the ear canal.

*Signs*

• Scratching at one or both ears.

• Skin around or behind the ear may be abraded from scratching.

• Excessive scratching may rupture a blood vessel in the ear and cause a haematoma to form (see page 143).

• Continual shaking of the head.

• Heavy, dark wax in the ear and down the ear canal can be seen on close inspection.

• Presence of minute mites, which can be seen by looking quickly down the ear canal with the aid of a pencil torch.

*Treatment*

Apply an oil-based ear drop containing an insecticidal agent to the ear canal; four drops twice daily for seven days into both ears. After three days, when the wax has softened, clean both ears thoroughly once daily before applying the drops.

Treat all dogs and cats in the household even if you are aware of only one animal showing signs of ear mites.

If difficulty is encountered in clearing up the problem, then all cats and dogs in the household should be washed in a diluted Malathion (maldison) solution, i.e. 15 mL (3 teaspoons) of Malathion (maldison) to 1 litre (1/4 gallon) of water, as the mites not only live in the ear canal but can also live on the body.

### Eclampsia (see page 185)

### Ectropion

Ectropion is the turning out of the eyelid, thus exposing the conjunctiva and making it susceptible to inflammation and infection. This condition is rare.

### Enlargement of mammary glands
(see page 159)

### Entropion

Entropion is turning in of the eyelid, which causes the eyelashes to rub on the surface of the eyeball (cornea), thus irritating it.

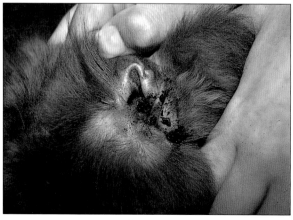

*Ear mites, causing heavy, dark wax in the ear.*

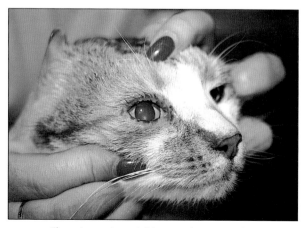

*Chronic conjunctivitis, causing entropion .*

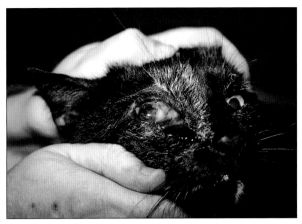

*Severe damage to the cornea.*

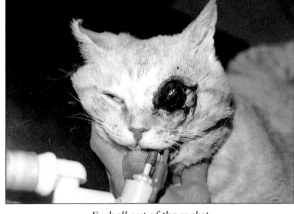

*Eyeball out of the socket.*

*This cat's right eyelids are closed because of an eye ulcer.*

*An eye with a bluish, opaque surface.*

*Cause*

Some kittens are born with this condition, often with both eyes affected. Chronic conjunctivitis and laceration of the eyelids can be the cause of entropion in adult cats.

*Signs*

• Weeping of the affected eye with a wet patch below it.

• Partial closure of the eyelids of the affected eye.

• Rubbing of the eye to alleviate constant irritation.

*Treatment*

Contact your veterinarian as this condition can be corrected successfully by surgery. In young kittens, the affected lid may be corrected by turning out the lid six or more times a day and by applying an eye ointment.

**Euthanasia** (see page 95)

**Eye diseases and problems**
(refer to the following)

Black spot on cornea (see page 134)
Blocked tear duct (see page 135)
Cataract (see page 135)
Conjunctivitis (see page 136)

Ectropion (see page 144)
Entropion (see page 144)
Eye injuries (see page 145)
Eye ulcers (see page 145)

**Eye injuries**

Any injury to the eyeball or eyelids should be regarded as serious and veterinary attention should be sought quickly. Damage to the eyeball may lead to permanent blindness and any break in an eyelid may lead to a loss of tears and a dry eye.

**Eye ulcers**

As the cornea or surface of the eye is exposed, it is more subject to injury than are other parts of the eye. In many cases injury is followed by ulceration.

*Causes*

• Injury.

• Foreign body.

• Dry eye (lack of tear production).

• Eyelids do not close completely.

• Infection.

• Entropion, i.e. turning in of the eyelid with eyelashes rubbing on the surface of the cornea.

145

*Signs*

The obvious sign is the sight of tears streaming down the cheek, with the eyelids partially or completely closed. The appearance of the cornea (i.e. the surface of the affected eye) can vary from clear to dull and hazy in a small area, to the whole surface of the eye being opaque and bluish-white in colour. Often the ulcer can only be seen by the veterinary surgeon using special techniques for examining the eye. Scar formation following corneal ulceration is common. Its effect on vision depends on the size, thickness and position of the scar.

*Treatment*

Early veterinary treatment will help minimise scar formation and maintain proper vision. You can help by cleaning and bathing the eye, using a clean wad of cotton wool soaked in hot water that is as hot as your hand can tolerate.

If a foreign body is present and can be readily removed, do so, otherwise leave it for the veterinarian to extract.

Place the cat in a shaded area or darkened room, as corneal ulcers are very sensitive to direct sunlight. Wind, dust and flies aggravate the problem.

Some shallow ulcers respond well to eye ointment, whereas those that do not or that are deep and extensive respond well to the third eyelid being pulled across the surface of the eye (cornea) and stitched to the inside of the upper eyelid. Thus the ulcer is covered by the third eyelid, which is left in place for two to four weeks.

### False pregnancy (see page 177)

### Feline AIDS (feline immuno deficiency virus) (FIV)

This disease is the same as the human variety, except that it is species specific. That is, the virus cannot be transferred from the cat to humans or to other species, such as the dog. Cases have been reported in Australia since 1988. The virus suppresses the immune system, making the cat susceptible to infection and suppressing its ability to destroy or control the infection.

*Cause*

Feline immuno deficiency virus (FIV). It has not been shown that the virus is transmitted sexually. It is thought that the virus is spread by biting. Male cats that are six years of age and over and are allowed to roam freely have the highest incidence of the disease. It may be transmitted from an infected stud to the queen at the time of mating if the skin at the back of her neck is broken when he grasps it with his teeth. The virus is highly transmissible and may be spread readily throughout a cattery or household where there are numerous cats.

*Signs*

• The common signs are weight loss, poor appetite, lethargy, temperature fluctuating from normal to high, and swollen glands (lymph nodes).

• The cat may be chronically unwell, with such symptoms as persistent diarrhoea, respiratory infections, mouth infections, disorders of the nervous system or repeated abortions.

• Other diseases, such as feline infectious anaemia (see below) or feline infectious peritonitis (see page 148), may develop because of the cat's depressed immune system.

• The signs of feline leukaemia virus infection are similar to FIV, but the viruses are different and are never found together in the same cat.

*Treatment*

A blood test is available to diagnose the disease. If the cat is antibody positive, then it has the disease. The disease may take two to three months to develop. If feline AIDS is suspected and a cat returns a negative result, then it should be retested in three months.

There is no treatment for feline AIDS. Cats that are infected and sick can be treated to ease their suffering and prolong their life, but they are a health threat to other cats. Any cats suffering from the disease that are diagnosed positive should be put to sleep. Cats that are positive but appear healthy may live comfortably for years before succumbing to the disease. These cats are also a source of infection to other cats.

*Control and prevention*

Households with large numbers of cats or catteries should have the cats tested and any positives should be put to sleep or isolated. A new cat should be tested before being admitted to the cattery or household.

### Feline infectious anaemia

This disease is caused by a small organism which attaches itself to the wall of red blood cells and eventually causes their destruction. FIA is found worldwide.

*Cause*

A small blood parasite, called *Haemobartonella felis*. The cat may carry the disease without showing any signs until it becomes stressed by an infection, surgery, pregnancy or any debilitating condition which lowers the cat's resistance. This then allows the disease to erupt, producing obvious signs.

How cats become infected is not completely understood. The possible routes of infection are cat bites, insect bites, blood transfusions or the

*A kitten with feline enteritis.*

*Dehydration leads to a loss of elasticity in the skin.*

mother's bloodstream via the placenta to the un-born kittens.
*Signs*
The incubation period is not known. The cat shows a high temperature, lethargy, weakness, poor appetite and weight loss. The mucous membranes (conjunctiva and gums) are pale and may become jaundiced as the disease progresses. Some cats recover and become carriers of the disease; others succumb and die.
*Treatment*
See your veterinarian, who can confirm the diagnosis by a blood test. Treatment involves specific antibiotics, multi-vitamins and, in severe cases, a blood transfusion.

### Feline infectious enteritis or feline panleucopenia
(see 'Vaccination program', page 87)

This viral disease is highly contagious in cats and is fatal in most cases. Ninety per cent of young cats which contract the disease die. Some cats die within twelve to twenty-four hours without any sign of illness having been observed. In these sudden death cases, the owner most often suspects poisoning. Less acute cases seldom survive longer than five to seven days.

The disease is widespread throughout most countries. The virus causing it can be destroyed by disinfecting the immediate environment, such as cages, with 0.5 per cent formalin.

The virus can survive for three months in the environment. Its incubation period in the cat is from three to ten days. Primarily, it is a disease of the young cat, but adult cats that have not been vaccinated are also susceptible.
*Cause*
A resistant virus that can be caught by direct contact with an infected cat or with its infected faeces,

urine, nasal secretion or vomitus.
*Signs*
• Fluctuating temperature.
• Severe depression.
• Diarrhoea, which may contain blood and shreds of the lining of the intestines.
• Vomitus, which is usually a white or yellow frothy fluid.
• Dehydration, signs of which are sunken eyes, rough unkempt coat, and loss of elasticity in the skin. Loss of elasticity can be tested by pulling a fold of skin at the back of the neck. When you let go, it should snap back into place; if it remains folded for a time it indicates dehydration.
• The cat may hover over its water bowl and drink occasionally.
• The cat is often hunched up with abdominal pain.
*Treatment*
Contact your veterinarian immediately. Antibiotics are of value to control the secondary bacterial infection which usually occurs with a viral infection. Antibiotics have no effect on the disease itself, which will run its course.

Your veterinarian will treat the cat according to its symptoms. Drugs to help control vomiting and diarrhoea, fluids given intravenously or subcutaneously to counteract dehydration may be administered. Good nursing is essential.
*Prevention*
The outcome of this disease is usually fatal, and prevention by vaccination is essential. There are two types of vaccine, either killed or modified live virus. The latter acts more quickly to give protection and immunity lasts longer.

The vaccination procedure for kittens, adult cats and queens is as follows:

Kittens — Vaccination with either killed or modified live vaccine at six to eight weeks, twelve to fourteen and sixteen to eighteen weeks of age.

147

Adults — An annual booster vaccination with either killed or modified live vaccine.

Queens — Vaccination of pregnant queens using killed vaccine in the last third of pregnancy will produce high levels of antibody in the first milk (colostrum). Provided the kittens suckle soon after birth, they will have strong temporary immunity. The use of modified live vaccine for pregnant queens is not recommended.

### Feline infectious peritonitis (FIP)

This disease is widespread throughout the world. The incidence of the disease is increasing. The disease is not well named as it suggests that it is localised to the abdominal cavity. This is not so, as the virus can affect the chest or the brain. It is more common in cats under three years of age living in groups.

*Cause*

A virus which lives in the environment for thirty-six hours. It is killed by the use of disinfectants such as chlorhexidine or benzalkonium chloride.

*Signs*

Lethargy, poor appetite, weight loss. If the peritoneum (lining of the abdominal cavity) is affected, it produces fluid, which eventually causes the abdomen to swell. If the pleura (lining of the chest cavity) is involved, it produces fluid, which causes laboured breathing. The breathing gets worse as the fluid increases.

There can be involvement of one or both eyes, with the most noticeable change being in eye colour. If the brain is affected, a variety of symptoms appear. Cats with the disease usually die within six weeks.

Fluid withdrawn from the abdomen or chest is a yellow to amber colour and if examined by the pathologist helps to confirm the diagnosis.

*Treatment*

Your veterinarian can treat the cat symptomatically, but in the end it usually succumbs to the disease.

*Prevention*

There is no vaccine.

### Feline leukaemia virus (FeLV)

This viral infection of cats is widespread throughout the world. It only lives for a few hours in the environment and is readily destroyed by household disinfectants. All cats are susceptible to this virus.

*Causes*

Cats spread the virus by sharing food bowls, grooming each other, incurring a bite wound and sharing litter trays, thereby coming into contact with contaminated urine and faeces.

Kittens less than twelve weeks old do not have a fully developed immune system, so they are more susceptible, as are older, sick or stressed cats.

Cats in multiple cat households or catteries are more likely to become infected. Similarly, cats that are allowed to roam free, especially uncastrated males, are also more susceptible.

*Signs*

Feline leukaemia is thought to be a disease of the blood cells, but more often causes lymphosarcoma, which is a cancer of the lymph system, or it may involve the intestine or other organs.

Depending on the type of leukaemia, symptoms include: weight loss, poor appetite, vomiting, diarrhoea, laboured respiration, anaemia, lethargy, weakness, failure to become pregnant, abortion, or birth of dead or weak, sickly kittens.

*Diagnosis*

Following exposure to the virus, some cats develop the symptoms and die, some recover and a small percentage become symptomless carriers shedding the virus intermittently.

Feline leukaemia virus is detected by a blood test. One positive test is not sufficient to diagnose your cat as having FeLV. Two positive tests three months apart are necessary to indicate that your cat will develop clinical signs of the disease and more than likely will die within two years. During that time your cat is a risk to other cats. It should be isolated, removed from the cattery and not used for breeding.

Two negative tests three months apart indicate that your cat is free of the virus. Annual tests and tests prior to mating will help to eliminate spread of the virus and control the disease.

*Treatment*

Cases have gone into remission with chemotherapy, but none has survived for any period of time. Euthanasia is recommended for cats that are confirmed cases.

*Prevention*

There is a vaccine available in the United States.

### Feline panleucopenia (see page 147)

### Feline respiratory disease
(see 'Vaccination program', page 87)

This disease complex is commonly yet incorrectly called 'cat flu'. The cause is not an influenza-type virus; most cases are caused by the feline rhinotracheitis virus or feline calicivirus.

### Feline viral rhinotracheitis (FVR)

This is a herpes virus which is widespread throughout the world.

*Cause*

Feline viral rhinotracheitis is a highly contagious

*This cat is suffering from acute conjunctivitis.*

*This cat has a watery discharge from the eyes.*

disease spread by direct contact with secretions from the nose, eyes or mouth of infected cats. It can be spread indirectly by the infected cat sneezing in the presence of a healthy cat. Infected droplets from a sneeze travel about 1 metre (3 ft). Also, a person can inadvertently transfer the virus to a healthy cat by touching it with hands contaminated with secretions from an infected cat.

*Signs*

The incubation period for the infection is four to six days, but it can be longer. Signs are temperature rise, lethargy, sneezing, discharge from the nose and eyes, sometimes inflammation and ulceration of the cornea, depressed appetite, drooling saliva from the mouth, coughing, dehydration, weight loss, and abortion in pregnant queens.

Recovery normally takes place in two to three weeks. Some cats are left with a chronic sinus infection. Periodically, they have bouts of sneezing thick, coloured mucus.

*Treatment*

Same as that for feline calicivirus (see page 149).

*Prevention*

Same as that for feline calicivirus (see page 149).

### Feline calicivirus (FCV)

This virus is widespread throughout the world. It may be found along with feline viral rhinotracheitis in the one cat.

*Cause*

The virus is spread by direct contact with secretions from the nose, eyes or mouth of infected cats. It may be spread indirectly by sneezing, contaminated feed bowls or the contaminated hands of some person who has been in contact with an infected cat. The virus can live in the environment for approximately a week.

*Signs*

The incubation period is about five to seven days.

Signs of infection are temperature rise, followed by lethargy, poor appetite, watery discharge from the eyes and nose, and dribbling from the mouth. Examination of the mouth reveals ulcers on the tongue.

Recovery normally takes place in a week, leaving some cats as symptomless carriers. Death can occur in young kittens or adult cats that develop complications which are neglected.

*Treatment*

Some cases that are neglected can be fatal. Good general nursing is very important. Clean away discharge from the eyes and from the nostrils to assist breathing.

If the cat's nasal passages and upper respiratory tract are clogged with thick mucus, an inhalation may help to improve breathing and give the cat some comfort. To do this, confine the cat in a well-ventilated basket and place a bowl of boiling water containing eucalyptus oil beside it. Cover the basket and bowl with a towel. Do this for ten minutes, twice daily.

The blocked nasal passages cause the cat to lose its sense of smell and consequently its sense of

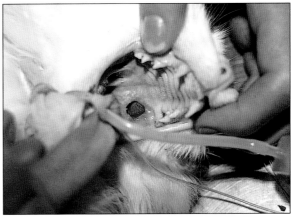

*An ulcer on the roof of a cat's mouth.*

taste. Provide food with plenty of flavour and odour. Warm up the cat's favourite food or add some hot water to it to heighten the flavour and odour.

Grooming helps the cat to feel better and aids in recovery. Keep the cat in a warm, well-ventilated, draught-free area.

See your veterinarian, who will treat the cat according to its symptoms, administering one or all of the following: antibiotics, fluids, eye ointment, vitamin supplement and drugs to help break up the mucus, clear the chest and nasal passages.

*Prevention*

The vaccines for FVR and FCV are combined in the one injection. They are available in the modified live virus or killed form.

The vaccination procedure for kittens, adult cats and queens is as follows:

Kittens — They can be given the killed or modified live vaccine at six to eight weeks, twelve to fourteen and sixteen to eighteen weeks of age.

Adults — Adult cats should be given a booster vaccination annually.

Queens — They can be vaccinated in the last third of pregnancy with the killed vaccine. This increases the level of antibodies in the colostrum, giving the kittens strong temporary immunity. Modified live vaccine should not be used on pregnant queens.

The viruses are readily killed by benzalkonium chloride or chlorhexidine.

The disease in boarding or breeding catteries can be prevented by insisting all cats are vaccinated prior to entry into the cattery and by keeping the cats in runs at least 1 metre (3 ft) apart.

If the cattery is enclosed, good ventilation is important to minimise the possible spread of feline respiratory disease.

More than 70 per cent of cats that recover from the infection are carriers and will intermittently shed the virus, especially when stressed.

In breeding catteries, isolate all new admissions for two weeks before allowing contact with other cats.

Some carriers have no symptoms of the disease, while others occasionally or permanently have discharge from the nose and/or eyes. If they are exhibiting signs of the disease, they should be isolated while in a cattery.

## Feline urological syndrome (FUS)

This condition (also referred to as feline urolithiasis) is common and can be fatal, especially in male cats. In the male and female cat the condition encompasses inflammation of the bladder and

*Continual licking around the penis may indicate feline urological syndrome.*

urethra, together with the formation of sand-like crystals in the urine. The crystals are mainly made up of a magnesium compound called struvite (see page 77).

In male cats the urethra is long, narrow and has a bend in it, which is readily blocked. The female cat's urethra is short, of a greater diameter and rarely becomes blocked.

*Causes*

The cause may result from a combination of factors:
• Infection.
• Alkaline urine.
• Excessive magnesium in the diet.
• Restricted access to water.
• Excessive dry food.
• Reduced physical activity.
• Restricted access to the place where the cat normally urinates, causing it to retain stale urine in its bladder for lengthy periods of time.

*Signs*

Common to male and female:
• Squatting frequently.
• Straining to urinate (often mistaken for constipation).
• Licking around the penis or vulva.
• Urinating in unusual places.
• Blood in the urine.

Peculiar to male and caused by partial or complete blockage of urethra:
• Crying in pain, especially when picked up.
• Lethargic.
• Swollen abdomen.
• End of penis, if protruding, may be red to bluish in colour.
• In shock.
• Not eating.

*Treatment*

Contact your veterinarian immediately; if delayed,

a blocked urethra can be fatal due to a build up of toxic waste products in the blood or to rupture of the bladder.

Your veterinarian will carefully anaesthetise the cat, pass a catheter (tube) up the urethra to the blockage, clear the blockage and then pass the catheter into the bladder. The catheter allows the urine to flow freely. The cat is treated with antibiotics, anti-inflammatory agents, fluids and urine acidifiers.

If the problem recurs immediately or sometime after the catheter is removed, a surgical procedure called a perineal urethrostomy is recommended. This procedure shortens and widens the male urethra, preventing a blockage from recurring.

*Prevention*
• Provide access to clean water.
• Increase fluid intake by adding water and a small amount of salt to the diet.
• Take the cat off dry food, even though dry cat food now has a reduced amount of magnesium.
• Provide access to clean litter tray or to the garden.
• Encourage exercise.
• Your veterinarian can provide a prescription diet which will dissolve the struvite crystals which have already formed in the bladder. After two to three months the crystals will be completely dissolved. The veterinarian will then prescribe another diet which will prevent crystals from forming by keeping the urine acidic and the magnesium level low. Keep your cat permanently on this prescription diet.

**Feline viral rhinotracheitis** (see page 148)

**Fish hook in lip** (see page 109)

**Fit** (see page 109)

**Flatulence** (passing wind)

To pass wind from the anus is a normal bodily function of the cat as a result of gas being produced during the digestion of food in the stomach and intestine. Frequently passing large volumes of foul-smelling gas (wind) is considered abnormal.

*Causes*
• Eating rapidly and gulping air with the food.
• Eating excessive amounts of grass or vegetables such as cauliflower and cabbage.
• Intestinal irritation due to change of diet, infection or worms.

*Treatment*
• Feed three or four small meals a day.
• Change the diet. Try different brands of canned and dry food. If you prepare the cat's food, cut down on the amount of vegetables in the diet and

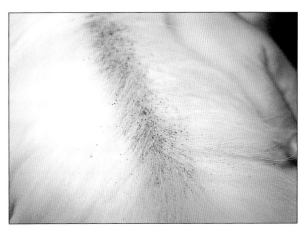
*This dark discolouration is flea dirt.*

check the quality of the meat that is included.
• Worm the cat.
• Have your veterinarian check the cat for some abnormality of the stomach or intestine. A drug to slow down peristalsis (intestinal movement), may be prescribed.
• Try giving the cat charcoal tablets obtained from your local pharmacy.

**Flea allergy**

This is one of the most common skin conditions in cats, especially in warm climates. Fleas also play a part in the tapeworm life cycle (see 'Worms', page 173) and in large numbers can cause severe anaemia.

*Cause*
The flea is a bloodsucker and bites the cat for that purpose. This causes a local allergic reaction, which irritates the cat. The cat bites or scratches the irritated area to get temporary relief. At the same time this aggravates the inflamed skin, which irritates the cat more, and so the cat bites and scratches more. Thus a vicious circle develops and the skin problem gets progressively worse. A cat's tongue is like rough sandpaper.

*Signs*
The skin is red, inflamed and irritated to the point where there may be small crusty scabs due to the cat scratching.

Hair loss around the neck and along the back towards the base of the tail, if evident, can vary from thinning to baldness.

The skin may be broken in areas due to scratching and licking. After years it becomes thickened, scaly and infiltrated with black pigment (melanin).

Brush the hair back along the cat's back and around the base of its tail. Look carefully and you will probably see fleas and flea dirt or excreta, which is really waste from digested blood. The excreta is seen as small black specks lying in the

*A sign of allergic reaction to a flea collar.*

coat and on the skin around the base of the tail.
*Treatment*
If the cat is continually scratching and biting, take
it to your veterinarian, who may give an injection
of cortisone to stop the irritation, to allow the skin
to repair itself and return to normal and for the hair
to grow back.

To help clear up the existing condition and
prevent it recurring, you must get rid of all the fleas.
Treatment involves the infested cat, other dogs and
cats in the household, and their environment.

Different types of treatment are:

1. *Insecticidal rinse (containing maldison)* Maldison
(Malathion) is very effective and lasts for approximately one week. When you dilute it with water as
directed and pour it on the cat, most of the rinse will
run off (because the cat's coat is partially waterproof). Shampoo the cat first or at least wet the coat
before applying the rinse.

Read carefully the directions on the label, particularly in regard to dilution and age for use. It is
important for the person washing the cat to have
minimal body contact with the Malathion. The
rinse has an odour to which the cat might object.
The task of rinsing may then become a difficult one.

You can allow the cat to drip dry or it may allow
you to use a hair dryer. Cats that lick themselves
after washing should be towel-dried to prevent
ingestion of excessive amounts of Malathion.

Most dog insecticidal rinses are poisonous to
cats.

2. *Insecticidal shampoo (containing pyrethrins and
piperonyl butoxide)* These do not have the pungent odour of the insecticidal rinse. They can be
used on kittens as well as on mature cats. The
shampoo kills fleas at the time of the wash, but it
does not have any long-lasting, residual effect. The
shampoo must be rinsed off thoroughly. It can be
used in conjunction with flea collars and sprays. If

you start to bathe kittens when they are weaned
from the mother, they usually become accustomed
to being washed.

Shampoos have a good cleansing effect on the
skin and coat, but they do not have a long-lasting
effect against fleas. They can be used on young
kittens, but some cats prove very difficult to wash.

3. *Insecticidal tablet or liquid* This is administered
twice weekly via the mouth or food. It is fairly
effective but should not be given in conjunction
with any other flea treatment.

4. *Insecticidal sprays (containing pyrethrins and
piperonyl butoxide)* The pressurised can-type makes
a hissing noise as the spray is released and frightens
the cat. The pump action-type is reasonably easy
and quick to apply.

Brush the hair back to expose the skin and spray
with a fine mist, holding the bottle about 15 cm (6
in) from the cat. Wipe any excess spray off the hair
with a towel, because if the cat licks the spray on
the coat it may salivate profusely. It is not toxic. It
will kill the fleas at the time of spraying and can be
used on the queen, her kittens and their environment, but it does not have a long-lasting effect.

5. *Flea collars* There are numerous brands of flea
collars that vary in their effectiveness and period of
action. Some collars are designed to expand and
allow the cat's head to slip free if the collar gets
caught on an object. If the collar gets wet, the
insecticidal product can be leached out, rendering
it ineffective.

Some cats are allergic to flea collars and develop
a severe inflammatory skin reaction underneath the
collar. When you put on a collar, check the skin
underneath it for about a week. If there is no
reaction, there is no need for further checking; if
there is a reaction, take off the collar and seek a
veterinarian's advice.

The collar is reasonably effective and easy to
apply, but it does not control fleas in the cat's
environment.

6. *Flea powders* There are numerous types of flea
powders which vary in effectiveness and length of
action. Some can be used on young kittens over
four weeks of age and can also be sprinkled on
their bedding. Flea powder is not as effective as
other products in treating adult cats, although it
may be used in conjunction with flea collars.

When applying the powder, brush it well into
the coat and then wipe the excess powder off the
surface with a damp cloth.

7. *Fleas in the cat's environment* The flea egg and
flea larvae live in debris shed from the cat (hair,
skin, etc.) onto bedding, carpets, door mats and the
cat's favourite sleeping places. Where possible,

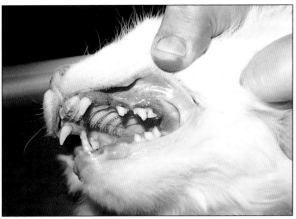

*Gingivitis: a red, inflamed gum.*

vacuum these areas, burning the contents of the vacuum cleaner, and use insecticidal sprays (pyrethrins and piperonyl butoxide) twice weekly on the areas where cats lie.

There is a relatively new product called Siphotrol (permethrin and methoprene) available in a pressurised can. Place the cans strategically throughout the house as directed on the label. Press the button on the can, and the contents are released in a mist which spreads throughout the house. The product claims that the flea eggs and larvae and even adult fleas in the house are eliminated for a period of up to eight months. (See 'Flea infestation of kittens and queen', page 194.)

### Fly strike

This problem is seasonal and more common in longhaired cats.

*Cause*

Blowflies are attracted to open wounds and more so if the hair around the infected wound is matted with pus. Hair matted with faeces around the anus is a prime target for fly strike. The blowfly lays eggs in the matted hair, the eggs develop into maggots, which invade the skin, anus and vagina, causing severe tissue damage.

*Signs*

Often the cat is lethargic, off its food. On close inspection, you will see maggots wriggling in the wound or around and even in the anus, and sometimes in the vagina.

*Treatment*

If the problem appears extensive, contact your veterinarian. In some cases of fly strike, where there is extensive tissue damage, toxins are produced which poison the cat and may prove fatal. Your veterinarian may need to anaesthetise the cat and cut away any dead tissue, as well as administer antibiotics.

*Prevention*

In spring and summer, longhaired cats should be checked regularly around the anal area. Hair around the anus and vagina should be cut short to prevent contamination with faeces. Cats prone to develop matted coats should be brushed and combed regularly. A weekly Malathon (maldison) rinse helpful.

**Foreign body** (see page 166)

**Fracture** (see page 109)

**Gingvitis**

*Causes*
* Bacterial infections.
* Irritant substances licked from a contaminated coat.
* Plaque and tartar on the teeth.
* Viral respiratory infections.
* Excessive vitamin A in the diet.

*Signs*
* Red, inflamed gum along the tooth-gum margin, which is usually in the region of the premolar and molar teeth, especially of the upper jaw.
* There may be evidence of bad breath and saliva, which may be blood-tinged, drooling from the mouth.
* The cat shows interest in food but is tentative or reluctant to eat.
* The teeth may be clean or covered in varying amounts of plaque and tartar.
* The gums often bleed if touched.

*Treatment*
See your veterinarian. If necessary, the cat will be given a general anaesthetic and its teeth will be cleaned with an ultrasonic descaler. Any loose or unhealthy teeth will be extracted.

Anti-inflammatory agents may be administered to reduce the redness and pain, and antibiotics to clear up any infection.

Encourage the cat to eat by feeding it soft food (canned) with plenty of flavour and odour. Do not feed liver to the cat, because of its high vitamin A content. Gingivitis often recurs; extraction of the premolar and molar teeth in severe chronic cases will often give a permanent cure.

*Prevention*
A regular six-monthly check-up by your veterinarian and ultrasonic descaling, if necessary, will help to prevent gingivitis.

**Grass eating** (see page 171)

**Hair ball** (see page 171)

**Heart disease**

The heart is a four-chambered, muscular pump, made up of special muscle fibres. The heart's

153

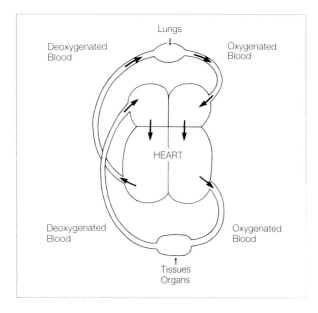

pumping action is controlled by electrical impulses released from a small node situated in the heart muscle, but this automatic control is overridden by other factors when a cat is excited or disturbed.

The function of the heart is simply to circulate blood to the numerous tissues and organs throughout the body. Basically, blood goes from the heart to the lungs, where the red blood cells are replenished with oxygen and their waste products are removed. The oxygenated blood then goes to the tissues and organs, where it exchanges its oxygen for carbon dioxide and other waste products. It is then said to be deoxygenated blood, and travels back to the heart and is again pumped to the lungs, where the waste products are removed and the blood is reoxygenated.

Heart disease and associated problems are uncommon in cats. In this regard, cats are unlike dogs and humans, who have a relatively high incidence of heart disease.

*Causes*

The cat may be born with a heart defect. Viruses and bacteria may also damage the heart muscle and valves. The causes of certain heart conditions, such as heart muscle wasting (cardiomyopathy), have not yet been finally determined.

*Signs*

The signs of a heart problem include:

• Laboured, rapid breathing and rapid heart rate following moderate exercise.

• Fatigue and poor exercise tolerance or general lethargy and reluctance to exercise or play.

• Coughing associated with movement, exercise or excitement, or a persistent, intermittent cough, together with drinking excess water and swelling of the abdomen.

(The above signs are not specific indicators of heart disease, but you should be suspicious if your cat exhibits them.)

• Heart murmur, detected with a stethoscope, is associated with incomplete closure of the heart valves. When the heart muscle contracts on a supposedly closed chamber, some blood leaks through the partially closed valves, thereby reducing the cardiac output, the oxygenation of the tissues and exercise tolerance.

Other heart conditions may be detected by your veterinarian using an electrocardiogram, enabling the evaluation of abnormalities in the heart.

*Treatment*

Treatment by your veterinarian will vary according to the type of heart disease diagnosed and its associated symptoms. The aim of any treatment is to improve heart function and to reduce fluid retention.

Good general nursing, such as protecting your cat from stress caused by excitement, overexertion, excessive hot or cold temperatures and humidity.

Make sure clean water is always readily available. Check with your local water authority as to what the level of sodium is in your water supply. If the level of sodium is above 150 ppm, use distilled water.

Your veterinarian can supply prescription diets that have a greatly reduced salt content. Reduction of salt content (sodium) in the diet helps to decrease fluid retention, thereby improving blood circulation and organ function, including the function of the heart. Avoid feeding the cat canned and dried foods that have a relatively high salt content to enhance their palatability.

If prescription diets are unavailable, you can prepare your own salt-reduced diet of rice plus lamb or beef or chicken.

### Heartworm

This disease is very common in dogs in most countries with tropical or subtropical regions, such as the US, southern Europe, Australia and India. The disease is rare in cats.

*Cause*

A worm called *Dirofilaria immitis* which lives in the right ventricle of the heart and the pulmonary artery. The pulmonary artery is the major vessel supplying the lungs. The worms can vary from 10-25 cm (4-10 in) in length.

The female worm produces microfilaria (larvae), which are released into the bloodstream. Certain species of mosquito ingest microfilaria when sucking blood from an infected dog or cat. The same mosquito, when biting another dog or cat, releases

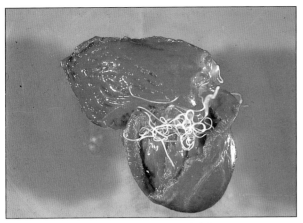

*A dissected heart, showing adult heartworm.*

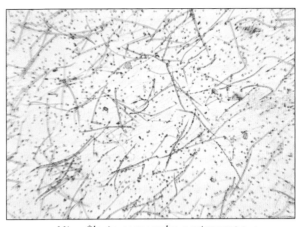

*Microfilaria, seen under a microscope.*

microfilaria into its tissues or bloodstream. Over a period of six months or more, the microfilaria find their way to the heart and pulmonary artery, and live there as mature adults.

Heartworm is not transferred directly from cat to cat, dog to dog or dog to cat. A cat or dog can only become infected by being bitten by a certain species of mosquito carrying the microfilaria.

*Signs*

Signs vary with the number of heartworms in the right side of the heart and pulmonary artery. Often there are no signs of the disease. Signs include lethargy, chronic cough, anaemia, laboured breathing, swollen abdomen and drinking excess water.

The heartworm may float free in the bloodstream and block an important blood vessel, acting like an embolism or clot, and cause death.

*Treatment*

Your veterinarian can diagnose heartworm by a blood test. X-rays of advanced cases usually show enlargement of the pulmonary arteries and right side of the heart.

Treatment involves intravenous injections of an arsenical compound to kill the adult worm, followed a month later by another type of drug to kill the microfilaria. This method of treatment is usually very successful.

Preventative treatment in the form of tablets is available, but it is not usual to give it to cats because the incidence of he artworm in cats is rare.

**Heatstroke** (see page 113)

**Hepatitis**

The liver plays an important role in digestion and in the production of proteins, fats, sugars, vitamins and

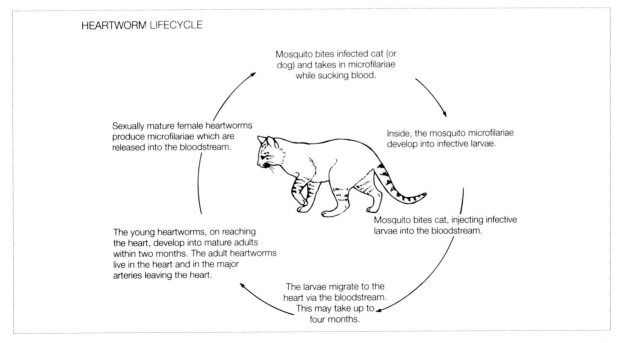

HEARTWORM LIFECYCLE

Mosquito bites infected cat (or dog) and takes in microfilariae while sucking blood.

Inside, the mosquito microfilariae develop into infective larvae.

Sexually mature female heartworms produce microfilariae which are released into the bloodstream.

Mosquito bites cat, injecting infective larvae into the bloodstream.

The young heartworms, on reaching the heart, develop into mature adults within two months. The adult heartworms live in the heart and in the major arteries leaving the heart.

The larvae migrate to the heart via the bloodstream. This may take up to four months.

155

*Jaundice: the yellow discolouration of the conjunctiva.*

in detoxifying poisons and waste products.

Hepatitis is inflammation or damage to the liver. The liver has tremendous powers of recovery, and unless the damage is overwhelming, the liver cells can regenerate and restore the liver back to normal function. Hepatitis in cats is not contagious to humans.

*Causes*

Trauma due to a motor vehicle accident or some other injury. Viral or bacterial infections. Poisons ingested or absorbed through the skin in sufficient quantity will damage the liver. Poor blood circulation to the liver due to heart disease. Primary and secondary cancer of the liver.

*Signs*

Not eating, vomiting, abdominal pain, diarrhoea, lethargy, urine dark in colour and jaundice (yellow discolouration of the conjunctiva and gums).

*Treatment*

Consult your veterinarian, who can diagnose the disease, and often its cause, by examination, urine tests, blood tests, X-ray and in some cases by an exploratory laparotomy (opening up the abdomen to examine the liver in detail). The treatment

administered by your veterinarian will vary according to the cause and symptoms.

At home you can assist in the recovery of your cat by:
• Providing clean, fresh water.
• Feeding four or more small meals per day.
• Making sure the food is fat free, such as lean meat, chicken or fish.
• Giving NO milk or dairy products.
• Giving a vitamin-mineral supplement high in the vitamin B group.
• Providing protection from the environment (heat and cold) and not allowing the cat to overexert itself.

### Hormonal hair loss

This condition occurs in both neutered males and females, although it is much more common in the males.

*Cause*

Unknown, but a hormonal imbalance is thought to be the cause.

*Signs*

The hair loss is equally distributed on both sides of the body, i.e. it has a symmetrical appearance. The hair loss is usually down the inside and back of the hindlegs, and extends along the abdomen and up the flanks. There is no sign of the skin being irritated or the cat pulling, rubbing or scratching out the hair. If you look carefully, the apparently bald skin is sparsely covered with very fine hair.

*Treatment*

Consult your veterinarian, who will put the cat on a hormone treatment. Some cats respond well to the treatment. In cases that respond, some require ongoing treatment to prevent the condition recurring.

### Hypervitaminosis A (see page 170)

### Hypothermia (see page 191)

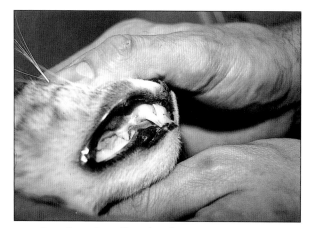

*Jaundice: the yellow discolouration of the gums.*

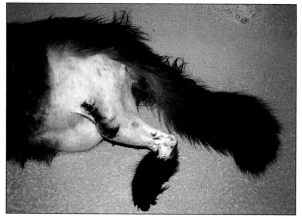

*Hormonal hair loss.*

### Infectious viral diseases
(refer to the following)

Feline AIDS (FIV)  (see page 146)
Feline calicivirus  (see page 149)
Feline infectious enteritis  (see page 147)
Feline infectious peritonitis  (see page 148)
Feline leukaemia virus  (see page 148)
Feline panleucopenia  (see page 147)
Feline viral rhinotracheitis  (see page 148)
Rabies  (see page 163)

### Infertility of queen (see page 185)

### Infertility of stud (see page 186)

### Iodine deficiency (see pages 74, 186)

### Kidney and bladder diseases and problems
(refer to the following)

Acute kidney disease  (see this page)
Cancer of the kidney  (see page 135)
Chronic kidney disease  (see page 158)
Cystic kidneys  (see page 138)
Cystitis  (see page 138)
Feline urological syndrome (FUS)  (see page 150)
Nephritis (kidney disease)  (see pages 157-158)
Urinary incontinence  (see page 170)

### Kidney diseases

The cat has two kidneys, which filter waste products from the bloodstream.  If the kidneys are not functioning properly, the waste products accumulate in the blood and have a toxic or poisoning effect on the cat. Waste product build-up in the blood may eventually be fatal.  If up to 75 per cent of each kidney is damaged, the cat can still function and enjoy a good quality lifestyle.

Chronic kidney disease is common, especially in cats over nine years of age.  Some surveys indicate that approximately 25 per cent of the cat population in that age group have some form of kidney disease.

Kidney disease or nephritis can be divided into two main groups, namely acute and chronic.

#### Acute kidney disease

This form occurs more frequently in younger cats (two to six years of age) and is characterised by sudden onset with obvious symptoms.
*Causes*
• Infection, both bacterial and viral
• Motor vehicle accidents, leading to:
   (a) direct damage to the kidneys;
   (b) shock which results in reduced blood flow, causing both damage to the kidneys and decreased filtration of the blood.
• Other diseases may cause damage to the kidneys

by reducing blood flow or by causing debris to accumulate in the blood, thus blocking the filtration system within the kidneys.
• Poisons, such as ethylene glycol (antifreeze), arsenic (insecticides and herbicides), thallium (rat poison) and a venomous snake bite, which may damage the internal structure of the kidneys.
• Certain antibiotics, for example neomycin and gentamycin, can cause kidney damage.
*Signs*
• Not eating, but may show interest in food by hovering over the food bowl.
• Drinking may be increased or decreased, depending on how toxic the cat is. The cat may hover over the water bowl.
• Vomiting.
• Lethargy.
• Dehydration. In cases that are fairly severely dehydrated, the skin loses its elasticity. When the skin is pinched behind the neck, rather than snapping back into place, it remains in a pinched fold.
• Urinating more frequently if the cat is drinking more.
• Coat looks harsh and rough; the cat stops grooming itself.
*Treatment*
Contact your veterinarian. Nephritis can be readily diagnosed by blood tests for urea and creatinine. Your veterinarian will treat your cat according to the cause and symptoms.  The treatment may involve:
• antibiotics,
• anti-vomiting drugs,
• fluid and electrolyte therapy given intravenously, subcutaneously (under the skin), or orally if the cat is not vomiting. It is more difficult to give the same volume orally than it is by other methods.

While the cat is not eating or drinking at home, it should be hospitalised for fluid therapy.  Otherwise, it will dehydrate and exacerbate the problem because of reduced blood circulation through the kidneys and concentration of toxins (waste products) in the bloodstream.

Regular blood tests for urea and creatinine can help the veterinarian assess the cat's progress.  A sign of recovery is when the cat starts to eat and drink.

Once your cat goes home, it is important that it should be given a balanced diet to reduce stress on the damaged kidneys.  A balanced diet containing a reduced amount of high quality protein, sodium and phosphorus will help to reduce the quantity of waste products produced and the workload on the kidneys.  Try to avoid giving your cat meat, eggs, cheese or bones. In addition, provide your cat with fresh, clean water and good nursing. Avoid exposing it to extremes of temperature.

Your veterinarian can provide you with a prescription diet that has been formulated by veterinary nutritionists for cats with kidney disease. The diet is highly palatable and readily accepted by most cats.

### Chronic kidney disease

This disease occurs more frequently in cats over the age of nine years. Approximately 25 per cent of cats over nine years have some form of chronic kidney disease. This disease can take months or years before symptoms are obvious enough to make the owner aware that the cat is seriously ill. The signs or symptoms are more subtle than acute kidney disease, and unless you are alert to the signs they may go unnoticed for some time.

*Causes*
- Infection: bacterial and viral.
- Other diseases such as diabetes.
- Congenital abnormalities, e.g. cystic kidneys.
- Cardiac disease.
- Other unknown causes.

*Signs*
As the disease progresses slowly over months or years, the signs correspondingly may also develop slowly or the cat may compensate and the signs may be hidden up to the point where it can no longer compensate and the signs appear suddenly.

The signs may be:
- Drinking excessively.
- Urinating excessively.
- Weight loss.
- Lethargy.
- Poor appetite.
- Coat rough and harsh due to lack of interest in grooming.
- Occasional vomiting.
- Bad breath.
- Anaemia.

*Treatment*
Contact your veterinarian, who can confirm chronic kidney disease by a thorough clinical examination and pathology tests. Often, one or both kidneys on palpation are hard, irregular in shape and larger or smaller than normal. A urine sample may indicate the presence of blood, a high level of protein and a low specific gravity, which indicates the urine is very dilute. A blood test which shows that the urea and creatinine levels are elevated indicates the extent of the damage to the kidneys and the cat's chances of recovery.

After treatment has been administered for a number of days, a second test is useful to determine if the levels have moved up or down. Treatment will vary according to the symptoms and cause, and may include:
- antibiotics to clear up any bacterial infection;
- anabolic steroids to aid in repair of damaged kidney tissue, to prevent weight loss and to stimulate weight gain;
- a vitamin supplement, because many chronic kidney disease cases are anaemic due to waste products in the blood affecting red blood cell production from the bone marrow.

Your veterinarian can provide you with a prescription diet containing a reduced amount of high quality protein, sodium and phosphorus. The prescription diet will reduce the workload on the kidneys, while supplying the nutritional requirements of the cat.

Most cats with nephritis have a poor appetite, so gradually introduce the new diet over a fourteen-day period. Start by mixing a small amount of the prescription diet with your pet's normal food, and gradually increase the amount of prescription diet food, at the same time decreasing the amount of the cat's normal food until it is eating only prescription diet food. Try to avoid giving meat, eggs, cheese or bones to your cat.

With proper dietary management, progressive chronic nephritis may be stopped or slowed down.

If your cat is not eating or drinking, it will dehydrate, which will make the disease worse. Your veterinarian will hospitalise your pet and give it fluids intravenously or under the skin to help flush the waste products out of the blood. This often gives the kidneys the opportunity to improve their function and makes the cat feel better, thereby stimulating it to eat and drink.

Chronic kidney disease sometimes gets progressively worse. In a human situation, the patient relies on a dialysis machine to survive while waiting for a kidney transplant. This treatment is not feasible for the cat. If your cat, after intensive treatment with fluid therapy in hospital, will not eat or drink and its urea and creatinine levels are still abnormally high, then you should give consideration to having it put to sleep.

### Kitten diseases and problems
(refer to the following)

Umbilical hernia (see page 191)

## Lice

Lice are not a common problem in cats.
*Cause*
Those cats most often affected are debilitated, with a dirty, matted coat due to a lack of interest in cleaning themselves.
*Signs*
They are found on the head and along the back of the cat. Lice have a brown head and a greyish body, and are found on the skin surface, not on the hair.

The cat is itchy and scratches itself, causing red, inflamed skin to shed dry flakes into the matted hair. Eggs are attached to the hair shaft and can be seen in good light.
*Treatment*
Clip any matted hair away and then shampoo to clean the coat before giving a 0.5 per cent Malathion (maldison) rinse. Repeat three times at seven-day intervals. Worming and nutritious feeding of the cat are also recommended.

## Lungworm

*Cause*
The lungworm, which is a small roundworm 7-9 mm (0.3-0.35 in) long, lives in the pulmonary artery of the lung. The cat becomes infected by eating lizards, birds or rodents carrying lungworm larvae.
*Signs*
Cats often have lungworm and show no symptoms. The usual symptoms are a persistent cough, sometimes associated with lethargy, poor appetite and weight loss.
*Treatment*
Lungworm can be successfully treated by your veterinarian. The disease in most cases is self-limiting.

## Lymphosarcoma (see page 140)

## Mammary (breast) lumps

There are three common types of lumps or swellings associated with the cat's mammary glands: enlargement of the mammary gland, mammary cysts and mammary tumours.

## Enlargement of the mammary gland

*Cause*
In unneutered females the cause is hormonal. It may occur in desexed males or females being treated with the hormone megestrol acetate, which is often used for skin problems in cats (page 166).
*Signs*
One or more mammary glands may be enlarged. The whole gland is swollen and firm, but not tender to the touch. The cat is otherwise healthy.

*Treatment*
In female cats that have not been desexed, it usually resolves itself. If it persists, desexing will bring about a reduction in the swelling of the mammary gland(s).

Discontinuance of the use of megestrol acetate for skin problems in desexed cats that also have mammary gland enlargement will usually bring about a reduction in the swelling, with the mammary glands returning to normal.

## Mammary cysts

*Cause*
Blockage of a duct within the mammary gland.
*Signs*
A dark-coloured, fluid-filled cyst in the mammary gland .
*Treatment*
Surgical removal of the cyst or complete excision of the mammary gland.

## Mammary tumour

*Cause*
Usually occurs in older female cats that have not been neutered. The tumours are usually malignant.
*Signs*
In the early stages, a small hard lump, approximately 0.5 cm (0.2 in) in diameter, can be felt in the mammary gland. At a later stage, the tumour may be the size of a walnut and the skin over the surface of the tumour may be ulcerated.
*Treatment*
Before resorting to surgery, your veterinarian will X-ray the chest to make sure there are no secondary tumours in the lungs. If the lungs are clear on the X-rays, the tumour is surgically excised. If the tumour is of such a size that it involves a large portion of the mammary gland, then the whole of the gland will be removed.

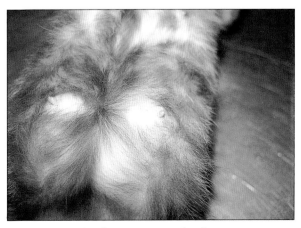

*Swollen mammary glands.*

159

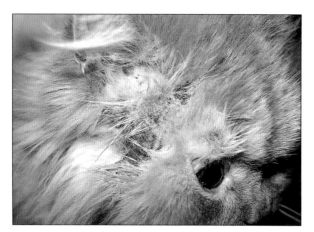

*Mange: hair loss, and crusty scabs.*

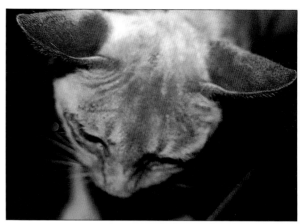

*Mange: the skin is thickened and corrugated.*

Histopathology on the lump will determine if it is benign or malignant.

### Mange

When people see a cat with hair loss and crusty, infected, thickened skin, they often refer to the cat as being mangy. There are many causes of this type of skin condition. Mange is a specific disease caused by a mite.

*Cause*

This condition is caused by the mite *Notoedres cati*.

*Signs*

Mainly found on the forehead. Hair loss, redness, crusty scabs, scratching. The damaged skin becomes infected and if it goes untreated, it becomes thickened and corrugated. It may spread to other parts of the body.

*Treatment*

See your veterinarian, who will confirm the diagnosis by scraping the skin deeply until blood is drawn. The scraping is looked at under a microscope to identify the mites.

Rinse the cat thoroughly in 0.5 per cent Malathion (maldison) and repeat in seven days. Any cats that the infected cat comes into contact with should also be rinsed thoroughly.

It is a good idea to treat the bedding or to get rid of it, although the mites can only survive for a short time off the cat. Your veterinarian may prescribe antibiotics, anti-inflammatory agents and a vitamin supplement.

### Mastitis (see page 185)

### Middle ear infection

The middle and inner ear structures are important for hearing and balance.

*Cause*

It is usually caused by a bacterial infection associated with inflammation of the middle and inner ear. There are several routes to the middle ear that the infection can take. It can pass along the external ear canal and through a ruptured eardrum, along the eustachian tube from the throat or via the bloodstream as a generalised acute infection localising in the middle ear.

*Signs*

• There may or may not be discharge from the ear.
• The head is tilted towards the affected side.
• There may be sideways movement (flickering) of the eyes.
• Usually the cat will have a drunken sway when it moves, and it will tend to circle in the one direction, sometimes falling over on its side.

*Treatment*

Take the cat to your veterinarian. The treatment may involve antibiotics, anti-inflammatory agents, surgical drainage and hospitalisation until the cat regains its balance. Response to treatment is sometimes slow. Some cases are left with a permanent head tilt, a tendency to wobble and deafness.

### Miliary dermatitis

*Cause*

Fleas, high fish diets.

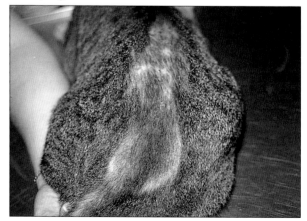

*The signs of miliary dermatitis.*

*Signs*

Numerous small scabs on top of a small thickening in the skin. The scabby lumps are along the back, around the neck and head, and on the lower abdomen. The cat's skin is most unpleasant to touch. Scratching aggravates the small, scabby lumps and causes hair loss.

*Treatment*

Take the cat off the fish diet and put it onto a lamb and rice diet. Consult your veterinarian, who may put the cat on antibiotics, anti-inflammatories, and hormone therapy.

Strict flea control is also important (page 195).

**Milk fever** (see page 185)

**Mouth diseases and problems**
(refer to the following)

Gingivitis (see page 153)
Overshot jaw (see page 86)
Plaque (see page 86)
Supernumerary teeth (see page 86)
Tartar (see page 86)
Tongue ulcers (see page 169)
Trench mouth (see page 170)

**Navel infection** (see page 191)

**Nephritis** (see page 157)

**Neurological dermatitis** (see page 162)

**Nutritional secondary hyperparathyroidism**
(see page 78)

**Obesity**

A cat's weight varies according to diet, exercise and type of breed. An obese cat is one that is obviously fat. It is more common in older cats, although less common in cats than dogs.

*Causes*

The primary cause of obesity is overeating. Secondary causes are lack of exercise, desexing and advancing age. The cat's genetic make-up will also have an influence on its weight, e.g. a Siamese is a cat of slender build, whereas a Persian is heavier. As the cat puts on weight, it tends to exercise less, setting up a vicious circle.

*Signs*

The average cat weighs about 4-5 kg (9-11 lb), although this varies greatly in different breeds. An obese cat looks and feels overweight. It may have a large abdomen that hangs down and protrudes outwards, the result of fat deposits under the skin, especially over the ribs and around the abdomen.

Obesity makes a cat susceptible to arthritis, joint and ligament problems, back problems, heart disease, breathing difficulties, diabetes, heat stress and constipation.

*Treatment*

Consult with your veterinarian to confirm that your cat is obese and that its obesity is not due to a medical problem.

Weight loss may be achieved by reducing calorie intake and increasing exercise. You can record your cat's weight by holding it in your arms and standing on a set of bathroom scales. Record the combined weight of yourself and your cat, then subtract your weight from the combined weight to find the cat's weight.

The amount of weight loss that you should aim for in your cat is from 100-250 gm (4-9 oz) per week.

Reduce your cat's calorie intake by reducing the volume of food gradually and by feeding it three or four small meals a day.

You can obtain from your veterinarian a prescription diet that is high in fibre, low in fat and calories, and completely covers your cat's nutritional requirements. The advantage of this type of diet is that the cat can eat the same volume of food and lose weight. The prescription diet is highly palatable and useful not only for achieving weight loss, but also for preventing weight gain.

Do not feed your cat snacks or other foods between meals. In relation to snacks, make sure

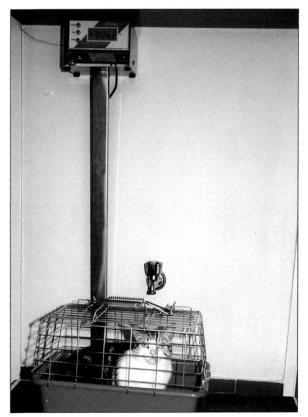

*Checking a cat's weight.*

the entire family is aware of your cat's weight reduction program. Encourage your cat to exercise. If it is an indoor cat, put it outside for a number of hours every day.

Weigh your cat weekly and record the weight gain or loss.

**Old age** (see page 94)

**Orphan kitten** (see page 188)

### Overgrooming (neurological dermatitis)

Some cats develop a fetish for continuously grooming themselves. Prolonged vigorous licking with the surface of the tongue, which is like rough sandpaper, causes the hairs to break and bald patches to form. If the licking continues, the skin becomes damaged.

*Causes*
• An allergic skin reaction to a flea bite or to some vegetation.
• Grazed skin.
• Anxiety created by some event such as a new cat or dog in the house or the owner going away and putting the cat in a boarding establishment.

*Signs*
Hair loss in areas where the cat can lick with its tongue, e.g. sides, flanks, lower abdomen. Often, the hair looks as if it has been shaved with a razor. Once the skin is broken, it irritates the cat, so it licks the area to alleviate the irritation. While it gets temporary relief, the licking further aggravates the skin and so the irritation continues.

A vicious circle develops and the initial cause is forgotten. The red, inflamed, ulcerated skin is looked on as the problem, while the initial cause, which ought to be included in the treatment, is forgotten.

*Treatment*
Try to identify the allergy or cause of the anxiety

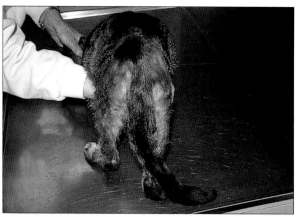
*Hair loss due to overgrooming.*

and remove it. Cats are fastidious about cleaning themselves, so the application of ointments and paints often aggravates the situation by attracting the cat's attention to the site of the problem.

If the skin is broken, consult your veterinarian, who may give antibiotic and cortisone injections to control infection and inflammation. The use of hormone therapy in many cases helps to alleviate anxiety without sedation.

If this fails, then an Elizabethan collar will physically prevent the cat from licking itself. Leave the collar on until the skin has completely healed and the hair is growing back. If the skin is 90 per cent better but there is some irritation still present, the cat will return to licking and very quickly will end up with the same problem again.

Make sure the cat is flea free.

**Overshot jaw** (see page 86)

**Paint on coat** (see page 113)

**Pancreatitis** (see page 140)

**Placental membrane** (see page 185)

**Plaque** (see page 86)

### Pneumonia

This is an infection and/or inflammation of the lung tissue.

*Causes*
There are numerous causes of pneumonia, namely viruses, bacteria, parasites or inhalation of foreign material. There are many predisposing causes, such as travelling, overcrowding and malnutrition, all of which lower the cat's resistance to infection.

*Signs*
The signs will vary with the suddenness of onset and the volume of lung tissue involved. Generally, the cat will be off its food and lethargic. Breathing is rapid and shallow. Often a cough, nasal discharge and a high temperature are associated with

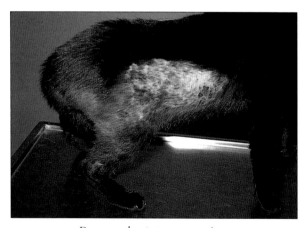
*Damage due to overgrooming.*

pneumonia. The breath may have a foul odour, and if you place your ear to the chest, moisture may be detected as the cat breathes in and out. The cat will sit in one place, not wanting to move or lie down.

*Treatment*

Consult your veterinary surgeon immediately. Keep in mind that good nursing is an essential part of any treatment. Keep the cat in a well-ventilated, draught-free area. Keep its temperature as even as possible, but not too high. Fresh water and nutritious, palatable food should be available to encourage eating and drinking. Electrolytes in the water are important as they help to prevent dehydration.

### Poisoning (see page 116)

### Puncture wound (see page 116)

### Rabies (see 'Vaccination program', page 88)

This is a highly contagious viral disease of warm-blooded animals and can be fatal. It is a disease of major significance because it is transmissible to humans. Rabies is widespread throughout the world, although Australia, the United Kingdom, Ireland, Japan, Hawaii, the Netherlands, Norway, Sweden and New Zealand are free of the disease.

*Cause*

A virus which is transmitted by the bite of an infected animal. The virus is found in heavy concentration in the saliva of the infected animal. Cats that contract rabies usually develop what is called the furious form, a sign of which is the tendency to attack, bite and scratch. The virus can be spread if a fresh wound is contaminated by infected saliva.

*Signs*

The period of time from being bitten to the symptoms showing can vary from weeks to months.

There are three phases of the disease. The first phase is characterised by a change in personality and a tendency to hide in dark places. This phase may be easily overlooked.

The second phase, the furious stage, develops two days after the first signs of the disease. This phase can last up to four days. The cat may suddenly attack, biting and scratching its victim viciously.

The third phase is the dumb stage, which develops over forty-eight hours. Paralysis starts in the hindquarters and progresses forward along the body until the cat is completely paralysed. **This is followed by death.**

Rabies can only be definitely determined by autopsy.

*Treatment*

If you suspect your cat has been bitten by a rabid animal, wash the wound thoroughly with soap and water, and take it to your veterinarian immediately. It is important to have available for the veterinarian information about the type of rabies vaccine your cat has had and when. This information will determine how the cat will be treated, provided it shows no symptoms of the disease. Once the cat has developed signs of rabies, treatment is useless and the only course open to the veterinarian is to put it to sleep.

The World Health Organisation recommends that unvaccinated cats known to have been bitten by a rabid animal should be put to sleep immediately because of the risk to humans and other animals.

If you suspect your cat shows signs of rabies, do not approach it. If it is in an enclosed space, lock it in and immediately contact your veterinarian.

*Prevention*

Every cat should be vaccinated in countries which are known to have rabies. This is in the interest of the cat, other animals and humans.

There are both killed and modified live virus vaccines to combat this disease. Some vaccines for dogs are unsuitable for cats. The vaccine is not available in countries that do not have the disease.

The vaccination procedure for kittens and adult cats is as follows:

Kittens — First vaccination at three months.

Adults — Booster vaccination annually.

### Rectal prolapse

*Cause*

Usually, this problem results from persistent diarrhoea and is more often found in young kittens than in mature cats.

*Signs*

A red, sausage-shaped, swollen mass usually about 4 cm (1.6 in) long protruding from the anus. The cat may strain and attempt to lick the prolapsed rectum.

*Treatment*

See your veterinarian immediately.

### Ringworm

Ringworm is a highly contagious skin disease caused by a fungus. It is not caused by a parasite or worm. The disease is more common in young cats and kittens. It is contagious to humans (especially young children) as well as to other cats and dogs.

*Cause*

The fungus *(Microsporum canis* or *Microsporum*

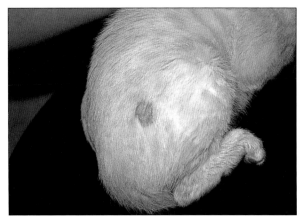

*The signs of ringworm.*

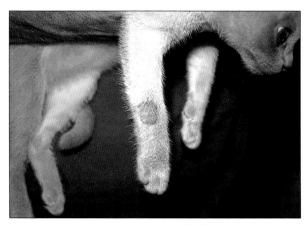

*Ringworm on the foreleg.*

*gypseum)* is spread by either direct or indirect contact. The fungus lives on hair, so the disease can be caught from loose hair shed by an infected cat. It can be spread by humans e.g. by using infected grooming equipment.

*Signs*

The ringworm may be anywhere on the body, but the common sites are the head and forelimbs. The lesions appear as a circular area of hair loss varying in diameter from 0.5-2.5 cm (0.2-1 in). There may be one or more lesions, which may or may not have a definite border. It takes approximately two weeks from the time of contact to the appearance of hairless patches. The skin in the bald patch has a dry, grey, scaly appearance.

*Treatment*

Wash the cat in a 0.3 per cent halamid (chloramine) solution twice weekly for three weeks to kill the fungus on the skin. Your veterinarian will prescribe griseofulvin tablets to be given for three weeks. Isolate the cat for three weeks. Vacuum areas where the cat lives, to pick up any loose infected hair. Soak grooming equipment in a 0.3 per cent halamid (chloramine) solution. Hair regrowth may take a month or more after successful treatment. Once a cat has had ringworm, it usually develops immunity.

Your veterinarian will make an initial diagnosis on the appearance of the lesions and any history of a family member having ringworm. The veterinarian can confirm that it is a ringworm by shining an ultraviolet light (Wood's lamp) over the suspicious area of skin in a darkened room. If it is ringworm, the lesion will glow a fluorescent green colour. A skin scraping with some hair can be sent to the laboratory for culture.

**Rodent ulcer**

Rodent ulcers often occur on one or both sides of the upper lip. It was thought many years ago that these ulcers were caused by a bite from a rodent. This is not true.

*Cause*

The cause is unknown. The ulcers that occur on the upper lip are usually opposite the canine teeth. It is not known if the canine tooth initiates the irritation. It is almost certain that the rough tongue of the cat promotes and stimulates the ulcers to develop. The correct name for them is *Eosinophilic granuloma*, because when examined in the pathology laboratory numerous cells called eosinophils are found at the site of the lesion.

*Signs*

They can occur on the upper lip, roof of the mouth, back of the throat, tongue and skin, and around the hindlegs and abdomen.

In the mouth they are usually circular, raised, with a rough surface and yellowish in colour. Those involving the lip are obviously ulcerated, thickened and hard to the touch.

The lesions on the skin are hairless, raised, with a rough fleshy red surface. They can vary in size from approximately 2-20 mm (0.08-0.8 in).

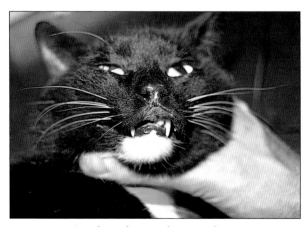

*A rodent ulcer on the upper lip.*

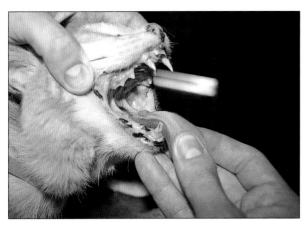

*A raised, circular lump on the tongue.*

*An ulcerated lip.*

*Treatment*

Consult your veterinarian. The treatment varies from the use of cortisone and/or hormone therapy to surgery, which involves surgical excision or cauterisation.

**Shock** (see page 116)

**Sick cat with poor appetite** (see page 78)

**Sinusitis (chronic snuffler)** (see page 166)

**Skin cancer**

Cats generally love to bask in the sun. Any cats with white ears are prone to sunburn due to lack of protective pigment in the skin. Chronic sunburn eventually leads to skin cancer.

*Cause*

Cats with white, unpigmented skin subjected to excessive burning by ultraviolet rays when basking in the sun over a period of time.

*Signs*

The edges of the ears are red, inflamed and begin to lose their hair cover. While the redness subsides somewhat in the winter, the edges of the ears become permanently red and practically hairless over a number of years. The skin flakes off, sores develop and the edges tend to curl and become itchy. Likewise, a sore may develop around the border of the nostrils. The cat scratches them, making the sores bleed. Owners often mistake the bleeding sores for fight wounds and treat them as such. The sores do not respond to conservative treatment and with time they become more extensive and chronic.

*Treatment*

Amputation of the ears at the base. Once the wounds heal and the hair grows back, the cat does not look unsightly. The hair protects the wound edge from the sun. The nose in the early stages can be cauterised. In a more advanced stage, radiation treatment is usually very successful, although the cancer may recur within three years.

If the cancer involves the nasal cartilage, the success of any form of treatment is very doubtful.

*Prevention*

Keep the cat out of the sun between 10 am and 4 pm. Apply an alcohol-based sunscreen to the nose and edges of the ears. Tattooing the nose and

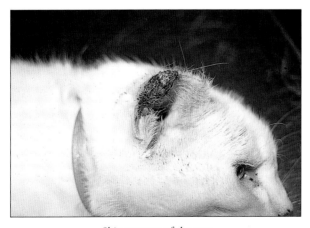

*Skin cancer of the ear.*

*Skin cancer, showing bleeding and a sore on the ear.*

*A front view of a cat which has had its ears amputated.*

*A side view of a cat with an amputated ear.*

ears of a young cat provides artificial pigment in the skin, which helps to guard it against skin cancer.

Selecting a kitten with good pigmentation of the skin, especially the nose and ears, is another way of avoiding the problem of skin cancer in your cat.

### Skin diseases and problems
(refer to the following)

Abscess  (see page 130)
Acne (feline)  (see page 132)
Cat leprosy  (see page 136)
Dandruff  (see page 138)
Flea allergy  (see page 151)
Fly strike  (see page 153)
Hormonal hair loss  (see page 156)
Mange  (see page 160)
Miliary dermatitis  (see page 160)
Overgrooming  (see page 162)
Ringworm  (see page 163)
Rodent ulcer  (see page164)
Skin cancer  (see page 165)
Stud tail  (see page 167)
Sunburn  (see page 165)

### Snake bite (see page 117)

### Sneezing

Sneezing is a fairly common problem in cats. There are two common causes of sneezing: one is allergies and the other is infections. In the cases of allergies, cats investigate their environment by sniffing, which often stimulates sneezing because they inhale house dust, pollens and numerous other irritants.

The most common infection of cats that causes sneezing is feline respiratory disease, more often referred to as cat flu (see page 148).

### *Allergic sneezing*

*Causes*
House dust, pollens or some other irritant.

*Signs*
Frequent sneezing or a spasm where the cat sneezes rapidly in succession a dozen times and then may not sneeze again for hours.  There is usually no discharge, but in some cases there may be a fine spray of clear fluid.  The eyes are usually clear, but they may be slightly watery.  The cat is otherwise healthy.

*Treatment*
Try to identify what the cat is allergic to in the house or garden. If the sneezing persists, see your veterinarian, who may prescribe antihistamines.

### *Foreign body*

*Cause*
Either inhalation of a foreign body up the nostril or ingestion of a foreign body, such as a blade of grass, which passes over the top of the soft palate and into the back of the nose.

*Signs*
The sneezing is continuous, vigorous and may involve sneezing rapidly in succession a dozen times or more, followed by a rest period.  There may be bleeding from the affected nostril.

*Treatment*
In most cases, the cat will need to be anaesthetised by your veterinarian to identify the position of the foreign body before removing it.  If a foreign body is protruding from the nose, remove it yourself.

### *Sinusitis (chronic snuffler)*

Following feline respiratory disease, some cats become 'chronic snufflers', i.e. they sneeze pus discharge from the nose off and on for years.

*Cause*
The mucous membrane lining the sinuses and nasal cavity may be permanently damaged following viral respiratory infections.  The damaged mucous membrane is then susceptible to bacterial infections.

*Skin cancer of the nose.*

*Skin cancer, showing a bleeding sore on the nose.*

*Signs*
Frequent, irregular bouts of sneezing. Thick pus discharge is sprayed from both nostrils. The discharge may be blood-tinged. The nostrils are usually partially blocked, causing noisy, snuffling breathing. The condition may appear to clear up, only to erupt again. This may continue throughout the cat's life. These cats are referred to as chronic snufflers.

*Treatment*
See your veterinarian, who may administer antibiotics and anti-inflammatory agents. The short-term results are good, but the sneezing and pus discharge usually recur.

A swab may be taken from the nasal pus to identify the bacteria and to find out the best antibiotic to use against that type of infection.

Another alternative is surgery to provide better drainage of the sinuses.

In some cases, treatment will control the infection but does not provide a permanent cure (see Feline respiratory disease treatment, page 148).

### Skin cancer (see page 165)
*Cause*
The cancer is caused by the sun. Cancer involving the mucous membrane inside the nostrils causes an irritation which stimulates sneezing.

*Signs*
A deep ulcerated sore on the nose involving the tissues and membrane lining the inside of the nostril. Usually, the sign is an occasional sneeze with no discharge or a fine spray of clear or blood-tinged fluid. The cat may rub or lick the nose.

*Treatment* (See above.)

### Spider bite (see page 117)
### Steatitis (see page 172)
### Stud tail
Occurs in entire (unneutered) male cats.

*Cause*
The male sex hormone testosterone is involved, but the exact cause is unknown.

*Signs*
More commonly seen in Persians. The skin on the top of the tail, just below the base, is red and exudes an oily secretion, sometimes matting the hair.

*Treatment*
Wash the cat in an antiseptic shampoo (e.g. Peroxyderm) or an antibacterial shampoo (e.g. chlorhexidene). If it looks infected, consult your veterinarian.

### Sunburn (see page 165)
### Supernumerary teeth (see page 86)
### Tartar (see page 86)
### Teeth problems (see page 86)
### Tick poisoning
Tick poisoning occurs in various parts of the world. Ticks are active in late spring and early summer. Some authorities think that cats are not as susceptible to tick poison as are dogs. The fact that cats spend much of their time grooming themselves suggests that ticks are removed in the grooming process before they have an opportunity to attach themselves to the cat's skin and inject their poison. This may explain why the incidence of tick poisoning in cats is not as high as it is in dogs.

There are various species of the tick, one being *Ixodes holocyclus*, which causes tick poisoning in cats and dogs on the east coast of Australia. The adult female tick varies in colour from grey to blue to brown. It is oval in shape and, depending on how engorged it is with blood, it will vary in size from 2-8 mm (0.08-0.3 in).

It is only the female tick which attaches itself to the host cat or dog, poisons it and eventually causes paralysis. The male tick does not attach itself to a

*Ticks.*

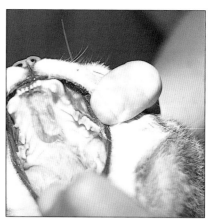

*Ulcers on the roof of the mouth.*

host. The primary hosts for *Ixodes holocyclus* are native animals such as possums and bandicoots, although dogs, cats, humans or any warm-blooded animal are suitable host substitutes.

The female tick lays 2000 to 3000 eggs, which hatch into larvae in about fifty days. The larvae attach themselves to a passing host and suck blood from it for five days before dropping off. The nymph, after a period of twenty to forty days, attaches itself to a second host, sucks blood from it for approximately five days and then drops off. Over a three- to ten-week period, the nymph develops into an adult tick. The adult tick attaches itself to a third host and sucks blood for six to twenty days. An adult female tick attached to a cat will poison it within four to six days.

*Signs*

The early signs are a change in the cat's voice to a croaky, husky meow. If the tick is around the face, there may be paralysis of the eyelids or lip on the side of the face to which the tick is attached. The pupils are dilated, the tongue may poke out of the mouth and the cat may vomit.

The hindlimbs become wobbly and the paralysis progresses to the chest muscles, often causing a grunting, distressed type of breathing. The cat becomes paralysed in both the front legs and hindlimbs. The cause of death is paralysis of the respiratory muscles, i.e. the cat actually dies from asphyxiation.

*Treatment*

If you find a tick on your cat, remove it immediately. Do not put methylated spirits, turpentine or other such preparations on the tick, because as the tick dies slowly, it will inject more poison into the cat. Do not grab the body of the tick and try to pull it off as it may break. Furthermore, in squeezing the body of the tick, you may stimulate it to inject more poison into the cat before you can remove it.

To remove a tick, first direct another person to hold the cat firmly but not tightly by the neck. If the cat is held too tightly, you may restrict its breathing further and cause it to struggle violently, thus making it more difficult to remove the tick.

Hold the hair away from the tick so that you can see where the head is attached to the skin. With a pair of tweezers, grasp the tick at its point of attachment to the skin and pluck it out. Examine the tick to see if you have removed all of it. If you have left part or all of the head in the skin, do not worry. It will not continue to poison the cat, but it will act like a foreign body, such as a splinter, and may cause swelling and inflammation of the skin around it. Dab some antiseptic on the site after removal.

Even if there is no sign of poisoning, observe the cat closely as the poison already in the cat's system may take up to forty-eight hours to take effect after the tick is removed. Search the cat thoroughly, as it may have more than one tick.

If your cat is showing any signs of tick poisoning, no matter how mild, take it to your veterinarian, who will hospitalise it, administer antitick serum by injection and treat the cat according to its symptoms. It is important for the cat to be kept cool as heat will aggravate its breathing difficulty.

*Prevention*

• Keep your cat out of the bush as much as possible, especially in late spring and early summer.

• Go over the cat in a methodical way every day, looking and feeling for ticks by rolling the skin between your fingers. Concentrate your search in the head and neck area, as 80 per cent of ticks are found there; the other 20 per cent could be found anywhere on the body.

It usually takes four to six days for a tick to poison the cat, so if you go over it every day, you have four chances of finding it, before the cat shows evident signs of poisoning.

• Rinse the cat once a week in a 1 per cent Malathion (maldison) solution.

• Longhaired cats should be clipped short in spring as ticks do not attach themselves as readily to short hair as they do to long hair. Also, clipping the hair short makes it easier to find ticks.

### Tongue ulcers

*Causes*

Tongue ulcers are often associated with viral respiratory infections, vitamin B deficiency, chronic kidney disease or the cat licking its coat which has been contaminated with an irritant substance.

*Signs*

• Dribbling from the mouth. The saliva may be tinged with blood.

• Often the cat's breath has a foul odour.

• The cat may show interest in food but refuse to eat.

• On opening the cat's mouth, you will see ulcer-ated areas of varying size on the tongue.

• There may be ulcers on the roof of the mouth.

*Treatment*

See your veterinarian. The treatment usually involves antibiotics, multi-vitamins and fluids if the cat is dehydrated as a result of not eating and drinking. The administration of anti-inflammatory agents is very effective in alleviating inflammation and pain. Any irritant substance is removed from the coat.

### Toxoplasmosis

Toxoplasmosis is a common disease of cats in the UK, US, Australia and Europe. Many infected cats have no apparent symptoms. This disease is emphasised because it is a health risk to humans.

*Cause*

• *Toxoplasma gondii,* a single-cell parasite, micro-scopic in size.

• Cats may become infected by eating other ani-mals whose tissues contain toxoplasma cysts, e.g. birds, rabbits, rodents or freshly killed, uncooked pork or lamb.

• Unborn kittens can acquire the infection in the uterus from their infected mother.

*Signs*

Cats that develop symptoms usually fall into two categories:

• Infected young cats, which often develop a rapid acute form, with one or more signs, such as a high temperature, rapid laboured respiration, hepatitis, diarrhoea and, in some cases, death.

• Infected older cats, which usually develop the slow chronic form, with one or more signs, such as weight loss, diarrhoea, pale gums, wobbliness and blindness.

The majority of infected cats show no signs of the disease. These cats over an approximate two-week period, shed millions of toxoplasma oocysts in their faeces, which after forty-eight to ninety-six hours are able to infect another animal or human, if ingested.

*Treatment*

Consult your veterinarian, who can make a definite diagnosis based on symptoms and pathology tests on blood and faeces. The cat can be treated with antibiotics, but it eventually develops immunity.

*Prevention*

• Do not feed cats raw meat. Feed canned or dry food. If feeding fresh meat, cook it thoroughly. Deep-freezing meat reduces the risk of toxoplasmosis.

• Try to prevent your cat from hunting (see page 64).

• Control vermin in your immediate environment.

### Toxoplasmosis and human health

Toxoplasmosis is widespread in humans throughout the world. In males and non-pregnant females, the symptoms are usually mild and are often confused with symptoms of glandular fever. In the case of a pregnant woman who contracts toxoplasmosis, the main concern is for the unborn foetus and how it may be affected.

*Causes*

• Eating raw or undercooked meat, especially pork or lamb.

• Handling fresh meat.

• Contact with cat faeces in the soil while garden-ing.

• Contact with cat faeces from litter trays.

• Children contacting cat faeces in sandpits.

• Handling cats that have toxoplasmosis. Keep in mind that the majority of infected cats show no signs of the disease.

• Cockroaches, flies and rodents carrying oocysts and contaminating food.

*Signs*

In males and non-pregnant females, the infection may go unnoticed or the symptoms may be lethargy, swollen glands and general aches and pains. The symptoms are often confused with those of glandular fever. In pregnant females who contract the disease, there is a risk of abortion, stillbirth or mental retardation and blindness in the baby.

*Diagnosis*

Cat owners (especially pregnant women) who are aware of toxoplasmosis often want to know if their cat has the disease and whether or not it is a risk to them or their family. The cat's faeces can be tested for oocysts or its blood for toxoplasma antibodies.

If the faeces show evidence of oocysts or the blood shows negative toxoplasma antibody titre, then the cat is a potential risk factor to the health of the pregnant woman, her unborn child and other members of the family. Positive antibody titre indicates that the cat is probably immune and is unlikely to shed oocysts. A blood sample should be taken from the pregnant woman by her doctor to ascertain the level of her antibody titre. A second blood sample is taken to determine if the level of her antibody titre is stable or rising. If the second antibody titre is the same or similar to the first blood test, it indicates that she is immune and toxoplasmosis is no threat to the unborn foetus.

*Prevention*
• Cook meat thoroughly before eating, especially lamb and pork.
• Wash your hands thoroughly after handling raw meat.
• Remove faeces from the cat litter tray daily. Oocysts in the faeces do not become infective for two to four days after being excreted by the cat.
• Clean the litter tray thoroughly with boiling water or disinfectants containing ammonia.
• Do not introduce a young kitten into the family if you are pregnant.
• Pregnant women should get someone else to clean the litter tray.
• Wear gloves when gardening.
• Avoid handling cats that eat raw meat or cats that are unknown to you. Always wash your hands thoroughly after handling any cat.
• Children's sandpits are a common place for cats to defecate. Cover the sandpit when not in use and remove the sand regularly. Children often playing in a sandpit should wash their hands thoroughly, especially before meals. Oocysts buried in sand or soil may be infective to humans for many months.
• Control rats, mice, flies and cockroaches.
• Vegetables, brought or home-grown, before being used in salads should be washed thoroughly.

### Travel sickness (see page 171)

### Trench mouth

This disease is often an extension of gingivitis, involving the gums and surrounding tissue at the back of the mouth.

*Cause*
High levels of bacteria in the mouth due to lack of oral hygiene, plaque and tartar on the teeth, and grooming habits.

*Signs*
• Dribbling from the mouth.
• Foul breath.
• If severe, eating poorly or not at all.

• Refusing to open the mouth and, if it is opened, the cat often cries out in severe pain.
• The tissues at the back of the throat and on either side are thickened and bright red in colour.

*Treatment*
See your veterinarian, who will administer a course of antibiotics and anti-inflammatory drugs. Regular teeth care and, if necessary, extraction of the upper and lower back molars often bring about a permanent cure.

### Umbilical hernia (see page 191)

### Urinary incontinence

This problem is not as common in cats as it is in dogs. Incontinence occurs when urine dribbles or leaks from the bladder and the cat is unaware of it happening.

*Causes*
• Spinal injuries or disease.
• Hormonal imbalance.
• The aftermath of prolonged cystitis or FUS.
• Ectopic ureter, which is a rare condition where the ureter empties into the vagina rather than into the bladder.

*Sign*
Dribbling urine.

*Treatment*
Consult your veterinarian.

### Vitamin A toxicity

*Cause*
Feeding cats on a high liver diet and/or cod liver oil and/or vitamin supplements high in vitamin A.

*Signs*
The cat develops a stiff neck and lameness in one or both forelimbs. This is due to excess bone growth affecting the neck and elbows. The cat is inactive and looks scruffy due to difficulty in grooming itself.

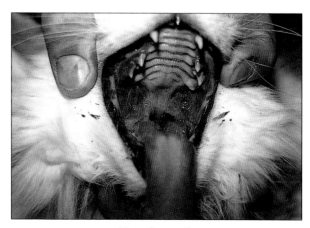

*Trench mouth.*

170

*Treatment*

Stop feeding liver, cod liver oil or vitamin supplements containing vitamin A. The cat will improve over a period of months, but will be left with some permanent disability.

**Vitamin B1 deficiency** (see page 75)

**Vomiting** (refer also to the following)

Foreign material  (see this page)
Hair ball  (see this page)
Infection  (see this page)
Obstruction  (see this page)
Overeating  (see page 173)
Sensitivity to food  (see page 173)
Travel sickness  (see this page)
Worms  (see page 88)

Do not confuse vomiting with regurgitation of food or gagging. Regurgitation of food usually takes place with little or no warning signs. The cat does not appear distressed and the regurgitated food appears to be undigested. Gagging is usually stimulated by a collection of mucus or foreign material (grass) in the back of the throat. The cat often makes a loud noise as it attempts to expel the cause of the irritation from the throat.

Unlike humans, a cat may vomit occasionally without anything being wrong with it. However, vomiting four to five times over twelve to twenty-four hours and often associated with some other symptom (such as lethargy, not eating and diarrhoea) is abnormal, indicating that you should seek veterinary advice.

*Causes*
• Foreign material
— eating grass,
— hair ball from self grooming,
— obstruction, e.g. bone in stomach or intestine.
• Infection.
• Worms.
• Constipation (see page 137).
• Travel sickness.
• Food — overeating and sensitivity to food.

*Signs*
Vomiting is characterised by restlessness, salivation, swallowing, contraction of the abdominal muscles, extension of the head and neck, and finally followed by expulsion of food, fluid or foreign material, which is often accompanied by a retching noise.

*Treatment*
FOREIGN MATERIAL
*Eating grass* A cat will eat grass to alleviate an irritation of the stomach. The grass stimulates vomiting, the idea being to clean out the source of irritation from the stomach. Occasional eating of grass and vomiting is acceptable, provided the cat otherwise is eating well and not losing weight. If the cat is eating grass and vomiting frequently in association with not eating well and losing weight, then you should have it examined by your veterinarian.

*Hair ball* The cat, when grooming itself, collects hair on the barbs at the back of the tongue. The hair is swallowed into the stomach, where it may pass into the intestine or it may accumulate in the stomach and form into a wad. The wad of hair lying in the stomach for a period of time irritates the lining of the stomach (gastritis), stimulating vomiting. Often, the cat will vomit the wad of hair, which is shaped like a sausage.

Some cats will vomit immediately after eating due to the wad of hair irritating the stomach and also because the wad may occupy a large volume of available space in the stomach.

See your veterinarian who, after examination and depending on the size of the wad, can administer a drug to make the cat vomit the hair mass.

It is a good idea to give cats that are prone to this problem a laxative paste or paraffin oil twice a week to assist the passage of the hair through the intestine and its elimination with the faeces. In this manner, the accumulation of hair in the stomach is prevented. Frequent grooming to remove loose hair from the coat is also an effective preventative measure.

*Obstruction (e.g. bone in stomach or intestine)*
Usually the cat is lethargic, refuses to eat, vomits frequently, shows signs of abdominal pain and dehydration. Take the cat to your veterinarian for treatment.

INFECTION
The signs may be similar to an obstruction, depending on the type, location and seriousness of the infection. If your cat is showing signs of lethargy, refusing to eat, dehydration (see page 140) in conjunction with vomiting, see your veterinarian, who will treat the cat according to the cause and symptoms.

WORMS
A heavy infestation of roundworms in the upper small intestine, especially in young cats, may cause vomiting. Occasionally, roundworms will be obvious in the vomit (see page 88).

TRAVEL SICKNESS
Travel sickness is not as common in cats as it is in dogs. Do not give your cat food or drink for twelve hours prior to travelling. If vomiting persists, see your veterinarian, who will prescribe a sedative in combination with an anti-vomiting drug, depending on the severity of the motion sickness.

171

*An appealing young crossbreed kitten.*

OVEREATING AND SENSITIVITY TO FOOD

Usually, cats that vomit following overeating or sensitivity to food are in good condition and are generally healthy. Of all domesticated animals, cats are still fairly primitive and tend to overeat and gulp their food as if it were their last meal for some time. This causes distension of the stomach and may stimulate the cat to regurgitate or vomit the food.

You cannot instruct the cat to eat slowly or to eat less. To prevent this problem arising, feed the cat three or four small meals per day, thereby decreasing the amount of food it ingests at any one time.

Some cats may be sensitive to additives in the food, especially the commercial preparations. Others may be sensitive to the temperature of the food, e.g. cold from the refrigerator. Make sure the food is served at room temperature.

Try a number of different brands and types of food and observe the response.

## Worms (parasites) (refer to the following)

Lungworm (see pages 91, 159)
Roundworm (see page 89)
Hookworm (see page 90)
Tapeworm (see page 91)

## Yellow fat disease (steatitis)

*Cause*

Excess amounts of unsaturated fatty acids in the diet. Foods that are high in unsaturated fatty acids are fish, cod liver oil, liver and horse meat. Cats fed exclusively on any of the above foods are susceptible to yellow fat disease.

*Signs*

Cats with this disease exhibit signs of pain when touched, especially in areas where there are deposits of fat, such as under the abdomen and in the pubic area. They may have a temperature, be reluctant to move and are irritable. The affected fat feels hard and lumpy.

*Treatment*

Stop feeding a diet high in unsaturated fatty acids. See your veterinarian, who will provide a vitamin E supplement to give to the cat (50 mg per day) and may administer an anti-inflammatory agent to alleviate pain. The cat should respond slowly to the treatment.

Commercially available canned fish for cats includes additional amounts of vitamin E. Cats fed exclusively on these canned foods should not develop the disease.

*It takes about six months for kittens to become fully independent.*

# BREEDING

***Queen and stud****: Reproductive cycle of the queen — Mating — Artificial insemination — Pregnancy diagnosis — False pregnancy — Management of queen during Pregnancy — Abortion — Birth — Post-natal care — Infertility in the queen — Infertility in the stud (tom)*
***Kittens****: Care of newborn kitten — Orphan kittens — Diseases and problems of newborn kittens — Collecting your kitten from the cattery — Training — Kitten care and your veterinarian.*
***Birth control****: Desexing — Alternatives to desexing.*

## QUEEN AND STUD

The cat's reproductive system is similar to that of other mammals, but cats in particular are prolific breeders for most of their adult lives. It is important for cat owners to have an understanding of the mating process, not only to ensure successful breeding but also to prevent the birth of unwanted kittens.

## REPRODUCTIVE CYCLE OF THE QUEEN

Cats are seasonal breeders. Their heat, season or oestrus cycle can vary from short and intense to long and less intense, from regular to irregular or to no obvious cycle at all.

The queen's ability to reproduce normally begins between seven to twelve months of age, but may be as early as five months. The queen's heat, season or oestrus period lasts for three to six days, although oestrus may last as long as ten days if the queen is not mated. For the following fifteen days, there is no sign of oestrus; this period is known as dioestrus. Altogether, the queen has an eighteen to twenty-one day cycle.

Ovulation in the queen does not take place spontaneously when the follicle ripens. It is thought that stimulation of the cervix during mating causes ovulation (release of the egg from the ovary), which usually takes place twenty-four hours after mating.

In the northern hemisphere, the breeding season extends from January until September. Within this period, the more intense breeding periods are February to May and July to August. In the southern hemisphere, the breeding season is from July to March, with the more intense breeding activity being in the months of August to October and December to January. The breeding season will vary according to the climate of the country in which the cat lives and whether or not it is exposed to light and warmth in an artificial environment.

The signs of oestrus in the queen are totally different from those in the bitch. There is no obvious swelling of the vulva nor any vaginal discharge and bleeding. On the other hand, there are marked behavioural changes in the queen. A cat that is normally content to stay inside will want to get out and will stay out sometimes for days on end. They can be more active to the point of being hyperactive and more vocal to the point of crying and yowling incessantly, as if in pain.

Often, when a cat is in oestrus, it is referred to as 'calling' or 'on call' because of this very obvious and sometimes disturbing vocal characteristic.

Cats that are usually cool and aloof may become noticeably more affectionate towards their owners. Often, they may roll on the floor, crouch with the hindquarters elevated and tail held to one side. The inexperienced cat owner, concerned about the cat's abnormal behaviour, often contacts the veterinarian, only to be told that is the normal behaviour during the oestrus period.

It is thought that development of the follicles on the ovaries is stimulated by a period of courtship, during which the female rejects the sexual advances of the male or males. This normally lasts for about four days after which the queen will allow a selected male or males to mate with her over a period of approximately twenty-four hours.

When ovulation occurs the ruptured follicles collapse and fill with blood to form into the corpus luteum, which produces a hormone that prepares the lining of the uterus to accept the fertilised eggs. If the eggs are not fertilised, the corpus luteum will regress and at the end of fifteen days will be non-existent as the queen comes 'on call' again. The queen's gestation period on average is sixty-five

*Cats mating.*

days, but it can vary from sixty to seventy days.

## MATING

This section refers to an organised mating rather than to the mating of free-roaming cats.

The queen should always be taken to the male, known as the tom or stud, because he feels more secure in his own environment or territory and will be able to give his full attention to serving the queen.

The mating area should be quiet so that the stud and queen are not disturbed prior to or during mating.

It is interesting to observe that in free-roaming mating, several toms may be attentive to the queen, but she selects the one with whom she is going to mate.

### Precautions for mating

Avoid the stress of a long journey, as it may dampen the queen's interest or cause her to go off heat.

Make sure she is up to date with her vaccinations against feline enteritis and cat flu, that she is wormed and has a certificate recently issued by your veterinarian to the effect that she has been tested for FeLV (feline leukaemia virus) and the results are negative.

Place the queen in a pen alongside the stud, to allow them to become accustomed to each other.

Once she is showing obvious interest in the stud, such as rubbing up against the bars in her cage, let her in with him.

### The mating process

The stud will smell and lick the queen, and she will adopt the mating position, crouching with her hindquarters elevated and tail held to one side. The stud will mount her, gripping the skin at the back of her neck with his teeth and holding onto her with his forelegs. This enables him to insert his penis into her vagina. Ejaculation usually occurs within twenty seconds and is often associated with a deep growl. The stud has small barbs on the tip of his penis, which may cause the queen some discomfort as he withdraws. She may scream and lash out at him.

## ARTIFICIAL INSEMINATION

This is not a common procedure for cats as it is not much in demand and there is some difficulty experienced in collecting semen. Semen can be collected using an artificial vagina or direct from the vagina of a queen immediately after being mated with a stud. The average volume of semen ejaculated into the vagina at any one mating is 0.04 mL.

The queen can be induced to ovulate by inserting an object such as a thermometer into the vagina

*A heavily pregnant queen.*

and mechanically stimulating the cervix. The semen is then deposited in the upper region of the vagina. It is essential that a veterinarian carry out the procedures for artificial insemination of the cat.

## PREGNANCY DIAGNOSIS

If the queen is pregnant, her nipples will enlarge and become noticeably pinker three weeks after mating. These signs will be more obvious if it is the queen's first litter.

Four weeks after mating, your veterinarian can palpate discrete golf ball-like swellings in the uterus. This procedure is not harmful to the cat or to the developing kittens if done carefully.

At five weeks, the abdomen increases in size.

At six weeks, the skeletal outline of the kittens can be detected by an X-ray. Prior to this, the kittens' bones are not formed enough to show up on X-ray.

At seven weeks, the heads of the kittens can be felt and the kittens show signs of movement.

In the eighth week, the queen's mammary glands may secrete milk two to three days prior to birth of the kittens.

## FALSE PREGNANCY

Sometimes referred to as pseudopregnancy or phantom pregnancy.

If the queen for one reason or another does not become pregnant following mating, she may show some signs of pregnancy lasting up to forty-five days. There may be enlargement of the nipples, mammary glands and abdomen. Rarely is there any milk production. Psychological changes associated with pregnancy may also be seen. After forty-five days the condition regresses spontaneously.

## MANAGEMENT OF THE QUEEN DURING PREGNANCY

The average gestation period for the queen is sixty-five days, but it can vary from sixty to seventy days. She does not require any special management, provided the pregnancy is normal.

### Nutrition

The volume of food during the first two-thirds of pregnancy need not be markedly increased. For good foetal development, it is important that there is no nutritional deficiency. A well-balanced diet, which can be provided by commercial rations (canned and dry food), is perfectly adequate.

Overfeeding can lead to a fat, lazy queen, which could cause problems at the time of birth. If she is on a high meat diet, then a calcium supplement is important, but it should not contain any phosphates (e.g. calcium carbonate, lactate or gluconate are quite satisfactory). A balanced vitamin-mineral supplement should be included in the diet.

The final third of the pregnancy period will see an increase in the queen's food intake until she is eating double by the eighth to ninth week. Three or four small meals a day will assist her digestion, as the growing foetuses take up a lot of room in the abdomen, restricting the normal expansion of her stomach.

### Exercise

Normal activities, including jumping, running and climbing, assist in maintaining good muscle tone, which is desirable for a smooth birth.

### Worming

The queen should be wormed at least once during her pregnancy, preferably in the last three weeks. She should be wormed against roundworm, hookworm and tapeworm. Seek your veterinarian's advice about the best worm preparation to use — one that is not detrimental to the mother or the developing kittens.

### Vaccination

Vaccinate against feline enteritis and cat flu in the last third of pregnancy using a killed vaccine, which will ensure that a strong temporary immunity is given to the kittens via the queen's colostrum (first milk). Live vaccine should not be given to pregnant cats.

### Housing

In the last ten days of pregnancy, provide a large cardboard box with one side cut down to such a height that it prevents the kittens from falling or crawling out but allows the queen to get in and out readily.

Place the box in a quiet area where the cat feels warm, comfortable and is out of draughts. Line the bottom of the box with newspaper or clean towels.

Provide water, food and a litter tray in close proximity to the box. If the queen's regular sleeping area (basket) is adequate, do not alter the situation.

### Prevention of abortion

Some queens continually abort. If the cause is narrowed down to a hormone deficiency, the queen may be given a series of hormone progesterone injections to help maintain a normal pregnancy. (See below for detailed information on abortion.)

## ABORTION

Abortion refers to the abnormal expulsion of a foetus, dead or alive, after the first three weeks of pregnancy until the full term. Abortion cannot be

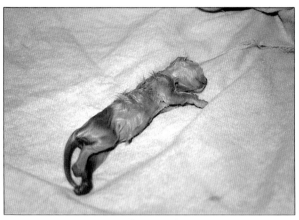

*An aborted foetus at full term.*

substantiated in the first three weeks of pregnancy for several reasons. It is difficult to diagnose that the queen is pregnant. If the developing embryo dies, generally it is absorbed by the queen rather than being expelled. Even if it were expelled, possibly it would not be noticed because of its small size and gelatinous nature.

If your queen aborts, several procedures should be followed:

• Other queens in the area where the abortion occurred should be moved to an isolated area.

• The foetus, foetal membrane and queen should be taken to your veterinarian, who will take a cervical swab from the queen for laboratory examination and perform a postmortem on the aborted foetus. A tissue sample may also be taken.

• The queen should be isolated in an area that can be disinfected readily at a later date. She should be kept isolated until the laboratory test results are known, generally in about two weeks.

• The general area where the abortion has taken place should be disinfected with Hibitane or a similar preparation.

• Wash your hands thoroughly before handling

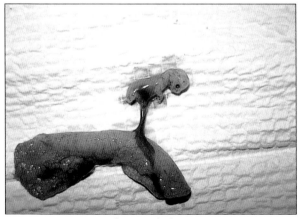

*A bacterial abortion.*

other cats, particularly pregnant queens.

The three most common types of abortion are viral, bacterial and hormonal.

### Bacterial abortion

Bacteria are easier to identify than viruses and do not spread as readily. The identification procedure is to swab the cervix of the queen and the aborted foetus, and then culture the swabs.

Some bacterial abortions can be prevented by having your queen swabbed prior to mating to determine if she has an infection, the type of infection, and the best antibiotic to be used for treatment, which should be given prior to mating and during pregnancy.

### Hormonal abortion

Queens that have a history of aborting, which is unrelated to infection or other known causes are suspected of having a hormonal imbalance. Hormonal abortions usually occur around the seventh week of pregnancy.

Progesterone injections, given by your veterinarian every seven days, commencing on the forty-second day of pregnancy and ceasing a week before the full term, should help to prevent hormonal abortions.

### Viral abortion

Feline leukaemia virus (FeLV) (see page 148) is one of the most common causes of abortion in cats. The majority of those that do abort show no signs of illness. All cats are susceptible to this virus. Cats spread the virus by sharing food dishes, grooming each other, incurring a bite wound and sharing litter trays, thereby coming into contact with contaminated faeces and urine.

Following exposure to the virus, some cats develop the symptoms and die, some recover, and a small percentage become symptomless carriers, shedding the virus intermittently.

Queens that are infected and become pregnant will either resorb the foetus, abort or give birth to weak, sickly or dead kittens.

If infected cats are treated, they should be confined in order to prevent spread of infection to other cats.

*Prevention*

Feline leukaemia virus is detected by a blood test. One positive test is not sufficient to diagnose your cat as having FeLV. Two positive tests, three months apart, are necessary to indicate that your cat will develop clinical signs of the disease and more than likely will die within one to two years. During that time, your cat is a risk to other cats and should

not be used for breeding. It should be isolated, removed from the cattery or put to sleep. Two negative tests, three months apart, indicate that your cat is free of the virus. Yearly tests and tests prior to mating will help to eliminate spread of the virus and control the disease.

## BIRTH

During the queen's pregnancy, many owners beset themselves with questions such as: how many kittens will she have? What sex will they be? Will they be normal? These concerns may be transient or they may set up nagging thoughts and worries that remain with the owner until the birth is over. In many cases, the kittens prove to be healthy and just what the owner wanted. Again, an owner witnessing the birth of the first litter of kittens may be disturbed by the queen's vigorous straining or by the sight of the afterbirth. However, any such feeling will be minimal if it is kept in mind that these situations are facets of the natural, normal process of birth.

*Precautions*

Keep the queen confined so that she cannot disappear and have her kittens in some obscure, inaccessible place. Have the necessary equipment available, such as scissors, thread, tincture of iodine, disinfectant, cotton wool and a clean bucket for hot water. The phone number of your veterinarian should be nearby in case you need to contact him/her.

*Signs that the queen is going into labour*
• Some queens will appear restless, getting in and out of the box frequently.
• The queen begins to make a nest from the bedding in the box.
• Milk may be readily expressed from the nipples.
• A temperature drop from 38.5 °C to 37.5 °C (101.2 °F to 99.5 °F), approximately twelve hours prior to birth.
• Loses interest in eating food.
• Grooms herself vigorously, especially around the vulva.
• Sixty-five days from the time of mating is the normal period to expect the queen to go into labour.

### Normal labour

It should be kept in mind at all times that the queen is an individual and may not follow precisely the normal labour pattern outlined below. Observe the queen's labour from a vantage point which does not disturb her.

*Stage 1*
This stage lasts twelve to twenty-four hours. The

queen is restless, getting in and out of the box, lying down to lick her vulva, looking at her flank and crying.

### Stage 2

Characteristics of the beginnings of this stage are that the queen lies down on her side, often with her head up, looking at her hindquarters. Visible straining is evident and the foetal membranes appear at the vulva.

The membrane (amnion) is rather like a bluish-white plastic bag lining the placenta and enveloping the foetus; when ruptured, it discharges a yellowish fluid. Not infrequently, the amnion ruptures before appearing at the vulva.

The normal presentation is head first, but it is not uncommon for a kitten to be presented tail first.

The kitten may be delivered within the amnion. The queen will lick vigorously at the sac, rupturing it, and then continue to lick the kitten, cleaning it thoroughly. While doing this, she will chew through the umbilical cord.

If the foetal membranes or amnion appear at the vulva and no further progress is achieved after ten minutes, seek veterinary advice.

### Stage 3

When the head of the kitten appears, immediately remove any foetal membranes that may be obstructioning the nostrils and mouth so that the kitten can breathe freely.

The umbilical cord is usually broken when the kitten is born. If it is intact and the queen does not break the cord by chewing through it, cut the cord using the following procedure.

Place a pair of scissors and thread in a dish of disinfectant. Tie the thread around the cord about 2 cm (0.8 in) from the body and knot it tightly. Cut the cord with the scissors 0.5 cm (0.2 in) away from the knot, between the knot and placenta. If the cord is broken at birth and is bleeding, it should be tied off. Thoroughly swab the stump of the cord with disinfectant. The cord will dry out and drop off within a short period of time, leaving a neat navel.

The placenta or afterbirth is usually passed with the kitten at the time of birth or shortly after. Make sure that a placenta is passed for each kitten born. If the afterbirth is not passed within eight hours of the last kitten, contact your veterinarian.

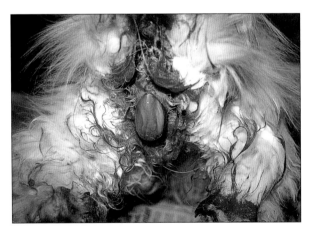

*The foetal membrane appears at the vulva.*

*The emerging foetus is enveloped in the membrane.*

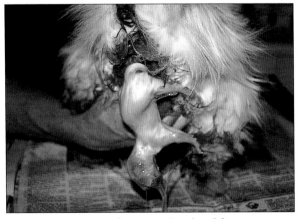

*A normal presentation, head first.*

*A not uncommon presentation, tail first.*

*A kitten delivered within the amnion, or membrane.*

The queen often chews through the umbilical cord and then proceeds to eat the placenta. This is quite a normal behaviour for the queen in the birth process. If she eats a number of afterbirths, it may cause vomiting and diarrhoea.

Once the first kitten is born, the others usually follow fairly quickly, so that all the kittens are born over a period of approximately three hours. Rarely does it happen that a queen will give birth to a number of kittens, then relax and go into labour twenty-four hours later and produce another healthy kitten.

### Abnormal labour

The queen's labour usually proceeds without a hitch; but sometimes complications occur. If they do, it is important to recognise them as early as possible and to take quick, knowledgeable action so that any danger to the life of the kitten(s) and queen is minimised. In such situations, the wisest course to follow is to seek the help of a veterinarian immediately.

When complications become apparent, some competent owners assist with the birth and cope successfully. However, there are always some people who do not cope and who either worsen the complications or create others.

*Kitten presented at the vulva*
If the kitten presented at the vulva is in the normal head-first position but the queen does not seem able to expel it, you might decide to examine it. If so, certain precautions should be taken. Your hands should be scrubbed thoroughly and a surgical glove, if available, should be worn. The area around the queen's anus and vulva should be washed with a non-irritant antiseptic such as chlorhexidine.

If the presentation is normal and the membranes are intact, break them to remove any obstructions around the kitten's nose and mouth, to help with its breathing. Also clear the membranes away from that part of the body visible outside the vulva so that you can assist the delivery. Using a clean towel to get a better grip, take hold of the kitten around the

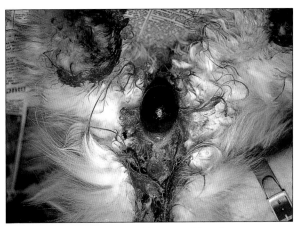

*This queen is unable to expel her foetus.*

181

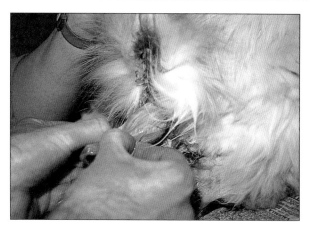

*When the hindquarters are presented, the kitten should be pulled outwards and downwards.*

shoulder area and slowly pull downwards and outwards. If the kitten will not budge, a twist to the left or right in conjunction with pulling will often bring about success. If there is no change, call your veterinarian.

*One leg presented at the vulva*

Before you put your finger into the vagina, make sure your hands have been scrubbed with non-irritant disinfectant and are lubricated, as it is necessary to prevent tissue damage and infection that may endanger the lives of the queen and kitten(s).

Feel for the other forelimb, pull it forward and then proceed to deliver the kitten.

*Hindquarters presented at the vulva*

If the hindquarters are presented, take hold of the kitten in the region of the hips and pull outwards and downwards. Avoid squeezing the abdomen, as this may cause serious damage to the kitten.

*No kitten present at the vulva*

Call your veterinarian if:

• the queen has been straining for more than an hour and no kitten has appeared;

• there are no obvious contractions and the queen is distressed, continually getting up and down, looking at her flanks and crying;

• after thirty minutes of obvious straining and contractions, the queen appears to give up, and her efforts for the following thirty minutes are weak and less frequent.

## POST-NATAL CARE

### First visit to the veterinarian

It is a good idea to take the queen and her kittens along to the veterinarian for a post-natal examination. Your veterinarian will check the queen to make sure no kittens are left in the uterus and no afterbirths have been retained. The queen may be given an injection of oxytocin to make the uterus

contract, thereby expelling any debris and helping to control haemorrhage. Her mammary glands will be checked to make sure she has adequate milk for the kittens. Tears or bruising of the vulva and vagina may necessitate an antibiotic injection.

The kittens are checked for general health as well as for any defects such as cleft palate and umbilical hernia.

### Care of the queen

Once the kittens have been born, there is sometimes a tendency to lavish attention and care on them, with a corresponding neglect of the queen. In this situation, it is well to remember that the kittens' viability depends on the health of the queen. The care of the queen after the birth should not be neglected and the following activities and observations should be established as routines.

*Cleansing*

If the queen's tail, vulva and hind-legs are matted with blood and discharge, the area should be washed to make her feel better and also to prevent the spread or growth of bacteria that may be harmful to the queen and kittens. Use an antiseptic, non-irritant wash such as chlorhexidene. Do not use harsh disinfectants as they may scald the skin, which may in turn cause the queen to reject the kittens. It is also important to wash off the remains of any soap, especially in the area of the mammary glands, because the taste may inhibit the kittens from suckling.

While the queen is being washed, place the kittens in a basket or box with a blanket or towel where she can see them, thus allaying any anxiety she may feel.

*Tears, bruising and swelling*

After the queen has been cleaned, she should be examined for tears, bruising and swelling. Lift the queen's tail out of the way so that the anus and vulva can be observed without hindrance.

Tears of any length or depth should be attended by your veterinarian, who will stitch the wound and protect the queen from infection with an antibiotic injection.

Swelling and/or bruising, if any, is normal and usually subsides over forty-eight hours. If the swelling is excessive and persists for longer or is accompanied by severe bruising, the queen is susceptible to infection, so consult your veterinarian.

Gentle, cold hosing of the swollen areas can have a threefold action. Firstly, it cleanses the area; secondly, the massaging effect of the water pressure will disperse and reduce the swelling; and thirdly, the coldness of the water will help to stop the bleeding that causes the bruising.

*A Brown Burmese with six-month-old kitten.*

*Two Ragdoll kittens.*

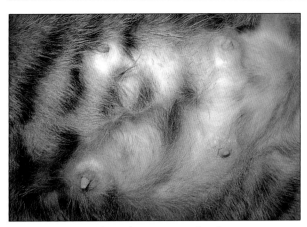

*Normal mammary glands.*

## Vaginal discharge

Small amounts of clear, serous discharge, sometimes blood-tinged, is normal up to a week after the birth. However, a constant drip of blood, a bloody brown discharge or pus coming from the vulva is abnormal. The queen should be examined by a veterinarian if this is the case.

## Mammary glands

Examine the nipples to see if they are normal. Express milk from the nipples to make sure that there is a satisfactory flow and the status of the milk is normal.

If one mammary gland is larger than the others, it may be due to the fact that the kittens have not suckled from it or there may be an infection of the gland, e.g. mastitis. If the mammary gland is infected, it is very painful to touch as well as being hot, swollen, hard and sometimes lumpy. It may be difficult to express the milk, which may be thick and discoloured. In acute cases, the queen will have a high temperature.

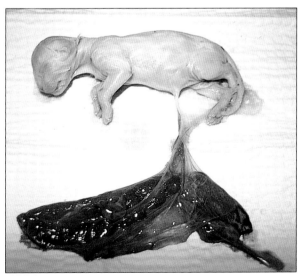

*The afterbirth.*

When treating the queen for mastitis, remove the kittens from her, apply hot compresses and consult your veterinarian, who will treat her with antibiotics.

## The afterbirth (placental membranes)

The afterbirth may be expelled with the birth of each kitten or immediately after. If the membranes have not come away from the queen within eight hours, contact your veterinarian.

If a placenta is visible, it may easily be removed by pulling on it with firm even pressure. The use of a piece of gauze or clean towelling will give you a better grip on the slippery membrane. If it is not removed in this way, an injection of oxytocin will be necessary to aid in separation of the afterbirth from its attachment to the uterus.

## Milk fever (eclampsia)

This problem is not common in lactating queens. It usually occurs in queens that have a large litter and the kittens are older than two weeks. The cause is due to the queen's calcium levels being depleted; the calcium is lost in the milk.

The symptoms are mild muscular twitching and wobbliness, progressing to severe, uncontrolled muscular twitching and spasm. The pupils become dilated and the respiration is rapid and shallow.

Contact your veterinarian, who will give the queen injections of calcium and cortisone, which will reverse the symptoms rapidly. The kittens may have to be removed temporarily from their mother (see 'Orphan kittens', page 188). The mother should be placed on a calcium supplement.

## INFERTILITY IN THE QUEEN

A queen that lives outdoors usually becomes pregnant at an early age (seven to eight months) and continues to produce a healthy litter of kittens at regular intervals for many years. The purebred queen that is kept in the controlled environment of a breeding establishment does not breed so well. The breeder may only allow the stud (tom) to mate with the queen once or twice, whereas in the free outdoor situation the queen may mate a number of times in twenty-four hours.

Prolonged foreplay is necessary for some queens to develop the follicle on the ovary from which the egg is released (ovulation) at the time of mating. A number of matings may also be necessary to stimulate ovulation in some queens.

Other known factors that affect the fertility of the queen are:

### Nutritional factors

Overweight queens or queens in very poor condition have a greater tendency to suffer infertility problems.

*Vitamin A deficiency* Unlike other species, cats cannot produce vitamin A from carotene in the intestine. Their vitamin A needs must be obtained from their diet; one such source is liver. A cat's daily requirement for vitamin A is 1600-2000 i.u. Queens on vitamin A-deficient diets may either fail to call or call irregularly.

*Iodine deficiency* Queens fed on a meat diet only may develop an iodine deficiency. If they are iodine deficient, queens may fail to call (cycle).

### Hormonal imbalance

During the normal breeding season, the queen may be cycling irregularly or not at all. The queen should be examined by your veterinarian to establish whether or not she has a hormonal imbalance. If she has, she may be successfully treated with hormone therapy.

### Psychological problems

A queen isolated from other female cats for prolonged periods may not cycle (call). If this is the cause, placing the queen with a group of regularly cycling queens may stimulate her to cycle regularly.

### Environmental factors

A queen needs approximately fourteen hours of sunlight per day to stimulate her to cycle regularly. With less then twelve hours of sunlight daily, she will not cycle.

### Infection

Any infection which has a debilitating effect on the queen, especially for a period of time, can stop her from cycling, e.g. feline infectious leukaemia virus (FeLV).

Many queens harbour bacteria in the reproductive tract; some are apparently harmless and others are known to be harmful or pathogenic. The latter are known to cause infection of the uterus.

Queens suspected of being infected should be swabbed by a veterinary surgeon, preferably when they are in oestrus (calling). The swab is cultured and, if the result is positive, the bacteria are identified and an antibiotic sensitivity test is done to determine the best antibiotic to use against the infection.

A queen may be suspected of having a uterine infection (metritis) if: there is pus discharge from the vagina; her heat (oestrus) cycles are irregular; she does not become pregnant after two or three matings; she gives birth to dead or weak, sickly kittens.

Following the results of swabbing, an infected queen is treated by your veterinary surgeon with the appropriate antibiotics.

*This cat is a Monorchid: only one testicle has descended.*

**Abortion** (see page 178)

## INFERTILITY IN THE STUD (TOM)

Known factors that affect the fertility of the stud (tom) are:

### Nutritional factors

Stud cats that are obese or suffer from malnutrition and are in very poor condition have a greater tendency to suffer from infertility problems.

A prolonged, severely deficient vitamin A diet can affect the testicles of the stud (tom), causing decreased testosterone (male sex hormone) production, which in turn decreases the stud's sexual drive and sperm production, which may lead to infertility.

### Congenital problems

Stud cats with small testicles that are hard on palpation usually have poor quality semen and a lack of libido because their testicle activity is minimal.

Sometimes a tom may have testicles that have failed to descend (cryptorchidism). This type of cat cannot be used as a stud because he is infertile.

The monorchid is a tom with only one testicle descended. He should not be used as a stud, even though he is fertile, because the condition is hereditary. This recommendation would still apply even if the other testicle, through the use of hormones, could be made to descend and develop.

### Psychological problems

When a mating is organised in a breeding establishment, the queen should always be brought to the stud. The stud needs to feel secure in his own environment, where he has marked the boundary by spraying urine and rubbing against objects to leave his scent. If he feels insecure in a strange

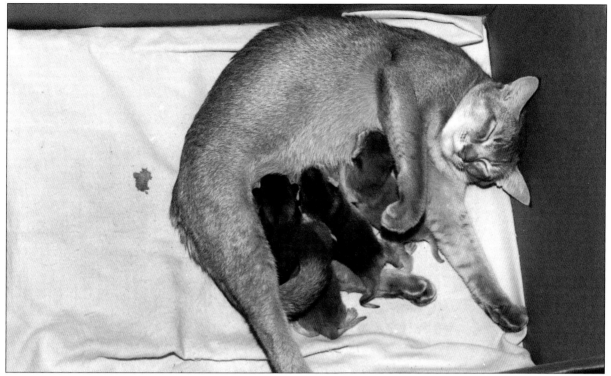

*A queen feeding her kittens.*

environment, he may be unlikely to mate with the queen.

### Infection

Any infected bite wound received on the testicles or penis from another cat can render a stud infertile. Other serious infections over a prolonged period which are generally debilitating can also lead to infertility.

## KITTENS

It is a thrilling experience to see your newborn kittens being licked and nuzzled by their mother as they suckle from her nipples. So far the queen has done most of the work. It is now up to those who assisted at the birth to do a little more.

A close watch should be kept on the kittens; what to do and when to do it will be determined primarily by the kittens' needs. The following guidelines may be accepted as basic to the immediate care of the newborn kittens.

### CARE OF NEWBORN KITTENS

As soon as a kitten is born, check to see that it is breathing. If necessary, clear away any placental membranes or mucus that may be blocking the nostrils or mouth. If the kitten is not breathing, it should be given oxygen therapy by means of a resuscitator unit or by mouth-to-mouth resuscitation. The kitten has only a very small lung capacity, so

use only short, shallow breaths, otherwise there is a risk of stretching or rupturing the lungs. Gently massage the chest with finger and thumb. Put the kitten in a head-down position, with the head lower than the rest of the body, thus allowing the blood to flow more freely to the brain. Vigorous rubbing of the kitten's chest with a towel will stimulate breathing.

If the kitten is still not breathing, grasp it firmly in your hand with its head protruding between your index and middle finger, then raise the kitten

*Contented kittens taking a catnap.*

187

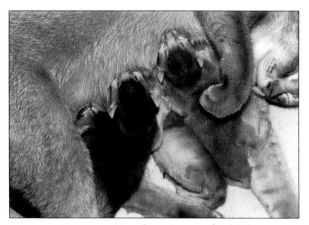

*Kittens suckle a few minutes after birth.*

above your head and proceed with an action as if you were going to throw it to the ground. Repeat the action four or five times. This action gets rid of the mucus from the nose and mouth, as well as stimulating respiration.

Allow the queen to break the umbilical cord, which is normally done at the time when she is licking, pulling and tearing at the foetal membranes around the kitten to free it. Usually, the stump of the umbilical cord is about 2 cm (0.8 in) long. Swab the end with tincture of iodine. In three to four days the cord will wither and drop off.

Premature breaking of the umbilical cord by anyone assisting at the birth may deprive the kitten of its maximum blood supply, thus starving the brain of oxygen, with subsequent brain damage. If the end of the cord is bleeding, tie it off with a disinfected thread to control haemorrhage.

If by chance the umbilical cord does not break, a ligature (knot) should be applied about 2 cm (0.8 in) from the kitten's body using thread soaked in disinfectant. The cord is then cut with scissors soaked in disinfectant 1 cm (0.4 in) from the ligature, between the ligature and the placenta. Swab the cut end with tincture of iodine. An alternative to cutting the cord is to break it using your fingers.

While the queen is still in the process of having more kittens, if she is interested in the kittens already born, licking and encouraging them to suckle, leave them with her. Otherwise, if she appears disinterested in the kittens place them in a box with a hot water bottle wrapped in a towel and leave them there until all the kittens are born.

If the kitten or kittens do not suckle the queen (do not mistake mouthing of the teats for suckling), the failure to do so may be caused by weakness or deformity of the kitten, or by the queen being cranky, or due to some other factor. Normally, the kittens will suckle within minutes after finding their way to the queen's nipples. If a kitten does not suckle within a couple of hours, then with one hand expressing milk from the queen's nipple and the other hand holding the kitten's head with its mouth partially open, place its mouth over the nipple. A good healthy kitten will start sucking immediately. Sucking can be stimulated by moving the kitten's mouth on and off the nipple.

Kittens suckle about every two hours in the first week. If they are getting adequate milk, they will be warm, relaxed and not crying. The kitten should almost double its weight in the first week.

Colostrum is the name given to the first milk that the queen produces. It contains antibodies which give the kittens temporary immunity against infection for six to sixteen weeks after birth. Colostrum is only produced by the queen for about the first twenty-four hours after the kittens are born, and the kittens can only absorb the antibodies from it for about the first thirty-six hours of life. In addition, colostrum has a high vitamin content and food value, and guards against constipation.

The queen licks the kittens around the anal and genital area, stimulating them to urinate and defecate.

## ORPHAN KITTENS

When kittens loses their mother at birth or shortly after, it strongly arouses our sympathy. Orphan kittens include not only those kittens whose mother died during or shortly after birth, but also those whose mother, for one reason or another, has no milk or cannot nurse her offspring.

### Bottle feeding

The kittens should be fed every two hours for the first week of life. Thereafter, the frequency of the feeds should be decreased and the amount increased, so that by the time the kittens are two weeks old feeding every four hours is sufficient.

*Inserting a teat into an orphaned kitten's mouth.*

In the first week at each two-hourly feed, the kittens should receive about 5 mL (1 teaspoon) of milk substitute, and this can be varied according to individual demand.

Two suggested formulas for substitute milk are:

1 cup evaporated or powdered milk mixed with boiled water and made up to double the strength recommended for babies

1 egg yolk

1 teaspoon Glucodin (sugar solution)

or

1/2 cup cow's milk

1 egg yolk

1 teaspoon Glucodin (sugar solution)

Note: If possible, express colostrum (first milk) from the queen's nipples and give it to the orphan kittens, either with the formula or separately.

Your veterinarian can supply you with a commercially prepared mother's milk substitute and an appropriate feeding bottle.

Warm the milk to body temperature before feeding. Hold the kitten firmly, with its head slightly elevated, and insert the teat of the feeding bottle into the kitten's mouth. Move the teat gently in and out of the mouth, expressing a small amount of milk to stimulate sucking.

The disadvantage of bottle feeding is that it is time-consuming (cleaning the bottle and teat and holding the bottle while the kitten is feeding).

## Foster mother

In many cases a foster mother is not readily available when urgently required. There is a greater possibility in a large cattery of one being available, as most queens will be having their kittens at approximately the same time. Most queens are good foster mothers and readily accept an orphan kitten. If a queen is available, place the orphan kitten with a litter of similar size kittens, otherwise, if the orphan is considerably smaller and weaker, it may not be able to compete for an adequate quantity of milk.

## Stomach tube

If the kitten will not take to bottle feeding or it is too time-consuming, try feeding it by stomach tube, which is quicker and ensures that the kitten receives adequate nutrition. The equipment required is simply a piece of soft plastic tube, 2 mm (0.08 in) in diameter and 15 cm (6 in) long, attached to a syringe.

Before inserting the tube, measure the distance with the tube from the kitten's mouth to a point two-thirds along the ribcage and mark it. This will

*A foster mother.*

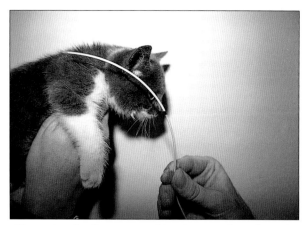

*Measuring the distance to a kitten's stomach, with a tube.*

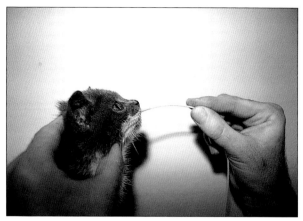

*Inserting the tube gently but firmly.*

indicate how far the tube has to go in to reach the stomach.

Insert the tube through the mouth gently but firmly, pushing the tube over the back of the tongue, which should guide it into the oesophagus (food pipe) and eventually into the stomach. When the mark on the tube touches the mouth, it indicates that the end of the tube has reached the stomach. Make sure the tube is in the stomach and not in the lungs before pressing the plunger on the syringe and delivering the substitute milk into the stomach.

The orphan kitten should be kept for about two weeks in a draught-free area at a temperature of 30°C (85°F). Kittens do not have the ability to control or regulate their temperature. In the normal situation of being fed by the mother, kittens are kept warm by contact with the mother's mammary glands and the other kittens, and by moving about.

Rubbing the kitten around the anal and genital area with a small amount of petroleum jelly will stimulate it to urinate and defecate. The kitten's faeces will give you an indication as to whether the

*A fourteen-day-old kitten with its eyes open.*

milk formula you are using is too rich or not. If the kitten has diarrhoea (fluid faeces), dilute the formula.

## DISEASES AND PROBLEMS OF NEWBORN KITTENS

### Conjunctivitis

Usually, kittens' eyes open seven to ten days after birth. At that time infection of the conjunctiva is usually noticed.

*Cause*
Usually staphylococcal or streptococcal infection.
*Signs*
• Eyelids stuck together.
• Pus oozing from the corner of the eyelids.
• Dry pus adhering to the edges of the eyelids.
*Treatment*
Warm bathing and gentle parting of the eyelids. Be careful not to pull the eyelids apart too abruptly because you may damage the rims. Once the eyelids are open, bathe them regularly to wipe away the pus and to prevent them sealing together again. If you are unable to part the eyelids or once parted there is evidence of heavy pus discharge, see your veterinarian, who will prescribe an antibiotic eye ointment.

### Diarrhoea

Diarrhoea may cause death in kittens if it goes unchecked, particularly in the first few days of life.
*Cause*
Diarrhoea may be caused by infection or by the queen's milk being toxic. In cases where the milk is toxic, usually the queen has a discharge from the vagina, indicating a uterine infection, the source of the toxins which enter the milk via the bloodstream.
*Signs*
Greenish fluid faeces, inflamed raw anus, crying, bloated abdomen and rough, harsh coat that tends to stand up.
*Treatment*
Treatment involves both the kittens and the queen. The queen should be treated by your veterinarian with antibiotics. The kittens may or may not require antibiotics, but ask your veterinarian to check them. Remove the kittens from their mother until her infection is cleared. Keep the kittens warm and away from draughts. Hand-feed them (see 'Orphan kittens', page 188).

### Hypothermia

Newborn kittens are unable to regulate their body temperature. They rely on body heat generated from the queen's body, including her mammary glands, the close proximity of the other kittens, general activity and on being in a draught-free, warm environment.
*Causes*
• Mother rejects kitten.
• Kitten removed from mother and placed in an unsuitable environment.
*Signs*
Initially, the kitten shows signs of increased activity, constant crying and is cold to the touch. Sucking is weak and little or no milk is ingested.

In a later stage, the kitten becomes weak, uncoordinated, stops crying and cannot or will not suck. Often, the queen rejects the kitten by pushing it away, further aggravating its hypothermia and causing the kitten to go into a coma. Shake the thermometer down as far as the mercury will go and then check the kitten's temperature. If its temperature is below 35 °C (95.5°F), hypothermia should be suspected.
*Treatment*
Slow, gentle heating can lead to complete recovery over twelve to twenty-four hours. Rapid warming can lead to shock and death.

### Navel infection

*Cause*
Infection, which may progress up the stump of the umbilical cord after it is severed or broken and into the abdominal cavity, causing peritonitis.
*Signs*
Indications of this problem are inflammation and redness of the stump of the umbilical cord, with pus discharge. The skin of the abdomen around the base of the navel is often bluish in colour.
*Treatment*
Involves your veterinarian administering antibiotics, fluids and keeping the kitten warm.
*Prevention*
Is related to the general cleanliness of the environment, the correct handling of the umbilical cord and swabbing the end of it with iodine after it is severed or broken.

### Umbilical hernia

Fatty tissue or the intestine passes through a hole in the muscles of the abdominal wall and presses against the skin, forming a swelling.
*Causes*
• A congenital defect. If an umbilical hernia is a congenital defect, the cat should not be used for breeding.
• The umbilical cord may be broken by the queen or by a person assisting at the birth. An umbilical hernia can be caused by pulling on the cord too vigorously, damaging the abdominal muscles where

191

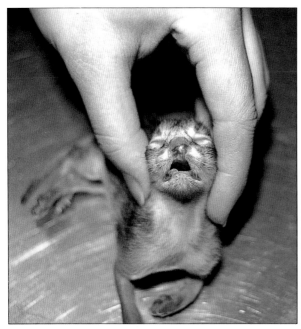

*A kitten with a hare lip.*

the cord is attached.
*Sign*
A swelling in the region of the navel, which may be up to 2 cm (0.8 in) or more in diameter.
*Treatment*
Many small umbilical hernias close up and disappear over a period of eight months. Nevertheless, it is wise to ask your veterinarian to evaluate the hernia and to recommend whether or not it should be corrected surgically.

If the hernia opening in the muscular wall of the abdomen is large enough, a loop of the intestine may become twisted in it and strangle itself, cutting off the blood supply to that portion of the intestine and necessitating emergency surgery to save the kitten's life.

## Deformities

CLEFT PALATE
This is an opening in the roof of the mouth which can vary from a slit-like opening in the midline to virtually the entire roof of the mouth being absent.
*Causes*
May be due to:
• unknown cause,
• an iodine deficiency in the queen during pregnancy,
• administration of cortisone in the early stages of pregnancy.
*Signs*
• Milk coming out of the kitten's nostrils.
• Unable to suck properly.
• Weakness and poor development due to lack of

nutrition.
*Treatment*
Take the kitten to your veterinarian to be humanely put to sleep.
HAIRLESS KITTENS
Do not confuse this problem with an overzealous mother licking her kittens frequently and vigorously, with resultant loss of hair.
*Cause*
It is due to a recessive gene.
*Sign*
The kitten is born hairless.
*Treatment*
The kitten should be put to sleep and the breeding program revised to avoid reproducing this deformity.
HARE LIP
May be associated with cleft palate, but not necessarily.
*Cause*
A genetic (inherited) characteristic.
*Sign*
The upper lip does not join in the middle.
*Treatment*
Euthanasia.
OPEN EYES
In this case, a kitten is born with its eyes open. Normally, kittens are born with their eyes closed and they do not open until seven to ten days after birth.
*Cause*
May be an iodine deficiency in the queen during pregnancy.
*Sign*
Kittens born with eyes open.
*Treatment*
The eyes must be kept moist. Contact your veterinarian, who may prescribe artificial tears and antibiotic eye drops or ointment. If the eyes are not treated, they will dry out, become infected and ulcerated, leading to permanent eye damage and possible blindness.

## Viral infection

Feline leukaemia virus and feline infectious enteritis virus are fatal, whereas the more common feline respiratory viruses usually are not.
*Cause*
The stress of pregnancy and parturition (birth) in queens that are carriers of a viral infection can cause the virus to multiply and the queen to release the virus in her secretions. Even though the kittens may have some immunity, one or all of them may succumb to the virus.
*Signs*
The kittens have watery eyes, conjunctivitis, nasal

*Kittens which have been removed from the queen.*

discharge, sneezing, blocked nose, lethargy and do not suck as vigorously.

*Treatment*

Consult your veterinarian, who will treat the kittens according to their symptoms. The treatment may include eye drops, antibiotics, fluids, antihistamines and good general nursing.

## Weaning

In general, start weaning when the kittens are about four weeks of age, but the precise starting time will depend on the size of the litter, the queen's milk supply and when you want the kittens to go to their new home(s).

As a starter for the weaned kittens, use prepared baby foods or canned cat food mixed with water to form a sloppy paste. Smear some of the food around the kittens' mouths or entice them to suck the food from the end of your finger. Once they show interest, introduce them to a flat dish or saucer containing the food.

Initially, they walk in the food and make a mess but soon they will get the idea of lapping it up. Once this is achieved, increase the consistency of the food to a more solid nature.

Provide the kittens with water or milk in a dish, but be careful as some may develop diarrhoea from cow's milk. If so, use a low lactose milk formula.

After a week the kittens should be eating solid food readily from a bowl. It is a good idea to feed them four times a day. At this young age the kittens should be exposed to a wide variety of taste and texture in foods, as some cats become addicted to the one type of food as they mature. In time, if you discover that the diet to which the cat has become accustomed does not cover all its nutritional requirements, it may be difficult to get it to change and accept more a balanced diet.

If the queen wants to feed them all the time during the weaning process, remove her from the kittens while they are being fed solid food. The kittens should be completely weaned over a four-week period, so that at eight weeks of age they are self-sufficient and ready to go to their new home.

By removing the kittens from their mother for periods during the weaning, the queen's milk production will decrease, so that when the kittens are fully weaned at eight weeks of age, she will not have uncomfortable, swollen mammary glands full of milk.

## Worming

The kittens and the queen should be wormed against roundworm, hookworm and tapeworm when the kittens are four weeks old. The kittens should continue to be wormed on another three occasions at two-weekly intervals and then every three months, the same as for all adult cats.

193

Make sure you use a worm preparation that covers all the intestinal worms mentioned. A worm paste may be easier to administer to kittens than worm tablets. The paste can be mixed with a small quantity of their favourite food or put directly into the mouth, or smeared around the mouth and on the hair of the forelegs for them to lick it off.

### Flea infestation of kittens and queen

Wash the queen in an insecticidal shampoo, as the stronger insecticidal rinses may have an adverse effect on the kittens.

Make sure she is thoroughly rinsed and dried, especially in the area of her nipples, so that the kittens do not ingest any of the insecticide and are not deterred from sucking by the unpleasant taste or smell of the insecticide.

Dip each kitten for a couple of minutes in a bucket of warm water so that its head is just above water level. While in the water, remove any fleas from the head. Dry the kittens thoroughly.

If the bedding is washable, give it a good scrub in the insecticidal shampoo and then rinse thoroughly. Otherwise, burn the bedding and renew.

## COLLECTING YOUR KITTEN FROM THE CATTERY

Before you collect your kitten from the cattery, it is very important to be prepared for its arrival in its new home.

### Buying a carry box or basket

Kittens and adult cats in particular generally do not like travelling in a motor vehicle. They often become agitated and run around inside the vehicle. They are potentially dangerous to the driver and may cause an accident. On arrival at the destination, when the door is opened, they may jump out and run away. If they are in a strange environment, they will become more frightened, continue running and may be lost forever.

The best solution is to buy a carry box, of which there are numerous types available. In some countries if you are driving alone in the car with your cat, it is an offence not to confine it to a carry cage or basket. The cardboard box variety is cheap, but a determined kitten or cat can force its way out or tear a hole in the box with its claws and escape. If the cat urinates while travelling, the cardboard becomes soggy and breaks open under the weight of the kitten or cat. When removed from the box, the cat smells and its hair is matted with urine and faeces.

The cane or wicker basket type (either with a lid on top or with a door at the front) is strong, although over a number of years the cane may deteriorate and break. The hinged-lid variety gives you better access for putting the cat in and taking it out. However, if the lid is not secured at both ends, the cat may be able to force its way out. One disadvantage is the cat is not able to see through the basket.

Cane baskets with a wire door at the front give the cat good visibility, but with some cats it is difficult to get them into that style of basket and to take them out, as they tend to retreat to the far end, away from the door. If the basket is soiled, it is difficult to clean.

The best type of box is one with a plastic base and wire top. Once the cat is put in the box, it is totally secure, and the cat is happy because it can see out. An obvious advantage, especially for long journeys, is that they are well ventilated. In the bottom of the box is a raised wire base or platform on which the cat sits. If it urinates or defecates, the cat is not left sitting in its own mess. The plastic base is waterproof, and is easily cleaned by hosing out and disinfecting. The hinged lid provides easy access for putting the cat in or taking it out. This type of box will last indefinitely.

When purchasing a cat carry box for your new kitten, keep in mind that it will develop into a strong mature cat, which you will have as a companion for approximately fourteen years. In that time there will be numerous occasions when you will need to transport your cat. So buy a carry box that will do the job and last for the lifetime of the cat.

### Necessary items for the arrival of the new kitten

- Plastic food dish.
- Plastic water dish. Those with a stable base are more desirable, otherwise the kitten may tilt the dish and spill its contents.
- A basket or bed. Do not buy an expensive one as you may find the kitten prefers to sleep in a discarded cardboard box. Buy a basket that can be easily cleaned.
- A litter tray complete with a top to prevent spread of litter when the kitten is scratching about. Obviously, this should be made of plastic for cleaning and disinfecting.
- Food — canned and dry.
- Litter.
- Collar — if a kitten has a collar with an identity disc, you have a good chance of recovering it if it is lost or injured.

Put the collar on so that you can just put two fingers under it. If it is too loose, it is liable to get

*A Silver Tabby American Shorthair.*

*A Blue Abyssinian.*

*Basic equipment for a new kitten.*

caught on protruding objects or the kitten is liable to flip it off with one of its paws and lose it.

Make sure the collar you purchase has an elastic strip sewn into it, which allows it to expand and slip over the head if the collar gets caught on an object. In twenty years of veterinary practice, I have not seen or heard of a cat strangling itself with such a collar.

When the kitten arrives at your home, keep it inside. Help it feel secure, offer it affection and provide it with a warm place to sleep. Put its basket and litter tray in a small room such as the laundry where it can be confined at night. Feed it at regular intervals (four times daily) with the food the breeder was using. If you want to change the diet, wait for a week and after that do it gradually.

Place the kitten frequently onto the litter tray. When it urinates and/or defecates, offer it a reward such as stroking it. Remove any faeces, but leave the litter for a day or two as the odour in the litter will reinforce in the kitten's mind that this is the place for its toilet.

After a number of days, when the kitten feels secure and happy with the environment inside the home, take it outside and let it explore the garden under close supervision. Make sure there are no other animals such as dogs or other cats in the garden to frighten the kitten away. Over a couple

of weeks, the kitten will develop a sense of belonging and also a sense of where its boundaries are, and will start to become protective about its territory.

Until the kitten is big enough to defend itself, do not leave it outside alone during the day. Even then, always provide an escape route to safety for it, such as a cat door giving access to the house or the laundry door left open. Always keep your cat confined at night as this is the time when it will tend to wander, with the risk of being attacked by another cat or run over by a motor vehicle.

## TRAINING

Never let the kitten jump onto kitchen benches as it is unhygienic. There are a number of diseases humans may catch from cats (see pages 93, 163, 169). If the kitten continues to jump onto the kitchen bench, give it a tap with a rolled paper, say the word 'no' and put it outside or into another room. Always coincide the reprimand with the undesirable act. Do not allow kittens onto or into beds, as this is also unhygienic.

Certain undesirable antisocial forms of behaviour can be related to anxiety or boredom. (See page 64.)

Once the kitten is old enough, it should be allowed to wander around your garden during the

197

day, giving it plenty of opportunity to perform its toilet habits outside, to climb trees rather than curtains and generally have a good time rather than scratch the lounge.

### Kitten care and your veterinarian

When your kitten is six to eight weeks old, make an appointment to see your veterinarian for a thorough and detailed examination of your pet and to discuss all aspects of pet-care including:
• behavioural problems (see page 66);
• birth control (see below);
• breeding (discussed in this chapter);
• fleas, lice and ticks (see pages 194, 159, 167);
• health problems (see pages 191-194);
• nutrition and feeding (see page 73);
• vaccination programs (see page 87);
• worms and worming (see pages 88-94).

## BIRTH CONTROL

When your kitten is having its final vaccination at sixteen to eighteen weeks of age, it is an opportune time to discuss birth control with your veterinarian, as females are desexed usually at five months of age and males at six months.

*Common terms used in breeding*

| | |
|---|---|
| Queen | a breeding female |
| Stud | a breeding male |
| Tom | an entire male (has both testicles); a free-range breeder |
| Neuter | a desexed male or female cat |
| On heat | the time when the queen is sexually attractive and will mate with the stud or tom |
| In season | same as above |
| On call | same as above |
| To neuter | to desex a male or female cat |
| To castrate | to desex a male cat |
| To spay | to desex a female cat |

### Desexing

The reason for desexing the female (queen) at five months of age is because she comes in season at six to nine months of age. The male (tom or stud) can be desexed later because he does not start breeding activity until about twelve months of age. Nevertheless, it is a good idea to have him castrated well before he develops male sexual characteristics.

Whether desexing be referred to as spaying, neutering, sterilising or castrating, the same surgical procedure for removal of the reproductive organs is followed. In the case of the female, the ovaries and uterus are removed; and in the case of the male, the testicles are removed.

*Surgical procedure for the female cat*

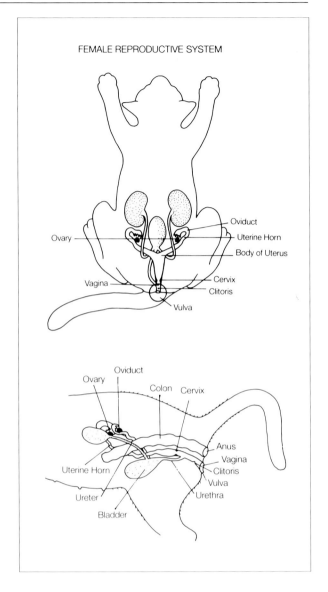

FEMALE REPRODUCTIVE SYSTEM

Ovary, Oviduct, Uterine Horn, Body of Uterus, Vagina, Cervix, Clitoris, Vulva

Ovary, Oviduct, Colon, Cervix, Uterine Horn, Anus, Vagina, Clitoris, Vulva, Urethra, Ureter, Bladder

• Make an appointment with your veterinarian.
• The female cat is not given food or fluid for at least eight hours before being presented to the veterinary hospital in the morning.
• The cat is given a general anaesthetic, the hair on the abdomen is shaved, and the skin is sterilised.
• The veterinary surgeon makes an incision about 2.5 cm (1 in) long in the skin and through the abdominal muscles to gain access to the abdominal cavity. Some surgeons prefer the flank approach, but most prefer the midline.
• The blood vessels supplying the ovaries and uterus are carefully tied off, then the organs are removed.
• The incision in the abdominal muscles is closed by stitching with dissolvable suture material. The skin incision is closed using non-dissolvable suture material, and the stitches are removed ten days after surgery.

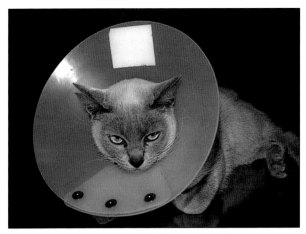

*A cat wearing an Elizabethan collar.*

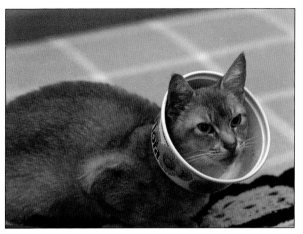

*A homemade Elizabethan collar.*

• Normally, the cat is kept under observation overnight and goes home the next day.

On arriving home, there is very little need for post-operative care. There are no signs of pain or discomfort; the cat eats normally and resumes normal activities. Leisurely activity is all right, but do not allow the cat to jump from a height or do anything strenuous which will put tension on the abdominal wound.

Most cats do not worry about the wound, but a few pull out the stitches soon after surgery, causing the skin wound to open up. If it does, it has to be restitched. However, if the skin wound does not open up and remains intact, just keep your cat quietly confined and the wound should heal as well as if the stitches were in place.

If you notice the cat pulling at the stitches, the only way to stop her is to put an Elizabethan collar around her neck. Your veterinarian can supply you with one, or you can make one from a small plastic bucket, flower-pot or ice-cream container. Leave the collar on twenty-four hours a day until the stitches are removed. While wearing the collar, the cat should be confined for her own safety. If she roams, she may be hit by a motor vehicle or have her head caught in the branches of a shrub or tree. The cat can sleep comfortably when wearing the collar, but you will either have to take the collar off to allow her to eat or leave the collar on and hold the food and fluids up to her mouth.

Some-times owners may ask the veterinarian about the feasibility of a tubal ligation. While this procedure is possible in female cats, keep in mind the difference in the purpose of the two types of surgery. Tubal ligation in humans is to prevent pregnancy while allowing a normal sex life. Removal of the uterus and ovaries in the female cat is designed not only to prevent pregnancy, but also to prevent her from coming in season and being sexually interested in or attractive to male cats. The problems of the queen calling and the tom hanging around fighting for her favours, urinating to mark his territory, howling and generally making a nuisance of himself, will disappear.

*Surgical procedure for the male cat*

• Make an appointment with your veterinarian.

• The male cat is not given food or fluid for at least eight hours before being presented to the veterinary hospital in the morning.

• The cat is given a general anaesthetic, the hair on the scrotum is shaved and the skin is sterilised.

• An incision is made in the scrotum to remove the testicles, from which testosterone, the male sex hormone, is produced. The blood vessels supplying the testicles are tied off before the testicles are removed. The scrotum is not stitched, and the wounds heal naturally.

• The cat recovers quickly and usually is allowed to go home the same afternoon.

Do not give the cat any food that evening, allow him only a small amount of fluid to drink and keep him quiet and confined. Keep your castrated tom

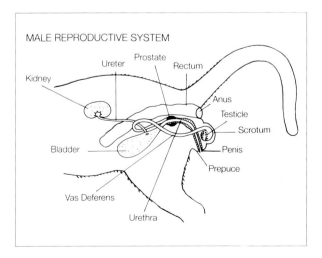

MALE REPRODUCTIVE SYSTEM

Kidney
Ureter
Prostate
Rectum
Anus
Testicle
Scrotum
Bladder
Penis
Prepuce
Vas Deferens
Urethra

warm, which is important in helping his body to metabolise the anaesthetic in his system. The next day, put the cat onto his normal diet and allow him free exercise.

If the young male cat is not desexed and develops into a sexually mature stud or tom, he usually has a scruffy appearance due to lack of grooming on his part. He sprays a particularly pungent urine with a distinctly unpleasant odour on objects to mark his territory. If allowed, he roams freely and spends most of his time seeking out queens on heat, and returns home only for food and rest.

While roaming and seeking sexual favours from queens on heat, he is often involved in fights with other cats. If wounded, an abscess may develop and go unnoticed for some days by the owner. At times, the tom, for no apparent reason, may be aggressive towards or remain aloof from the owner.

In most cases, after desexing, the tom sheds all his unpleasant characteristics and changes into a nice companion to have around the home. Furthermore, he no longer helps to produce unwanted kittens that contribute to the stray cat problem.

Keep in mind that if you have a sexually mature male cat castrated, it will take about a month for the testosterone (male sex hormone) to be eliminated from his system and consequently about a month for his male characteristics to subside. Some sexually mature castrated males retain some level of the male characteristics; that is why it is important to castrate a tom before he reaches puberty.

Some owners are concerned that their tom might go into a psychological decline after being castrated. A tom does not know that he has been castrated. Certainly his male characteristics will change, but there is no reason to believe that he will go into a 'psychological decline'.

Sometimes the veterinarian may be asked about performing a vasectomy on the male cat. Keep in mind that the vasectomy would only stop the stud or tom from producing kittens. It would not put a stop to those unpleasant male characteristics associated with howling, fighting, urinating and courting.

*Points of view for consideration before desexing*
Some owners maintain that, by allowing their queen to come in season and have a litter of kittens before being desexed, it makes her a more contented cat. There is no known medical or psychological evidence to support this notion.

Other owners do not want their cat desexed because it will put on too much weight after desexing. Certainly, it might have a slight effect on weight, more so in the case of the tom who once

he becomes a neuter is not so active, but generally, weight is determined by genetic make-up, the quantity and type of food eaten, and the amount of exercise taken. If the young cat is active, fed correctly and the parents are slim, then the owner need not worry about the cat getting fat after desexing.

Some owners express the opinion that they would like to breed from their queen to involve their children in practical sex education and in rearing the kittens. However, in many cases the birth of kittens often takes place at night, and consequently goes unnoticed. Even though queens are excellent mothers, they do require some assistance during the rearing stage of the kittens.

When the queen first comes on heat at six to nine months of age, she may be too immature physically to become pregnant. Her pelvis is often not developed well enough to allow for normal birth of the kittens; consequently, they may have to be delivered by caesarian section. The ideal age to start breeding with the queen is at about eighteen months, although it is a fact that she will come in season a number of times from the approximate age of six months.

In most countries there are too many kittens and not enough homes to accommodate them. This fact is borne out by the number of animal welfare shelters and stray cats in existence. Before breeding, make certain that you have found homes for the kittens.

## ALTERNATIVES TO DESEXING

### Confine your cat

When the queen comes in season, lock her up so that she does not have access to a male. Unlike the dog (bitch), the cat shows little visible physical signs of being in season. There is no swelling of the

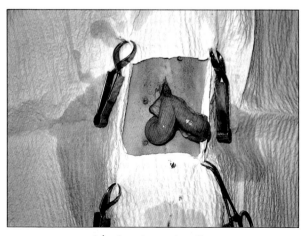

*A hysterectomy operation.*

vulva or bleeding from the vagina. Usually, there are quite obvious behavioural changes, such as being more vocal, more affectionate and crouching with the tail held to one side.

The success of this approach depends on your being able to recognise when the queen is in season, which you may not be aware of if you are inexperienced. If the queen is confined to the house or apartment, it may shriek and howl persistently when in season. This is characteristic particularly of the Siamese breed.

To sum up, confining the cat is not very successful in the long run.

### Contraceptive pill or injection

The contraceptive pill is not generally used to stop the queen coming in season. However, if you prefer to use the pill, consult your veterinarian for details of correct dosage and time for administration. If a cat is on the contraceptive pill for a lengthy period, a side effect may develop in the form of a cystic infection of the uterus, called pyometron. This infection can be life-threatening and is only cured by a hysterectomy if the infection is recognised early enough.

The long-acting contraceptive injection is given every five months. This stops the cat coming in season in the intervening five-month periods. The injection has the same side effect as the pill.

The pill or injection method of birth control often fails because owners forget either to give the pill or to arrange the injection at the appropriate time.

# ACKNOWLEDGEMENTS

I wish to express my grateful appreciation of the support given me by my father, Eric Hawcroft. His assistance in planning, research and proofreading, demanding of both time and effort, was invaluable. His constant encouragement motivated me to complete this book.

My sister, Judy Shields, had the task of typing, retyping and deciphering my handwriting and notations. She accomplished it in a spirit of cheerful cooperation and with much admired accuracy.

I would like to thank my wife, Jan, and children, Melanie, Samantha, Damien and Edwina, for their encouragement, patience, understanding and general support. I would like to thank my partner, Dr David Loneragan, and all the staff at Gordon Veterinary Hospital: Dr Andrew Morgan, Dr Sue McMillan and the nurses, Jenny Reber, Helen Mead, Kim Tupper and Diane Spalding, for their advice, patience and assistance.

My special thanks to the following cat breeders for their helpful advice, and for their assistance in providing photographs:

> Bambi and Brian Edwards (Bajimbi Cattery)
> Nonie English (Rubaiyat Cattery)
> George and Julie Kennedy (Nile Cattery)
> Sue Parker (An Cala Cattery)
> Sandra Weaver-Hall (Obanya)

Other people, institutions and companies who, in one way or another, have made a contribution, which I appreciate very much, are:

Ruth and Ron Bell-Searby (Bilbell Cattery); G and D Farthing (Candelsha Cattery); Elizabeth Flower; Alan Jackson; Jill Martyn (St Arok Cattery); Kay Pauling; Pfizer Agricare Pty Ltd (Dr Paul Macqueen); Ann Rockell; Royal Agricultural Society Cat Control, Sydney; Dr Jeffrey Smith; University of Sydney Faculty of Veterinary Science; Josephine Wing; Mrs Watman; Pat Page; Pets International Pty Ltd.

## PHOTOGRAPHY CREDITS

Dorothy Holby: pp 11, 12, 17, 27, 28, 30, 38, 46 (top & bottom), 47, 48, 55, 56, 62, 67, 68, 79, 80, 99, 100, 106,111, 112, 121, 122, 127, 128, 141, 142, 172, 184, 195
Sally (Barnett) Klein: endpapers, title page, pp 6, 18, 26, 34, 36, 37, 39, 42, 49, 50, 52, 54, 61, 105, 183, 196

# INDEX

# VACCINATION RECORD

# NOTES